THE GLASS CONSUMER

Life in a surveillance society

Edited by Susan

NCC National
Consumer Council
Making all consumers matter

First published in Great Britain in June 2005 by

The Policy Press
University of Bristol
Fourth Floor, Beacon House
Queen's Road
Bristol BS8 1QU

Tel +44 (0)117 331 4054
Fax +44 (0)117 331 4093
e-mail tpp-info@bristol.ac.uk
www.policypress.org.uk

© National Consumer Council 2005
Reprinted 2006

British Library Cataloguing in Publication Data
A catalogue record for this book is available from the British Library

Library of Congress Cataloging-in-Publication Data
A catalog record for this book has been requested

ISBN 1 86134 735 9 paperback

Cover design by Qube Design Associates, Bristol
Front cover: photograph kindly supplied by Robert Cocker
Printed and bound in Great Britain by Hobbs the Printers Ltd, Southampton

Contents

Notes on contributors

Perri 6 is Professor of Social Policy at Nottingham Trent University. He has published extensively on privacy issues, including such works as *On the cards* (1996), *The future of privacy*, 2 volumes (1998), research on public attitudes to data sharing between public services for the Cabinet Office (2002), for the Information Commissioner on identity cards (2003) and, for the OECD, on the demand for privacy-enhancing technologies. He is currently conducting new empirical research jointly with Professor Christine Bellamy and Professor Charles Raab on the relationship between partnership working between public services, data sharing and privacy.

Christine Bellamy is Professor of Public Administration and Associate Dean for Research and Graduate Studies in Business, Law and Social Sciences at Nottingham Trent University. She has written on information policy and e-government for many years, and is the author (with Professor John Taylor) of one of the first standard texts in this field. She has also written on the subject of e-democracy. With Professor Perri 6 and Professor Charles Raab she is currently running a major ESRC-funded study on data sharing and privacy in multiagency working in public services. She is a past Chair of the Joint University Council, the national subject association for Public Administration and Social Policy, and is a member of the Academy of Learned Societies in the Social Sciences.

John Borking is Director of Borking Consultancy (j.borking@xs4all.nl) and an associate board member of the Dutch Data Protection Authority (www.cbpweb.nl) accountable for technology assessments, as well of the Netherlands Gaming Control Board in The Hague. He is also an ICT arbitrator and mediator (www.sgoa.org). Before 1994, he was director of the Association for ICT Providers and from 1974 until 1986 was senior legal counsel and company secretary of Xerox Corp in Amsterdam and London.

Martin Evans is Senior Fellow at Cardiff Business School. He previously held professorial posts at the Universities of Portsmouth, Glamorgan and the West of England. His industrial experience was with Hawker Siddeley and then as a consultant to a variety of organisations over 30 years. Martin's specialist areas include direct marketing, consumer behaviour and marketing research and information and he has over 160 publications plus 7 books, mostly in these areas. He is an academic prize winner at the International Marketing Communications Conference, the Academy of Marketing, the Learning and Teaching Support Network (LTSN) and Institute of Direct Marketing. He is a Fellow of both the Chartered Institute of Marketing and Institute of Direct Marketing.

Harriet Hall is a solicitor with extensive experience in consumer policy work in the field of financial services. She is a member of the Financial Services Consumer Panel. This body advises the Financial Services Authority on its policies and activities from an independent consumer point of view. It also reviews and comments on wider developments in the financial services sector. From 1993 to 2000, she was the legal officer of the National Consumer Council and in this role commissioned and wrote numerous reports on the availability of financial services for disadvantaged consumers and on regulation and self-regulation in the sector.

Dr Susanne Lace is a Senior Policy Officer at the National Consumer Council (NCC) in the UK. Susanne leads the NCC's work on information issues. She is a member of the European Consumer Law Group and a member of the Editorial Board of the *Journal of Consumer Behaviour*. Prior to joining the NCC in 2001, she worked as a lawyer, researcher and academic at several institutions in the UK and Germany, including the law firm Addleshaw Goddard, the Institute for the Study of the Legal Profession at Sheffield University and the Max-Planck Institute for Foreign and International Criminal Law in Freiburg.

Jonathan Montgomery is Professor of Health Care Law at the University of Southampton and Chair of the Hampshire and Isle of Wight Strategic Health Authority. His publications include *Health* *care law* (Oxford University Press, 2nd edn, 2003) and (with Priscilla Alderson) *Health care choices: Making decisions with children* (IPPR, 1996). He is a member of the Medical Ethics Committee of the British Medical Association and of the Ethics Advisory Group to the Care Records Development Board (part of the NHS Programme for Information Technology). The views expressed in his chapter are entirely his own and do not represent the views of the committees on which he serves.

Charles Raab is Professor of Government in the University of Edinburgh. He has published extensively on information policy, including privacy protection, public access to information, e-government and e-democracy. He is co-author (with C.J. Bennett) of *The governance of privacy: Policy instruments in global perspective* (Ashgate, 2003). His ESRC-funded 'Virtual Society?' project investigated data protection in the context of European and global changes in processes and concepts. With Professor Christine Bellamy and Professor Perri 6, he is currently conducting an ESRC-funded study on data sharing and privacy in multiagency working. He served on the Advisory Board for the Cabinet Office (Performance and Innovation Unit) report, *Privacy and data sharing: The way forward for public services* (April 2002), and is on the editorial boards of six academic journals in the information policy field.

Introduction

Susanne Lace

It is your birthday and your post has just landed on the mat. Among the offers for loans and charity appeals (where did they get your name from?) you see that Sainsbury's has sent you a personalised birthday card, offering a free box of chocolates. Your car insurer also extends an invitation, to take part in a trial where your premiums will vary depending on the journeys you make. They will track your movements by satellite.

Later, you dine in a local restaurant. Looking up, you notice a CCTV camera — when did they install that? You drive home, passing a series of speed cameras on the way.

This is a current, not a future-based, scenario. We are all 'glass consumers': others know so much about us, they can almost see through us. Our everyday lives are recorded, analysed and monitored in innumerable ways but mostly we do not realise, or think nothing of it. When we are aware, we may even welcome it — CCTV may make us feel safer, we may appreciate discounts received as supermarket loyalty cardholders.

Yet our lives are subject to forms and levels of scrutiny that raise hugely important issues, which question the kind of society we want to live in. The significance of what has been dubbed the 'personal information economy' resonates across the consumer landscape, from food to finance, education to the environment.

This introduction discusses why this economy is of fundamental and growing importance: its operation increasingly will define our experience and choices as consumers, yet its impact is insufficiently understood and inadequately addressed. While debates such as those on identity cards capture extensive media coverage in the UK, the everyday, pervasive ways information use affects consumers lie largely unexplored. But it is in the back offices of public and private sector organisations, where our personal information is relentlessly processed, our worth or risk abstracted from our profiles, that our opportunities in the future will be determined.

The chapter begins by sketching the personal information economy, some of the key issues it raises and the contents of each subsequent chapter. The National Consumer Council's (NCC) recommendations are to be found in the conclusion, which sets out its manifesto for change. But first, how can we begin to assess the significance of the personal information economy?

Personal information: friend or foe?

The rise and rise of personal information

Estimates suggest that details of the average economically active adult in the developed world are located in around 700 major databases (Davies, 2002). The level of information held can be quite staggering. Experian, for example, a market-leader in credit checking and providing consumer data, holds detailed records on 45 million consumers in the UK and 215 million consumers in the US. By 2002, 16 million people in the UK had returned in-depth postal lifestyle and shopping surveys to them (Collinson, 2002), providing exhaustive details of their private lives. The list industry itself (where companies sell lists of consumers' details to other organisations) was valued in the UK in 2001 at £2 billion (Lawrence, 2002).

The appetite for this depth of data shows no sign of declining – if anything, it is growing. Drivers are numerous, from the desire of governments to control and manage populations, to the breakdown of monopolistic forms of enterprise. And all this is facilitated by the declining cost, increasing power and convergence of technologies.

Product diversification and the availability of personalisation in goods and services has moved in tandem with governments releasing massive quantities of anonymised data to the private sector. Information may then flow back into the public sector, perhaps through the use of geo-demographic tools (which map the economic and social profile of areas). This interdependent mixing of public and private sector agendas definitively hallmarks the personal information economy.

Such mutual back scratching has immense appeal. Information

can allow governments to better control risks and promote more informed policy, from targeting crime (including terrorism) to charting deprivation for regional development policy. In the private sector, personal information underpins attempts to increase sales and minimise losses, from customising and personalising goods and services to controlling fraud, measuring credit risk and deciding in which areas to invest. Personal information fuels economic growth.

As Perri 6 notes in Chapter One of this volume, the exploitation of personal information has spurred GDP growth since the decline of heavy industry in the UK. It has facilitated greater competition and has opened up markets that were less available to previous generations. Harriet Hall's chapter (Chapter Six) argues that before the electronic manipulation of personal data, many consumers would not have been able to access credit or buy insurance. The use of personal information has helped improve the living standards of many.

As consumers, we may experience benefits most tangibly in new forms and (improved) products and services, better customer service and increased efficiency and convenience. And, as Jonathan Montgomery's chapter (Chapter Seven) reminds us, better information management in sectors such as healthcare will not only save clients time and distress – it may also save lives.

So it is not too surprising that one of the most talked about ideas within public sector reform in the UK at present centres on the use of personal information. The personalisation of public services has been promoted as an extremely potent (albeit a highly contested and ambiguous) idea that could be as influential as privatisation was in the 1980s and 1990s in reshaping public provision (Leadbeater, 2004). Some believe that personalisation potentially could redistribute power within the public sector, enabling users to help transform the design and delivery of services (Parker, 2004).

But if personal information is to be used more creatively, it is even more important that it is used sensitively and fairly, appreciating its broader impacts. Discussion of the personalisation of public services often has been conducted at a conceptual level. If it is to work on the ground, it now needs to link into the broader debates around the personal information economy that this book explores.

The limits of current discourse

In itself, policy on personal information has yet to catch up with the complexity of information use. Debates have taken shape largely through rights-based advocacy, focusing on threats to privacy. But all too often, the social value, and the broader risks, of information use are forgotten as positions become entrenched, swinging from a denial of benefits to a denial of risks. As Scott McNealy (Sun Microsystems' chief executive officer) infamously said: "You have zero privacy anyway – get over it".

This is especially challenging following the events of '9/11'. Privacy arguments now play in an environment where the fear of terrorism tends to trump privacy concerns. And, while in relation to crime and terrorism the adage seems to be "you never can be too careful", this is not how information risks are approached.

In the past, the NCC also had couched personal information issues primarily in the language of privacy and data protection rights – yet this has proved to be of limited analytical value when faced with the casualties of the economy, such as growing food deserts and the withdrawal of banks from deprived areas.

While privacy and fair information principles still retain considerable value in guiding the appropriate collection and use of data, the NCC now believes that the social importance of this economy demands a wider canvas, one that recognises the huge benefits personal information use can bring but also the broader risks. In the future, we must not fall lazily into one-sided appraisals of developments – some of the risks of information use may present opportunities.

This book is therefore grounded in an appreciation of risk and how risk can be channelled. The ultimate goal of the NCC is to offer an alternative, consumer-centred way forward in negotiating and constructing policy on the use of personal information.

Impacts on consumers

It is often easier to detail the benefits of using personal information than to recognise and evaluate the risks. Throughout this book, authors will outline and discuss the challenges facing consumers.

The aim at this stage is to draw out some of the ways information use can harm consumers and some of the issues this raises. Overall, some of the most challenging risks revolve around injustice, loss of dignity and control of information, and threats to consumers' chances in life.

We are where we live; we are where we surf

Personal information can be used to sort and sift populations more intensively and efficiently than ever before, enhancing the life chances of some and retarding those of others. The more accurate (and often commercially rational) use of information may allow a shift in risk exposure, a transfer of group-pooled risk to settle risks more squarely on the individual shoulders of consumers. And, while individualised risk models may benefit those whom organisations classify as good risks, those who present greater risks (whether because of poverty, ill-health or anything else) can lose out.

In the private sector, for example, groups valuable to companies may receive special attention and special deals while others receive less information and inferior service (Lyon, 2003). Such disparities might be experienced on quite a mundane, hidden level – as when call centres use postcodes to single out wealthier customers and divert them to specially trained workers (while others wait in queues, to be answered by automated systems). As Hinde (2000, p 5) argues:

> If you are one of the favoured few, you will be wooed by special offers, perks and discounts. If you're outside the charmed circle, because you don't earn enough or because you're too old or because you live in the wrong neighbourhood, then it's tough luck.

So even if information does not create inequalities in the first place, it can reinforce or deepen them.

Consumers' information may be poorly handled

Information can be inaccurate or handled poorly, causing people significant harm. In 2003, the UK Criminal Records Bureau wrongly identified at least 193 job applicants as having criminal records (*The Economist*, 2004). The US Public Interest Research Group (PIRG) reported findings in June 2004 that one in four credit reports in the US contained errors serious enough to deny consumers credit – damaging their ability "to buy a home, rent an apartment, obtain credit, open a bank account or even get a job" (PIRG, 2004).

While legislation such as the 1998 Data Protection Act (DPA) in the UK should tether data use to fair information principles (to help ensure data are collected and used appropriately), such legislation may be poorly understood or blamed for other corporate failures. For example, during the writing of this book, poor information-handling practices (including misinterpretations of the DPA) have been implicated in several deaths – from the murder of two girls in Soham, to the deaths of two pensioners whose energy supply was disconnected in the middle of winter. This is the flipside of good information use – poor practices can affect our chances in life and even compromise life itself.

Information overload

Shenk (1997) notably wrote about 'data smog', the surfeit of low-quality information that was comparable in its emergence and effects to the pollution of rivers and seas by excess fertilisers, or to the health problems caused by a diet too rich in calories. In the past, information was scarce, but we had now reached the point of saturation and needed to limit our use of it. Silicon circuits have evolved much more quickly than human genes.

Interestingly, the NCC's research has shown that consumers are very concerned about the amount of marketing material and calls they receive. In 2004, 79% of the public agreed with the statement that "the sheer amount of marketing material I receive irritates me". Members of our Consumer Network, people who report their experiences as consumers to the NCC, have also reported considerable anger at the number of direct marketing calls they receive at home. One consumer wrote: "I know that people are trying to earn a living but it is hard to be polite when you have had a long day at work, bombarded with telephone calls, only to find that your 'quality time' is spent talking to people wanting to sell you something".

Unlike in the US, where the recent introduction of the 'Do Not Call Registry' (which allows consumers to prevent direct marketing calls at home) has been outstandingly popular, similar services in the UK are less widely known and used.

But we still know relatively little about the distribution and effects of data smog – and particularly whether the affluent are more likely to be affected, as marketers use consumers' personal data to market more effectively to them.

We are our profiles; we are who we were

Information overload is perhaps one of the most obvious manifestations of the use of personal information. It is more difficult to appreciate, and quantify, how our personal development may be affected by pervasive and hidden information use.

When researching the book, the Queen's words at court in *Alice's adventures in Wonderland* often came to mind: "Sentence first – verdict afterwards!". The use of information to profile individuals does risk treating people as suspects, as guilty until proven innocent (Crompton, 2004).

Recently, for instance, when countering criticism about crime prevention proposals to monitor the children of criminals, from birth to teenage years, UK Home Office Minister Hazel Blears protested: "About 125,000 kids have a dad in prison. We need to track the children who are most at risk.... I don't think it is stigmatising those children by targeting them" (*The Guardian*, 2004, p 5).

In this, the move to what William Gibson (2003) has termed 'absolute informational transparency' is apparent. Earlier, this was visualised as the life of the glass consumer. The properties and capacities of glass – fragility, transparency, the ability to distort the gaze of the viewer – mirrored our own potential vulnerability.

Some commentators, including regulators, have voiced concerns that people's development might be stunted by the operation of the personal information economy (Thomas, 2004). The fluidity of our personalities and our capacity to change and move on may be compromised.

Concern and lack of knowledge

We are still learning about how organisations collect and use information. It is not easy to find out more – many organisations provide little useful information about how they collect and use personal data. Few consumers have much idea about this. The NCC's research in 2004 found 58% of people admitting they did not understand how their personal information was collected and used by organisations.

Yet market research consistently reveals that people are concerned about privacy and about information use. There is considerable anthropological and sociological evidence that human beings have always needed a degree of privacy (Bennett and Raab, 2003, p 13), even though it is almost impossible to quantify whether we had more or less of it in the past. Homing in on present-day research, Bennett and Raab have summarised research findings as follows (2003, p 57):

In broad-brush terms, the most common finding in survey after survey is that privacy is regarded as a very important personal value, and is felt to be strongly threatened by new information and communication practices and technologies used in commerce and government. Levels of public trust in organizations which process personal data are variable but sometimes very low, as is confidence in existing protective instruments. There are more specific fears that privacy is at risk in the online environment, but worries persist about the protection afforded to personal data in more traditional, offline, transactions.

Certainly, consumers' reactions to developments that they perceive threaten their control over their information are important – the development of e-commerce has been slowed by such concerns. Will other markets and services (including e-government) similarly be challenged in future?

Outlining the chapters

This book sets out to promote an ambitious, sophisticated manifesto for the personal information economy, taking in but exploring broader terrain than privacy.

It brings together a number of leading authors to investigate key issues. Consensus was not sought – authors were given licence to discuss their own views, knowing that they may disagree among themselves. Chapters were commissioned to stimulate debate and help the NCC think through its agenda for change. The NCC's recommendations are therefore included in a separate, final chapter.

Part One: Orientations

The book is organised into four parts. The first opens with *Perri 6's* overview of the personal information economy, exploring its development and importance. It is hard to overestimate the importance of personal information: global retail organisations take investment decisions based on the most finely grained analysis of consumers' data. In the public sector, the detailed profiling of people supports the major reforms in public services.

Yet while 6 acknowledges the benefits of the economy, he also warns of the risks and builds a framework detailing those risks. Traditionally, much attention has been focused on risks of intrusion when considering consumers' information (with related privacy claims) but less attention has been paid to risks to life chances that arise from the ways the economy works. Looking to the future, he thinks it likely that conflicts around the collection and use of consumers' data will become more diverse; they will be less focused on narrow questions of privacy and more developed around big distributional issues about the impacts of the personal information economy.

In the second chapter, *Charles Raab* critically explores existing regulation and instruments for protecting consumers' personal information in the UK. In spite of several decades of regulatory activity, he finds the efficacy of regulation is far from clear, as the tools employed are outstripped by the complexity of the world. Personal information cannot be protected sufficiently at the level of a single national jurisdiction (especially online) and nations such as the US do not have comprehensive legislation, leaving consumers with a patchwork of protection.

Even within the UK, it is difficult for the regulator (the Office of the Information Commissioner) to take a lead and consumers are less powerful than they would need to be in order to present a countervailing influence comparable to the public or private sector appetite for personal data. Raab concludes that we need to build a new and more joined-up framework of protection that conceives of privacy more broadly, recognising its social value and the contribution groups within civil society can bring to the debate.

In the next chapter, *John Borking* focuses on one tool to protect consumers' information: privacy-enhancing technologies (PETs). He discusses how PETs might be used pre-emptively to protect data. He is upbeat about their potential, discussing how some forms of PET can help prevent unnecessary data collection and can design good information-handling practices into information systems. PETs may also empower consumers, by building in access to their data and allowing them to make choices about how their information is used. However, we still need to know more about what works, to improve the technology and to encourage its use.

Part Two: Contexts

Having explored the development of the personal information economy and the limits of current protection against information risks, Part Two moves on to explore the value and use of personal information to both the public and private sectors. *Martin Evans* discusses how vital information is to the private sector, as the personalisation of marketing and of products and services intensifies.

He shows how companies are using information about consumers from ever more diverse sources but he is concerned about the number of companies that do not take good information-handling practices seriously. The growing flow of information between the state and private sector is also worrying. In a similar vein to Raab, he laments consumer ignorance about the workings of this economy, which questions the economy's legitimacy. He argues that much more needs to be done to raise consumers' awareness of information issues and to win companies over to the importance of responsible information use.

Christine Bellamy, Perri 6 and *Charles Raab* then take up the thread of public sector interest in personal data, considering the reasons behind its appeal. Imperatives on the public sector to use personal information are increasing, most notably from the government's modernisation agenda. Risk management is key to this: some of the most developed uses of techniques such as data sharing and matching are associated with initiatives that measure risk to prevent or manage various social ills such as abuse, fraud and other crime.

However, public officials are often under pressure to downplay the risks of information use and many of the key policy issues (such as what circumstances justify using personal data without consent) have yet to be resolved adequately.

Moving forward, the authors recommend several reforms, from the expansion of the use of Caldicott Guardians (senior professionals who oversee how staff use personal information) to increasing sanctions for the violation of data protection principles.

Part Three: Case studies

Part Three extends the discussion through case study explorations of two sensitive areas, financial services and health. *Harriet Hall* recognises how the use of personal information can expand overall access to credit and insurance. However, the chapter focuses on impacts that are potentially exclusionary, to understand better the distribution of the risks and benefits of personal information use – and to consider the scope for creative solutions to new forms of exclusion. She therefore discusses what is known about the adverse effects data use can have on access to credit and insurance and analyses the success of policy responses.

Jonathan Montgomery takes stock of how personal information is now handled in the National Health Service (NHS) and assesses its future plans. He argues that shifts in the structure of health services and the replacement within the NHS of the paradigm of confidentiality with that of data protection should not be seen as damaging. Health service organisations have greater power to protect patient confidentiality than individual professionals could have done.

Nevertheless, it is not yet clear how a comprehensive national system for patient access to health records will be achieved, or how quality in relation to confidentiality will be assured. While standards of information governance are emerging, there is no overall framework for quality assurance and complaints mechanisms are fragmented. An integrated quality assurance system is needed, led by a single champion for patients' interests – effectively, an internal information commissioner for the NHS.

Part Four: NCC's agenda

Part Four sets out the NCC's agenda and recommendations. The NCC believes that the importance – the value, risks and opportunities – of the personal information economy needs to be appreciated more widely. It is worrying that insufficient attention is paid to the role of personal information in reinforcing social exclusion. This crucially identifies the need to generate a much greater awareness of the importance of information use, which particularly recognises risks and their distribution.

We also need to continue to make the case for practical improvements to the way personal information is treated. The chapter sets out a series of recommendations, which range from the reform of data protection legislation to the promotion of privacy impact assessments and PETs.

Taken together, the chapters in this book bring home the significance of the personal information economy – and how much remains to be done to tackle its challenges. In this, we need to recognise the limits of past work and broaden our focus, particularly recognising any impacts on consumers' chances in life.

The NCC is keen to catalyse change, to move beyond dogma by promoting an enlightened personal information agenda. This book maps our way forward.

References

Bennett, C.J. and Raab, C.D. (2003) *The governance of privacy: Policy instruments in global perspective*, Aldershot: Ashgate.

Collinson, P. (2002) '"This is your life" in Big Brother: someone somewhere is watching you', part one of a *Guardian* supplement, 7 September, p 6.

Crompton, M. (2004) 'Proof of ID required? Getting identity management right', Speech to the Australian IT Security Forum, Sydney, Australia, 30 March.

Davies, S. (2002) '"Private virtue"' in Big Brother: someone somewhere is watching you', part one of a *Guardian* supplement, 7 September, pp 4-5.

Economist, The (2004) 'Move over, Big Brother', *The Economist Technology Quarterly*, 4 December, p 26.

Gibson, W. (2003) 'The road to Oceania: reflections on the world since George Orwell' (www.gbn.com ArticleDisplyServlet.srv?aid=7200).

Guardian, The (2004) quote reported in the *Society* section, 18 August, p 5.

Hinde, S. (2000) 'Should rich shoppers get to jump the queue?', *Daily Express*, 23 October, p 5.

Lawrence, F. (2002) '"Checkout at the data supermarket" in Big Brother: someone somewhere is watching you', part one of a *Guardian* supplement, 7 September, p 8.

Leadbeater, C. (2004) *Personalisation through participation*, London: Demos.

Lyon, D. (2003) 'Introduction', in D. Lyon (ed) *Surveillance as social sorting: Privacy, risk and digital discrimination*, London: Routledge.

Parker, S. (2004) 'Personalisation and public services', Scope Disablism Summit, London, 15 July.

PIRG (Public Interest Research Group) (2004) 'One in four credit reports contains errors serious enough to wreak havoc for consumers', Press release, 17 June.

Shenk, D. (1997) *Data smog: Surviving the information glut*, San Fransisco, CA: Harper.

Thomas, R. (2004) 'Show and tell: is market competitiveness hindered by data protection law?', Speech to the Royal Society of Arts, London, 8 June.

Part One: Orientations

1

The personal information economy: trends and prospects for consumers

Perri 6

Introduction

At least for the last 30 years or so, and perhaps for longer, we have lived in a personal information economy (6, 1998). We have, of course, been 'information societies' since writing was invented in ancient Sumer: human societies of any complexity can hardly be organised on any basis other than information. But the centrality of personal profiling is a much more recent phenomenon.

Personal information is increasingly the basic fuel on which economic activity runs. Getting control and being able to make intensive use of vast databanks of profiles on individual consumers, citizens, clients and subjects gives an organisation a degree of resource-based power comparable to that possessed by the oil-producing countries until the 1980s. Companies offering geo-demographic profiling data are the 21st-century equivalents of the great energy companies of the 20th, but subject to much more competition than were the old energy giants.

This phenomenon is not confined just to direct marketing or credit rating. Today, for example, huge global retail corporations make their investment decisions on strategy, products and the location of outlets based on the most finely grained analysis of their consumers' incomes, wealth, preferences, mobility and behaviour. The 'loyalty card' phenomenon has little to do with fidelity, because those who take one card will almost certainly take others from rival chains: rather, such schemes provide very detailed profiles on the buying behaviour of named and closely tracked individuals. Financial services companies sustain their profitability only to the extent that they can successfully target their ever wider ranges of products to ever more tightly defined small niche markets of savers and borrowers. The 'marketplace of one' may be an unattainable goal, save perhaps for the very rich for whom service offerings have always been fully personalised. Yet the commercial world is investing huge sums in its pursuit.

The charitable world is no different: fundraising for donations and legacies today uses data mining and warehousing methods indistinguishable from those used by all other financial services (Farr, 2002) – for that is what fundraising now is. In the government sector, too, the detailed profiling of clients underpins all the major changes in public services (6 et al, forthcoming).

Close analysis of profiles of individuals, which are increasingly pooled between agencies, is the basis of crime mapping, intelligence-led policing, risk assessment in child protection and mental health services, initiatives to combat benefit and tax fraud, and the targeting of joint public health initiatives. Plans for electronic integrated health and social care records, the data systems underpinning Britain's Connexions card for young people, and the proposed data systems for identifying speeding drivers using digital registration number recognition systems are but the latest extensions of this programme. Identity cards, should the British government commit itself to their introduction, will add only centralisation of some of these data into an overarching population register (6, 2003) to what is already a model of public services redesigned around the collection, analysis and mining of vast banks of increasingly integrated personal profiles. The 'war on terror' declared in 2001 has extended the commitment of governments to the use of these techniques on sets of identified data from ever wider sources, including more commercial ones, than were previously routinely available to the police and security services (Lyon, 2003b).

Building the personal information economy has not been the work of decades but of perhaps two centuries, and governments have played an active role in shaping it. In the 18th century, the first governmental steps were taken in population profiling, creating what has been called the 'avalanche of statistics' that supported the public health and taxation policies of both Enlightenment-era Britain and the closer controls of the absolutist monarchies of the continent: central statistical offices were not only invented then but quickly became central to governance in the post-feudal era (Hacking, 1990; Porter, 1999). If Kafka's bleak satires on the late Austro-Hungarian bureaucracy betokened a concern with the scope of profiling, they prefigured the development of a genre of dystopian anxiety about governmental surveillance running through the 20th century, not only in the totalitarian regimes. Commercial profiling of consumers on a grand scale and the centrality to commercial strategy of the manipulation of those data is, however, an artefact of the age of the mainframe computer, rising affluence leading to greater diversity in consumer preferences, and the decline of monopolistic systems (comprising either single national giants or else small local proprietors in limited competition with each other), in everything from automobiles through groceries to savings from the 1960s onwards.

The decisions by governments from the 1970s through to the 1990s to release to the commercial sector huge quantities of personal data, albeit in technically anonymised forms but classified down to the street level, collected through the Census and many other surveys, have created the basis on which the geo-demographic profiling sector has turned itself into an industry as economically basic as energy or food production. New information technologies have made possible methods of warehousing, mining, matching, analysis, manipulation and integration of data that Kafka's bureaucrats genuflecting before the great repository of 'the files' could scarcely have imagined.

The personal information economy has brought both great rewards and real risks for consumers in both public and private sectors. It is almost inconceivable that the rates of GDP growth that marked the period since the decline of heavy industry, the rise of services, the liberalisation of trade and currencies and the deepening of competition since about 1970 could have been sustained without the development of the personal information economy. Product diversification, greater flexible specialisation with its small production runs for niche markets, greater competition, the availability of personalisation in goods and services for the wider middle class, the growth of whole professions involved in the processing of personal information sustaining white collar employment growth and social mobility during the post-war years, have all rested on the steady development of the personal information basis. To the extent that these things have given consumers today a measure of market power that their grandparents could not have conceived, as well as supporting growth in incomes and employment, the personal information economy must be accounted a gain.

Yet the rise across the democratic world since 1970 of data protection regulation reflects the depth of unease with which people have reacted as citizens to their situation as consumers (Bennett, 1992). Successive surveys have shown their high and rising levels of concern about the character and use of their records, even as such surveys have suggested that much of the public is willing to accept that privacy must on specified occasions be overridden in pursuit of other goals (see Bennett and Raab, 2003). Despite differences between countries, common sets of principles agreed by 1980 have informed the laws of most, governing the control of the purposes for which personal information may be collected and used, the quality of those data, the length of time they may be held, the extent to which they may be disclosed and the extent to which citizens and consumers have the right to know what is held on them and to apply for the correction of errors or the deletion of irrelevant matter. In no country have those principles become precise and tightly limiting algorithms, and in every country there are exemptions providing for a variety of organisational imperatives in both public and private sectors, to the chagrin of some privacy activists (Davies, 1996). Nevertheless, privacy regulators have become important public officials in many countries, able to assert a degree of independence from the executive. Their profile has been raised since the beginning of the 1990s as access to the Internet has become affordable to large numbers of people in the developed world and as privacy concerns about the capture of personal information in online transactions have led to more complaints, campaigns and adjudications. Even the US, famously a country with no general data protection law and with a powerful business lobby opposed to such regulation that is able to call on deep reserves of popular suspicion of government regulation in its aid, has seen the Federal Trade Commission in the 1990s using its powers to strike down 'unfair' trading practices in pursuit of greater privacy protection (Regan, 2003). The increasing importance of human rights law in Europe and many other parts of the world as a kind of quasi-constitutional constraint has bolstered the importance of data protection law, since both the United Nations and the European conventions include a qualified 'right to private life', which has been relied on in litigation in a number of important cases.

This chapter examines the nature of these concerns. The next section presents a taxonomy of the types of privacy risks and styles of risk perception. Then, the argument turns to the concepts used in making claims for privacy protection before examining the emerging patterns of both settlement and absence of settlement between privacy and competing governmental and commercial imperatives. Finally, some reflections are offered on the prospects for the politics of the protection of consumer privacy in the personal information economy of the 21st century.

Risks

Popular concerns about and interests in privacy[1] have been famously distinguished as those relating to demands for solitude, intimacy, anonymity and reserve (Westin, 1967). For many goods and services, perhaps the most important of these are anonymity and reserve – the claims, respectively, that records of our behaviours and speech not be identifiable as related specifically to ourselves and that as little as is necessary is recorded about our behaviours and speech. Reserve is of central importance mainly in connection with access to data from our telephone calls, faxes and e-mails other than those exchanged with formal organisations in the course of legal and proper transactions with them where it might be said that we waive our claim to reserve. However, the advent of the use of closed circuit video recording in shops and government offices that are used by the public also raises concerns about the relevance and meaning of solitude – that is, the claim not to be observed by others – in such settings before and after we have performed our transactions. Underlying each of these are aspirations for greater control over the collection, use and disclosure of information about us (Margulis, 1977).

Organisational *collection, use* and *disclosure* might give rise to different perceptions of privacy risk. I have suggested (6, 1998)[2] that it is helpful to distinguish between several distinct ways in which people might define their concerns about privacy risks. First, people may be concerned about *injustice*. For example, they may fear that information about them that is inaccurate, or out of date, or kept for too long and not now relevant, is being taken into account, and this may lead to their being wrongly denied state benefits, credit, insurance cover, a mortgage or employment, or even being given the wrong medical treatment or having a child taken into care wrongly. Second, they may fear that they *lack control* of information about them, because they cannot find out what is being held on them, or because they cannot effect consent or refusal of consent to collection or use or disclosure, or because they do not know by what means and from what sources information is gathered about them, or because they suspect that the purpose for which data are being collected and used has changed without their being informed or consulted. Third, people may be concerned about *loss of dignity* involved in being profiled in detail in the first place, or about the intrusive manner in which information is collected or the stigmatising way in which they are required to identify themselves. Fourth, they may simply experience lack of privacy as *inconvenience*, because they must make substantial effort to find out what has been collected about them or what is done with the information and to secure correction[3]. Each of these can be found in either mild or more extreme forms[4].

Although there are shifts over time in the distribution of these ways of framing privacy risks among consumers, these are much less significant than the differences between social groups. By and large, the ways in which consumers frame privacy risks are the result of their general situation, the degree of power that they have in relation to the public or commercial services with which they have to deal, their abilities including their articulacy and their self-confidence in seeking redress, and their bonds to other people in similar situations. For example, those who are both articulate and confident in their abilities to correct mistakes, who can go elsewhere if they are dissatisfied (therefore, those who mainly use private rather than public services), and who represent sufficient value to organisations providing these services that it is in those organisations' interests to retain their custom, and who have links to others in their position, are much more likely to frame privacy issues as matters of inconvenience. By contrast, more or less isolated long-term benefit claimants are more likely to think of the privacy risks they face in dealing with public authorities in terms of indignity (6, 2002a, 2002c, 2005).

It is a fair question to ask: do we know anything about trends in the probability, severity and distribution of actual privacy risks? For those are the three key dimensions on which any risk should be assessed (Royal Society Study Group, 1992; Stern and Fineberg, 1996). Unfortunately, it is very difficult to quantify the exposure of consumers on these measures. Take probabilities first. For much of the collection, use and disclosure of personal information is – ironically – veiled by considerations of commercial confidentiality in the private sector and the exemptions for national security, detection of crime and fraud control in the public services; no reliable or meaningful statistics are published even by companies and agencies that issue their codes of practice about their own compliance with them; certainly, such numbers as companies do issue are not available on a comparable basis. Numbers of complaints either to organisations or to regulators probably measure confidence in those organisations' capacity to provide redress more than they measure incidence of perceived violations of data protection principles. What can be said is that the scale of investment in the development of client data systems, and the warehousing, mining and analysis of these suggest that, over recent decades, practical limitations on data collections and use have sometimes been somewhat relaxed. As data protectors are only too well aware, this is hardly a satisfactory state of affairs, for many data-matching algorithms (see Chapter Eight) in common use are known to generate large numbers of both false positives and false negatives, requiring a good deal of subsequent checking of individual records to winnow them out, which no doubt is not always successful. Where data matching is a basic tool in decision making, therefore, the possibility of misidentification leading to specific injustices remains a matter of concern.

Indeed, data protection laws have not generally sought to proscribe collections but only to require transparency about their purposes.

By and large, not only the stated aims of data protection laws but also the organisational capabilities of regulators have been directed to limiting disclosures to third parties by original purposes, consent where appropriate or the legitimate scope of legally defined exemptions. Yet we have no meaningful statistical indicators of their success in reducing the probabilities of disclosure risk. Some cross-nationally comparative research would be particularly valuable, if it could identify differences between national regulators in the strictness with which they control the specification of purposes.

In some countries such as Australia, laws have regulated the manner in which internal manipulations of data are conducted, for example, by controlling the use of data-matching algorithms: the Privacy Commissioner is given powers to issue guidelines, which do not have the status of law but are used in audit. The present guidelines require that alternatives to data matching must be exhausted first, the public should be informed of its use, the Commissioner should be given the opportunity to comment on the protocols before use, decisions taken relying on matches should be subject to a 14-day period for objections, matches not used must be destroyed, and the data matching must be subject to time limits (see www.privacy.gov.uk/datamatching/index.html). Again, however, we lack evaluations of the privacy impact of and compliance with such detailed governance of the manner of manipulation of data.

Turning to severity or level of harm, again we have few quantitative indicators. To some degree, the harms that matter differ according to one's situation. Here, we can find some assistance in the classification offered above of the ways in which consumers frame privacy risks, for people perceive as most severe the harms that their framing recognises. In general, data protectors tend to regard risks that they define as injustices as the most severe and most deserving of regulatory action. Typically, the substantive injustices in question – wrongful denial of credit or insurance, or taking the wrong person's child into care – of course are not themselves privacy risks, but financial, employment-related risks or else abuses of professional power. By contrast, risks that can more readily be framed as control, dignity and convenience are more clearly principally informational in character. Because policy makers and data protectors alike have considered that they have limited prospects of controlling the scale of data collection and use, because the legitimate purposes for these activities can be written so widely, they have tended as a result to regard considerations of dignity as they arise in connection with the sheer quantity of information in personal profiles as being a lower priority, and presumably therefore of lesser severity. By contrast, their main efforts in respect of enhancing consumers' capacity to exercise control have taken the form of pressure on companies and agencies to provide consumers with details of what is held about them, and, to a lesser extent, to encourage the use of types of consent at least of the 'opt out' variety.

Of the three standard measures used in risk characterisation and assessment, we know least about the distribution of privacy risk. A common view, but one not based on actual research, is that the better off face greater risks from commercial organisations, because they are of greater interest to them, while the worse off, being the principal clients of public services, face greater levels of risk from government. Yet there are important business sectors, such as the sub-prime lending market, which target those on very low incomes and about which data protectors have had concerns for many years, principally about the sources from which companies in this field acquire their data about potential clients and their financial circumstances. Also, there are some important elements of law enforcement, including those engaged in detection of tax fraud, that pay great attention to the better off (for a fuller discussion of the distribution of privacy risks see Bennett and Raab, 2003).

Recent decades have of course seen major innovations in the means of protecting against some privacy risks. Risks to anonymity in particular have been addressed by a number of so-called privacy-enhancing and privacy-enabling technologies (see Borking, Chapter Three, this volume) and a growing but still niche sector has emerged in many markets that is prepared to offer consumers their benefits. However, it has proved more difficult to introduce technological solutions to the risks to, for example, reserve and intimacy, that are at once effective and also politically and legally acceptable. True, most reputable online retailers offer secure payment environments. Yet law enforcement agencies remain deeply worried that the use of encryption, Internet anonymiser sites and the like should be subject to legal regimes that allow them to access and decrypt information when they consider that they may need it: many countries have legislated for key escrow institutions that empower police, security and tax fraud investigation officials to obtain keys subject to some kind of authorisation, whether executive or judicial. There is limited scope for consumer-controlled technologies to prevent companies from disclosing their records to others: alerting systems are certainly possible, but it would be difficult for consumers to be confident that they are always alerted when a new category of disclosure is proposed. More traditional regulatory action remains the principal instrument by which reserve can be protected.

It would be wrong to conclude from this that data protection law and regulation is generally ineffective in controlling privacy risk. Rather, it is important to develop reasonable expectations. Unlike utility price regulators, data protectors have to regulate almost every organisation in a country. Yet they have fewer resources with which to do so than, for example, health and safety or environmental regulators. Since neither consumers nor regulators necessarily know when privacy violations have occurred or by whom they have been committed, it is difficult to allocate resources according to the severity or even typically by priority categories of risks. Data protectors cannot hope to rely on adversarial methods and enforcement, nor yet on extensive provision of advice, training and support to particular organisations – the two conventional regulatory strategies (Hawkins and Thomas, 1984; Hutter, 1996). Rather, they are forced to make sparing use of enforcement for the most egregious cases, to encourage the private sector to develop its own training and advice systems, and to focus on wider but shallower 'culture-building' strategies (6, 1998), using less targeted communications to raise awareness and challenge attitudes. Moreover, data protectors need to be both adroit and determined to regulate a set of risks that are more often latent than manifest in the public consciousness, and when regulators depend on quasi-constitutional human rights or European Union Law to defend their legitimacy against frequent challenges by governments and business alike.

This suggests some standards by which to measure the efficacy of data protection regulation. One might be the degree to which regulators have succeeded in institutionalising commitments to the protection of privacy to the point that they can withstand the turbulent periods when the legitimacy of privacy regulation faces sustained challenge from deregulatory interests in business and security imperatives in government. Others might include the extent of public recognition and understanding of the risks and confidence in the scope for and efficacy of redress and perhaps the regulators' ability successfully to embarrass major corporations discovered to be in breach of data protection principles. By these standards, data protection regulation in recent years might be counted a comparative policy success. For, despite business challenges during the 1990s and internal security departments' efforts to access ever more consumer data after September 2001, even in the US, privacy protections for consumers continue to be legislated (Gellman, 2002). In Europe, there have been only rather limited derogations from Article 8 of the European Convention, and business lobbying in Brussels for watering down of the 1995 Directive, which forms the basis of all members states' national data protection laws, has yet to be very successful. Large majorities of survey respondents profess themselves concerned about their privacy, aware of the legislation and the existence of redress[5]. Unfortunately, data protectors have yet to convince sufficiently great proportions of the population of their efficacy in securing that redress. In the UK, a number of high-profile cases of improper disclosures by banks and utilities and by NHS bodies have been taken up by the Commissioner, have attracted national newspaper attention and the Commissioner's interpretations of the law have been successfully enforced. Yet public scepticism has not abated.

Do we then have less privacy than our predecessors? In many ways, of course, we have more. Village life is a setting in which everyone knows everyone else's business. Data protection laws were simply unavailable to consumers in most countries before about 1970. We have no statistics with which to make comparisons, but it is at least reasonable to think that such laws have curbed disclosures between companies and agencies. Encryption and pseudonymous identifiers are powerful new tools. On the other hand, of course, we live in 'surveillance societies' (Gandy, 1993; Lyon, 1994, 2001) in which vast quantities of data are captured about us at almost every moment of our lives by every organisation with which we deal and many which we do not know to be dealing with us, and are analysed, matched, mined and inferences drawn from them on an industrial scale. If we have curbed disclosure, we have at best channelled use and provided means for the legitimation of the collection of personal information.

Life chances

The personal information economy is reshaping the lives of consumers in ways that run far beyond the concerns of data protection or indeed individual information privacy.

Above all else, the records that organisations hold on each of us are exercises in classification and sorting (6 with Jupp, 2001; Lyon, 2003a). For the purposes of banks, insurance companies, employers, benefits agencies or child protection teams or indeed retail companies, the most important task for a client record is to indicate the assessment of risk that we each present to them in their dealings with us, and the assessment of the value that we are believed to represent, for on this basis they make their decisions about what they will offer us, what they will deny us, how they will treat us. The ways in which they define their systems of classification, how they handle 'borderline' cases, and what kinds of classifications they are prohibited by law from taking into account (for example, information about race, religion, or for some purposes gender, disability, or trades union membership; or, under data protection law, information that is 'too' old) therefore have huge consequences for our life chances. Moreover, the investments they make in those systems define the degree to which the classifications are institutionalised (Zerubavel, 1991; Douglas and Hull, 1992; Gandy, 1993; Bowker and Star, 1999).

To some degree, of course, companies and public services have always worked in this way, as Mary and Joseph knew when they fled Herod's Census and his related policies on childcare. The 'redlining' of areas within which banks and building societies would not grant mortgages was common in the 1950s and 1960s and the subject of some protest. The coming of the personal information economy has, however, brought about qualitative changes. The capacity of contemporary information technologies to process huge quantities of data, and to handle much more finely grained classification systems has meant an end to the crude redlining approaches of some decades ago. Technologies available now enable banks and insurance companies to tailor interest rates, extent of coverage and premia much more precisely to their assessment of the risk that individuals present to them, either using tens or even hundreds of thousands of categories or simply distinct calculations using algorithms for each individual case. In the name of 'customer relationship management', data mining techniques are now in use that enable huge masses of data to be analysed very quickly to support individualised decision making (Gandy, 2002; Danna and Gandy, 2002; Rygielski et al, 2002). In the retail sector, too, the availability of fully identified purchasing data from loyalty card systems enables the careful targeting of offers to households, not only on the basis of their preferences as they are revealed by their buying, but also on the basis of their postcode and certain other key indicator purchases that reveal a good deal about their income and wealth. As retail companies both themselves offer financial services or go into partnership with financial services even in some loyalty card schemes, the possibilities for ever more tightly individualised offers are increasing[6]. Banks, insurance companies, other new kinds of financial services companies and the credit rating companies from which they take and to which they provide personal data are increasingly central in the personal information economy, because their determinations are used by many other companies too.

Second, developments in miniaturisation and information storage have largely ended the need to dispose of older data for reasons of space. Therefore, organisations are less likely to 'forget', and perhaps therefore also to 'forgive' behaviour by individuals in their past, and may continue to take account of such information for longer periods than previously (6 with Jupp, 2001; Blanchette and Johnson, 2002). Of course, data retention longer than is necessary for purpose would be a breach of data protection principles, but it is often difficult to determine from the notified purposes just how long it really is necessary to retain data.

The consequences of these developments are still uncertain. If indeed longer memories lead to less forgiving decision making, then this may well have an effect on the chances of upward social mobility. In the UK and many other countries, rates of social mobility seem to have fallen in recent decades in any case, for a variety of reasons perhaps including falling average rates of economic growth, higher levels of competition, rising credentialism in educational qualifications, the capacity of the middle class to protect their less bright children from experiencing downward mobility (6, 2001), house prices rising in real terms over decades, increasing urban congestion, and so on. As these big determinants of social mobility afford less scope than in previous decades, the role of these 'passport' services in assessing individuals' credit, mortgages, insurance and employment liability becomes more important in defining the patterns of mobility within the reduced overall rate. If they choose to use their more detailed personal profiles to support less 'forgiving' determinations, then both the distribution and perhaps the rate of social mobility may be still more adversely affected.

Recent debates about whether, how far, when, and under what terms insurance companies might be allowed to ask for, require, and take account of genetic testing data, and the risk of the emergence of a 'genetic underclass', are in essence only extensions of this general social policy concern.

At the more micro level, there are reasons to be concerned about the impacts of the ways geo-demographic profiling data systems place great weight on postcodes in determining our status. It is true, of course, that from a person's postcode, an analyst in possession of even fully anonymised geo-demographic data can tell a good deal about their likely income, wealth, employment status, household size, and so on. However, as people become aware of this fact, they have incentives to behave differently and in ways that reinforce both limited social mobility and social exclusion. For if one finds that having an address in a given area attracts a lower credit rating or higher insurance premia or reduced cover, then one has good reason to leave that area as soon as one's income rises sufficiently to make it affordable to do so, even if that might mean paying a higher proportion of one's income in housing costs. This can quickly lead to the spiralling downward of areas, as those left behind are progressively less affluent and now lack social ties to better-off neighbours, which we know also matter for social mobility (Wilson, 1997).

It is not only through organisational decision making about

individuals or households partly on geographical grounds that the personal information economy directly affects life chances. When large retail corporations carry out investment appraisals on proposals for opening up new outlets in particular areas, they pay particular attention to what they know from their own data – for example, from loyalty card data from outlets in immediately surrounding areas where they already have outlets – and from data acquired from geo-demographic profiling tools, in order to estimate comparative profitability. The 'food deserts' that mark some inner city areas, in which no large supermarket chains are prepared to invest, are in part the product of this kind of detailed mining of large banks of personal data. Such areas typically slide downhill in many ways.

Perhaps none of this might matter if one effect of the availability of these data were that other companies or specialist divisions of generalist companies were better able to focus on 'downmarket' consumers and areas. To some extent, perhaps, there are some optimistic signs. Some high street banks have shown themselves willing to extend some categories of lending to people whom previously they abandoned to the sub-prime specialist lending sector. In many other fields, and especially in retail and insurance, however, there is little sign that the personal information economy is empowering the downmarket sector in ways that might offset the incentives to concentrate on people and areas that present the best risks. In the personal information economy, the risks that we present to large organisations as consumers, employees or citizens constitute the measure of our 'merit', and the basis of a distinct kind of meritocracy. This meritocracy is, actuarially, vastly 'fairer' than were the crude systems of redlining that it replaced. The question about it concerns not its actuarial unfairness but rather, 'how unforgiving and rigid do we want that meritocracy to be?'.

Companies have of course always sought to limit their risk, and, within some limits, no doubt it is entirely reasonable that they should. The advent of the personal information economy has increased both their capability for reducing their exposure and the efficiency with which they can do so, effectively transferring more risk to consumers as a consequence of knowing those consumers much better. The result may or may not be more profitable – that may depend on just how congested the market becomes in serving people who present the best risks. A likely consequence seems, however, to be a marked increase in the rigidity of our society, as consumers have to compete much more fiercely for the expensive goods and services used as the classificatory passports to the reduced numbers of chances for social mobility. For at the heart of the personal information economy is the drive to increase profitability in conditions of increased competition, specifically by reducing risk, rather than by extending risk-taking into new markets. Indeed, in general, the contemporary economy increasingly seals off risk-taking activity into quite separate institutions – venture capital firms, specialist insurers, separately financed companies, specialist protected labour market institutions backed by statutory and charitable funds, and so on – from those which service mainstream markets and for which risk-reduction is strategically central.

Claims

In response both to the privacy risks and risks of growing rigidity in the allocation of life chances, consumers and their advocates have advanced their claims to protection and limitation using a variety of concepts.

Ideas of confidentiality achieved legal recognition in the 19th century in common law systems. However, it is a strictly limited notion, constraining only third-party disclosures and leaving collection and use of data untouched.

Data protection is today the most common framework for defining legal restrictions broadly on the manner in which the personal information economy should operate. Always a misnomer – since the aim is to protect people, not information – it is also less a single concept than a rubric for a set of principles of governance (see Raab, Chapter Two, this volume). Moreover, as we saw above, although it does address collection, data protection law has been much less invasive in its regulation of the quantity and detail of profiling than it has been in dealing with unwarranted disclosures.

Picking up concepts in German constitutional jurisprudence, it has been argued that individuals should have a 'right of informational self-determination', or a right to determine the use and disclosure of data about themselves, which can be limited only in specified ways or else for given purposes. In practice, of course, this general principle amounts only to a general presumption, and the exemptions and limitations on the 'right' are as great in Germany as in most European counties. For example, a German can no more invoke the right as a defence to a charge of trying to falsify their tax records or driving licence than a British citizen could invoke the 1998 Human Rights Act in those circumstances. The main effect of the constitutional court's use of the concept has been to give constitutional, and not merely statutory, status to the right of subject access, or the right to know what is held about one and consent where statute requires this in any case. We do not and cannot 'own' data about us held by organisations in the same way that we own our household effects, with full rights to amend or destroy them.

Another version of the concept of self-determination is the claim sometimes made that data protection regulation would be unnecessary if all organisations had to pay individual consumers for the rights to collect, analyse, match, mine, store and disclose their personal information, for then, it is suggested, each of us would set the price on our personal information that reflects our need for income or reduced prices for goods and services and our valuation of our information (Cairncross, 1997)[7]. One problem with this is that almost none of us knows the true value of our information, not least because companies do not necessarily know it in advance of collecting and experimenting with data. More practically, the numbers who would not trade, and would instead opt out, might be sufficiently great to threaten the critical mass of many commercial data sets. Moreover, putting a price or an incentive on consent might reduce the degree to which that consent is genuine and voluntary. Indeed, one might actually feel that an organisation was *less* trustworthy in handling one's personal information if the only assurance it could offer was that the organisation had bought the rights to it. In monopoly settings, of course, prices offered might be very low indeed and well below the true value. It also raises issues of equality since if the poor were sufficiently confident to charge for their information, they would charge less: high levels of differential pricing might not be generally acceptable.

The concept of privacy remains perhaps the key item in popular vocabulary by which consumers conceive the ways they might want to see regulation of the personal information economy. Even apart from the near impossibility of defining it or even delimiting the human or consumer interests in it, it remains unsatisfactory. Rooted in considerations of the limited accountability of the individual, the concept of privacy does not really address the social policy questions to which contemporary systems of classification and risk assessment give rise. For example, when those opposed to permitting life insurance companies in Britain campaigned for an extension of the industry moratorium on requiring or taking account of data from genetic tests, they did so in the name of privacy, as did those in the US who secured some state-level laws to that effect. But privacy considerations alone are threads too slender on which to hang a convincing argument for greater risk pooling in the commercial insurance sector than would be warranted by strict actuarial fairness. In the same way, privacy arguments seem to offer little to those who want to object to differential interest rates or to postcode discrimination in supermarket investment. Social policy arguments cannot be credibly grounded on civil liberties considerations alone. Finally, there is a presumption that privacy is something in which we all share a more or less general interest. Yet the big distributional questions about the consequences of the personal information economy for mobility, meritocracy, equality and social rigidity are ones in which, for example, rich and poor groups of consumers have sharply conflicting interests: indeed, the advent of the personal information economy has brought those conflicts into starker relief.

It seems likely that in the coming decades, the vocabularies by which we debate the regulation of the personal information economy will become more diversified. In particular, we shall need much more precise ethical concepts with which to debate the informational issues of equity, rigidity and merit, and with which to frame rival principles for the allocation of risk to those of actuarial fairness.

Prospects

It is reasonable to assume that, short of a general economic collapse in the West, the personal information economy will define consumers' experience in the 21st century, and that its effects will become steadily more far-reaching in this century as they did in the second half of the last. Indeed, it has brought great and undoubted benefits to many consumers.

In many commentators, however, the phenomenon has elicited either impotent rage against an economic or technological order they see as destroying all hope for privacy, or, which is but the obverse of the same coin, a fatalistic resignation that 'privacy is history'. Both reactions seem misplaced.

First, consumer organisation is a growing power across the developed world. If much of the 20th century was marked by total wars between nations and class conflicts within them, the 21st seems set to be marked by terrorist conflicts internationally around ethnicity, 'culture' and religion, and also by conflicts between producer and consumer interests in an economic sphere itself increasingly transnationalised. Mass and organised consumer protest against disclosures has, in recent years, forced major global corporations such as Lotus, Microsoft and Doubleclick to apologise and reverse course; there have also been cases where such companies have made out-of-court settlements to individual plaintiffs. In other areas far from privacy concerns, such as environmental impact or labour standards, companies like Shell, McDonald's and Nike have come under huge consumer pressure. It is true that consumer movements remain less organised, less united, less powerful and less capable of imposing sustained sanctions on companies and especially governments than were the trades unions at the height of their power to disrupt markets in the 1920s or at their most legally protected in the 1970s. Like trades union action and every other kind of popular protest against the prevailing form of economic activity and governance, consumer counter-mobilisation is subject to cycles of waxing and waning (Hirschman, 1982). Such movements do not overthrow economic orders, but can sometimes successfully insist on more effective regulation against particular risks.

A certain conventional wisdom has grown up in recent writings about what is still too often thought of as 'the information society', that conflicts over privacy will be central lines of fracture in the 21st century. To be sure, privacy conflicts will continue to be important: they are in many ways the artefact of the emergence of the personal information economy. Yet the claim of unique centrality seems too close to a linear extrapolation from the battles of today to be entirely plausible. The personal information economy came to maturity in the context of a global programme of deregulation, opening up of markets and the transfer of risk away from taxpayers to consumers and workers and, to a lesser extent, investors. The result in much of the West, where there was still a working class benefiting from protection, was growing inequality: in much of the South, there are signs of the reverse, for liberalisation tends to benefit the absolutely poor in poor countries[8]. It has taken a full 30 years for signs of an egalitarian backlash to develop against this liberalisation, but it is now expressed in anti-globalisation protests, in a variety of environmental and animal rights movements and in the burgeoning of political solidarity grounded in religions. Just as the great global liberalisation of the 19th century was rolled back by the tide of nationalism (Held et al, 1999; Hirst and Thompson, 1999), so today counter-currents are beginning to emerge (Castells, 1997). Liberalisation has been at the heart of the agenda for the use of personal information to produce ever smaller risk pools and ultimately to individualise risk entirely and transfer it to consumers, and actuarial fairness has been its core normative concept. Its core framing of individual information issues has been around specific injustices – arguing that more accurate profiling would actually reduce those risks, not increase them – and inconvenience – arguing that technological fixes such as real time online subject access would reduce these problems.

If we are to expect counter-currents against liberalisation generally, then I believe that we should expect that, when they show up in the organisation of consumer movements in the coming decades, they will focus on the distributional issues of mobility, rigidity, the extent of forgiveness in decision making and the extent to which the use of personal information permits solidarity in the consumption of the systems of protection that define our life chances. Such movements tend to frame individual information issues as being at least as much around dignity and control as they are about justice or convenience. It seems unlikely that in such a setting, consumer activists will choose to continue to rely exclusively on the relatively limited concepts of justice and 'fair information principles', although these will no doubt be important in the narrow politics of privacy, especially in the US (Culnan and Bies, 2003), where the prevailing political culture constrains the scope for other kinds of politics, except in religious and environmental fields.

Even if the liberalisation of risk and its basis in the use of personal information is curtailed in some respects, it seems unlikely that the great economic transnationalisation of the late 20th century will be reversed. In response to the growth in transnational flows of personal information, the nature of information regulation has changed from the early years of national data protection authorities focusing principally on their national markets and national consumer organisations. Regulation is itself increasingly transnationalised, through the European Union (EU), in the EU's 'Safe Harbor' agreement with the US, and more informally through the councils of the Organisation for Economic Co-operation and Development (OECD) and the International Conference of Data Protection Commissioners with its private online communications system for coordination between members (6, 2002b). It remains to be seen how far the regulation of the social policy questions about equity and solidarity can be and will be transnationalised in the same, partially 'bottom-up' way.

In sum, then, it seems plausible that the political conflicts around the collection, use and disclosure of consumers' personal information will become more diverse and less focused than they are today on narrow questions of privacy and also more developed around the big distributional issues about the impacts of the personal information economy, but conducted at increasingly transnational level. If these speculations are even roughly right, then they present major challenges for businesses, for regulators, and indeed for consumer movement organisations, which will have to work in quite new ways.

Notes

[1] Subjective concerns and objective interests – if interests are indeed objective, which is greatly contested – may not of course coincide. This is not the place to enter the quagmire that is sociologists', philosophers' and lawyers' debate about 'the' meaning of privacy. Those

who have the stamina for it might start with Margulis (2003); Westin (1967); Schoeman (1992); Wacks (1989); DeCew (1997); Michael (2004); Feldman (1997).

[2] My argument there was that these were distinct objective kinds of risks. I have since reconsidered this view: I now think that these should be regarded as subjective frames with which people perceive a wide variety of privacy risks. However, I continue to take the view that some privacy risks are much *more readily* framed as, for example, injustice or indignity risks than others: this point is developed below. That is to say, perception of risk is rarely entirely divorced from legal or scholarly (which I treat, for the present purpose, as 'objective') classifications. The argument was recast in: Performance and Innovation Unit (PIU) (now the Prime Minister's Strategy Unit) (2002); in 6 (2002c); and in 6 (2005).

[3] There are other ways of framing privacy risk, but I have argued that the other principal categories of frames are more rarely found among consumers and are more likely to be found among, for example, police officers, data mining staff, civil servants responsible for policy or for handling personal data in order to identify potential abusers of services, or among privacy activists. See PIU (2002); 6 (2002c).

[4] It is common, following Westin's work, to conduct and analyse data from public opinion surveys in the US with the Harris Equifax organisation over several decades, to distinguish between the privacy unconcerned, privacy pragmatists and privacy fundamentalists: see, for example, Harris Interactive and Westin (2002). However, this taxonomy is rather coarse, not least because in most surveys designed and analysed using this approach, the vast majority of the population turn out to be pragmatists, but this obscures important differences in their patterns of risk perception, their patterns of trust, and the ways in which they would and would not be prepared to see some privacy concerns overridden by other imperatives. For critiques, see 6 with Lasky and Fletcher (1998). On patterns of risk perception, see 6 (2002a); PIU (2002); and 6 (2002c).

[5] These data are collected in Britain in surveys conducted in most years for the Information Commissioner, and summarised in the Commissioner's annual reports, available at www.dataprotection.gov.uk

[6] Most schemes, such as the UK's Nectar consortium, say that financial and purchasing data are not pooled between retail and banking companies, but rather little is known about the way in which aggregated data are shared and whether they are coded down, for example, to the postcode level.

[7] Ironically, only three years later, Cairncross published a book arguing that privacy was doomed in any case, and that its death was a price worth paying for reduced levels of crime, suggesting that she had limited confidence in her own earlier prescription (Cairncross, 2000).

[8] Liberalisation opens up the Western markets to commodities that poor people in poor countries can produce more cheaply than poor people in rich countries: it is for this reason that agricultural protectionism is the most damaging barrier to globalisation. Clearly, other policies have to be in place in order to enable the poorest to take advantages of the opportunities: see OECD (2003); Killick (2001). For the general argument, see Legrain (2002); Jay (2000); Micklethwait and Wooldridge (2000).

References

6, P. (1998) *The future of privacy, volume 1: Private life and public policy*, London: Demos.
6, P. (2001) 'Profiles, networks, risk and hoarding: public policy and the dynamics of social mobility and social cohesion', Paper specially commissioned for the Performance and Innovation Unit seminar on 'Social Mobility', London, 20 March.
6, P. (2002a) 'Strategies for reassurance: public concerns about privacy and data sharing in government', London: PIU, Cabinet Office (available at www.number10.gov.uk/piu/privacy/papers/perri6.pdf).

6, P. (2002b) 'Global digital communications and the prospects for transnational regulation', in D. Held and A. McGrew (eds) *Governing globalisation: Power, authority and global governance*, Cambridge: Polity Press, and Oxford: Blackwell, pp 145-70.

6, P. (2002c) 'Who wants privacy protection, and what do they want?', *Journal of Consumer Behaviour*, vol 2, no 1, pp 80-100.

6, P. (2003) *Entitlement cards: Benefits, privacy and data protection risks, costs and wider social implications*, Wilmslow: Office of the Information Commissioner.

6, P. (2005) 'What's in a frame? Social organisation, risk perception and the sociology of knowledge', *Journal of Risk Research*, vol 8, no 2, pp 91-118.

6, P. and Jupp, B. (2001) *Divided by information? The 'digital divide' and the implications of the new meritocracy*, London: Demos.

6, P. with Lasky, K. and Fletcher, A. (1998) *The future of privacy, volume 2: The public use of private information*, London: Demos.

Bennett, C.J. (1992) *Regulating privacy: Data protection and public policy in Europe and the United States*, Ithaca, NY: Cornell University Press.

6, P., Bellamy, C. and Raab, C.D. (forthcoming) 'Joined-up government and privacy in the United Kingdom: managing tensions between data protection and social policy, Parts I and II', *Public Administration*.

Bennett, C.J. and Raab, C.D. (2003) *The governance of privacy: Policy instruments in global perspective*, Aldershot: Ashgate.

Blanchette, J.-F. and Johnson, D.G. (2002) 'Data retention and the panoptic society: the social benefits of forgetfulness', *The Information Society*, vol 18, no 1, pp 33-45.

Bowker, G.C. and Star, S.L. (1999) *Sorting things out: Classification and its consequences*, Cambridge, MA: Massachusetts Institute of Technology Press.

Cairncross, F. (1997) 'Privatising privacy', *Analysis*, programme transcript, London: BBC Radio Four.

Cairncross, F. (2000) *The death of distance: How the communications revolution will change our lives*, London: Texere.

Castells, M. (1997) *The power of identity: volume II: The information age: Economy, society and culture*, Oxford: Blackwell.

Culnan, M.J. and Bies, R.J. (2003) 'Consumer privacy: balancing economic and justice considerations', *Journal of Social Issues*, vol 59, no 2, pp 323-42.

Danna, A. and Gandy, O.H. (2002) 'All that glitters is not gold: digging beneath the surface of data mining', *Journal of Business Ethics*, vol 4, pp 373-86.

Davies, S. (1996) *Big Brother: Britain's web of surveillance and the new technological order*, London: Pan.

DeCew, J.W. (1997) *Privacy: Law, ethics and the rise of technology*, Ithaca, NY: Cornell University Press.

Douglas, M. and Hull, D. (eds) (1992) *How classification works: Nelson Goodman among the social sciences*, Edinburgh: Edinburgh University Press.

Farr, L.M. (2002) 'Whose files are they anyway? Privacy issues for the fundraising profession', *International Journal of Nonprofit and Voluntary Sector Marketing*, vol 7, no 4, pp 361-7.

Feldman, D. (1997) 'Privacy related rights: their social value', in P. Birks (ed) *Privacy and loyalty*, Oxford: Oxford University Press.

Gandy, O.H. Jr (1993) *The panoptic sort: A political economy of personal information*, Boulder, CO: Westview Press.

Gandy, O.H. Jr (2002) 'Data mining and surveillance in the post-9.11 environment', Paper presented at the International Association for Media and Communications Research Conference, Barcelona (available at www.asc.upenn.edu/usr/ogandy/IAMCRdatamining.pdf).

Gellman, R. (2002) 'Perspectives on privacy and terrorism: all is not lost yet', *Government Information Quarterly*, vol 19, no 3, pp 255-64.

Hacking, I. (1990) *The taming of chance*, Cambridge: Cambridge University Press.

Harris Interactive and Westin, A. (2002) *The Harris poll*, New York, NY: Harris Interactive.

Hawkins, K. and Thomas, J.M. (eds) (1984) *Enforcing regulation*, Boston, MA: Kluwer-Nijhoff.

Held, D., McGrew, A., Goldblatt, D. and Perraton, J. (1999) *Global transformations: Politics, economics and culture*, Cambridge: Polity Press.

Hirschman, A.O. (1982) *Shifting involvements: Private interest and public action*, Oxford: Blackwell.

Hirst, P. and Thompson, G. (1996) (2nd edn, 1999) *Globalisation in question*, Cambridge: Polity Press.

Hutter, B.M. (1996) *Compliance: Regulation and enforcement*, Oxford: Oxford University Press.

Jay, P. (2000) *The wealth of man*, London: Weidenfeld and Nicholson.

Killick, T. (2001) 'Globalisation and the rural poor', *Development Policy Review*, vol 19, no 2, pp 155-80.

Legrain, P. (2002) *Open world: The truth about globalisation*, London: Abacus.

Lyon, D. (1994) *The electronic eye: The rise of surveillance society*, Cambridge: Polity Press.

Lyon, D. (2001) *Surveillance society: Monitoring everyday life*, Buckingham: Open University Press.

Lyon, D. (ed) (2003a) *Surveillance as social sorting: Privacy, risk and digital discrimination*, London: Routledge.

Lyon, D. (2003b) *Surveillance after September 11*, Cambridge: Polity Press.

Margulis, S.T. (1977) 'Conceptions of privacy: current status and next steps', *Journal of Social Issues*, vol 33, no 3, pp 5-21.

Margulis, S.T. (2003) 'Privacy as a social issue and behavioural concept', *Journal of Social Issues*, vol 59, no 2, pp 243-61.

Michael, J. (2004) *Privacy and human rights: An international and comparative study with special reference to developments in information technology*, Aldershot: Dartmouth.

Micklethwait, J. and Wooldridge, A. (2000) *A future perfect: The challenge and hidden promise of globalisation*, London: Heinemann.

OECD (Organisation for Economic Co-operation and Development) (2003) *Globalisation, poverty and inequality*, Paris: OECD.

PIU (Performance and Innovation Unit) (2002) *Privacy and data-sharing: The way forward for public services*, London: Cabinet Office.

Porter, D. (1999) *Health, civilisation and the state: A history of public health from ancient to modern times*, London: Routledge.

Regan, P. (2003) 'Privacy and commercial use of personal data: policy developments in the United States', *Journal of Contingencies and Crisis Management*, vol 11, no 1, pp 12-18.

Royal Society Study Group (1992) *Risk: Analysis, perception and management*, London: Royal Society.

Rygielski, C., Wang, J.C. and Yen, D.C. (2002) 'Data mining techniques for customer relationship management', *Technology in Society*, vol 24, no 4, pp 483–502.

Schoeman, F. (1992) *Privacy and social freedom*, Cambridge: Cambridge University Press.

Stern, P.C. and Fineberg, H.V. (eds) (1996) *Understanding risk: Informing decisions in a democratic society*, Report of the Committee on Risk Characterisation to the Commission on Behavioral and Social Sciences and Education of the National Research Council, Washington, DC: National Academy Press.

Wacks, R. (1989) *Personal information: Privacy and the law*, Oxford: Oxford University Press.

Westin, A. (1967) *Privacy and freedom*, New York, NY: Athenaeum.

Wilson, W.J. (1997) *When work disappears: The world of the new urban poor*, New York, NY: Alfred A. Knopf.

Zerubavel, E. (1991) *The fine line: Making distinctions in everyday life*, Chicago, IL: University of Chicago Press.

2

Regulatory provisions for privacy protection

Charles Raab

Introduction

The protection of personal data has moved higher on the policy agenda in business and the public sector in recent years. In part, this reflects a realisation in many countries and international organisations that an apprehensive, albeit poorly informed, public is less likely to embrace online transactions in electronic commerce and electronic government than the proponents of these innovations would wish (Raab, 1998, 2001). Insofar as the processing of personal data is also construed as a privacy issue, data protection goes beyond the instrumental value of protection for winning public trust for e-commerce and e-government (and e-voting as well), and bears closely upon central human rights and human values. This, too, has elevated privacy's status on policy agendas.

Innovations in selling goods and providing public services using electronic means, as well as in electronic payments and other systems, generate a need to authenticate and verify individual identities, entitlements and personal circumstances. Workplace and public-place surveillance through a variety of modern information and communication technologies (ICTs) brings to the surface new conflicts over anonymity, identity and proper behaviour, threatening often highly prized values and conceptions of citizenship, labour, the self and society. Privacy is associated with dignity, selfhood and personality – the importance of which, however, is questioned in postmodernist debate – all of which are deemed to be potentially at risk when personal data are not protected, although privacy can be considered a social and collective value as well as an individual one. Its erosion diminishes society; its protection is a matter of public policy as well as practical activity on many fronts.

Regan (1995, 2002) has gone the furthest to develop the theory of privacy as a value for entities beyond the person (see also Schoeman, 1992). Regan (1995, p 221) argues that privacy serves important functions beyond those it performs for a given person, so that there are social interests in privacy that do not depend on the individual's subjective perception of its value. As a collective value, privacy cannot easily be provided to one person without its being enjoyed by others, and a certain minimum degree of privacy may be indivisible because of the way information and communication systems are designed. Beyond this, individual privacy may only be truly achievable in a society in which privacy is considered socially valuable and which reflects that esteem in its collective decision making. A further move would be to consider privacy not only as a collective or social value but also as an *egalitarian* one (Bennett and Raab, 2003, ch 2).

Unequal distribution of privacy could be seen as a societal issue, to be addressed by remedial or preventive policy options and by considering who should be responsible for adopting them. But privacy-as-social-policy has not yet seriously seeped into the bloodstream of the privacy policy community. Therefore, the 'social democracy of privacy protection' remains out of focus, although Lyon (2001) highlights the way in which social sorting creates or reinforces situations of inclusion and exclusion, advantages and deprivations, and discrimination.

The inroads made on privacy in 'surveillance societies' (Flaherty, 1989), perhaps especially since '9/11' (Lyon, 2003), leave privacy protection in a fragile condition. Beyond the realm of national and international security, privacy and its associated values are widely perceived to be under threat from the application of ICTs that process personal information on a more intensive and extensive scale than ever before, especially with the advent of the online environment. The increasing use of ICTs in a host of governmental functions, and in the worlds of work, leisure and consumption, brings new dilemmas for privacy protection. The conventional safeguards confront powerful public policy and commercial interests that press for more personal data to be collected, analysed and shared.

In the public sector, these pressures stem from policy initiatives to combat terrorism, illegal asylum seeking, child abuse, and benefit and financial fraud, among other objectives. Innovative applications of ICTs in public transport, health, social services and policing, sometimes involving DNA databases, video surveillance, biometric tools and identity cards or documents, have implications for privacy. The UK is typical of many countries in that its policy and administrative agenda seeks to improve public services in ways that entail information policies featuring data sharing and data matching, as discussed elsewhere in this volume. The improved delivery of public services through 'joined-up', 'information-age' government also relies on the increased sharing and matching of personal information (Bellamy et al, Chapter Five, this volume); the reconciling of this with the policy and statutory aim of privacy protection has been the focus of recent government deliberation (PIU, 2002). These are among the most prominent UK policy departures that, whatever their good intentions, may also limit the extent to which privacy claims and rights can be effectively asserted. The limitations are partly practical, but are also moral and political in nature, given that privacy is often construed as flying in the face of democratically elected government; but that is only one reading of the relationship between privacy and democracy (Raab, 1997a).

In the private sector – although the distinction between the private and public sector is blurred in many cases   database marketing, consumer profiling and targeting are some of the leading business practices that raise acute issues for the protection of identifiable personal information. The commercial value of collections of personal data, especially when processed with sophisticated analytical tools, is increasingly realised as a major business asset. Especially when finely categorised and profiled, lists of potential customers enter lucrative markets among sellers of goods and services (Gandy, 1993). The effectiveness of established regulatory principles and practices in safeguarding individuals against the threats of privacy invasion now meets novel challenges. The capability of new wireless and mobile technologies to track and monitor individuals in their various roles as consumers (as well as tracking the goods they handle and purchase), employees, communicators, motorists, pedestrians and sports fans is perhaps establishing a new battlefield for many privacy conflicts of the future. Camera phones are an example of how new surveillance or privacy issues proliferate rapidly: by 2006, an estimated two thirds of all telephones sold in Europe will have cameras embedded in them (Harvey, 2003).

New situations are therefore created in which understandings and practices concerning a range of issues addressed – however inadequately – by 'first generation' laws and systems of data protection are now comprehensively challenged. Moreover, the global transmission of personal data for commerce, the administration of public services and law enforcement presents novel problems alongside older ones that have not yet been surmounted. These relate in part to jurisdictional uncertainty in terms of the application of legal remedies for complaints. They also relate to the often incomprehensible complexity of information processes that face the consumer or citizen who is concerned about what happens to his or her data, where to go to find out, and how to obtain redress of grievances or harms; many surveys reveal the widespread but understandable ignorance of large proportions of the public about information systems, processes and flows (for example, MORI, 2003).

In the UK as elsewhere, data protection holds a precarious position in this context of rapid change, and doubt is cast, both generally in society and within the policy and regulatory communities for data protection, upon the robustness and efficacy of the principles and protective instruments that have constituted information privacy regimes, and that have become an important feature of the relationship between business or government, on the one hand, and, on the other, individuals as customers, consumers and citizens.

Principles of privacy protection

The importance of privacy protection concerning personal information has been realised in the policy agendas of many states. It has also gained a position of some salience in the information processes of business and government, perhaps especially concerning electronic transactions, and in the consciousness of consumers (or citizens) and the organisations that support their claims and rights to information privacy. More specifically, over the past 30 or more years, a consensus has emerged on the rules for the proper safeguarding of personal information (Bennett, 1992). A common set of 'fair information principles' has been propounded in international instruments (CoE, 1981; OECD, 1981; CEC, 1995), and is reflected in the legislation (for example the UK's 1998 Data Protection Act [DPA]) and standards or codes of practice (for example CSA, 1996) that form part of the practical regimes of information privacy protection around the world. These principles, with variations in number, wording, and emphasis in different documents, set forth norms for responsible processing, where processing is widely defined to include the collection, organisation, use, retention, disclosure and destruction of personal information. To paraphrase the version of the principles incorporated in the 1998 DPA, a data controller (that is, one who processes the personal data of living individuals) must ensure such data are:

- obtained and processed fairly and lawfully, and processed subject to general conditions, either under consent, or under necessity, for a limited number of general reasons;
- used only for the specified and lawful purpose(s) for which the data are collected and used;
- adequate, relevant and not excessive for the specified purpose(s);
- accurate and, where necessary, kept up to date;
- retained no longer than necessary for the specified purpose(s);
- processed in ways that respect the data subject's rights, including the right of subject access (the right to see information held about one);
- subject to appropriate technical and organisational measures to prevent unauthorised and unlawful processing, accidental loss of, destruction of or damage to the information; and
- not transferred outside the European Economic Area (EEA), except to countries where levels of data protection are deemed adequate.

Agreement on common principles, however, has not obviated contentiousness, as well as differences, in the making and implementation of policy in this field, both within one country and transnationally. Severe disagreements have arisen because the concept of privacy is a philosophical quagmire and has been variously construed (Westin, 1967; Schoeman, 1992). Beyond that, regulators and the regulated have contested the practical embodiment of the principles in specific rules governing data processing. Whether, for example, data subjects should have to opt-in or opt-out to the processing of their data; how long is too long with regard to the retention of data; and when the sharing of data is permissible across public sector organisations (a question of supreme importance in the aftermath of the 2003 Soham murders case), are only some of the grey areas in the principles and in the law that is predicated on them. It is a sobering thought that the resolution of these dilemmas and the clarification of ambiguous rules may not only be crucially important for the working of the economy and of government, or for the conduct of private lives (including the fun-and-games of camera phones), but for the safeguarding of lives themselves.

What constitutes 'adequate' data protection in non-EEA countries is another area of contestation; it also points up the difficulties that have arisen because of divergence across states in their implementation of the common principles (Bennett, 1992; Bennett and Raab, 2003). In the European Union (EU), a major attempt was made to narrow these differences through the harmonising effect of a Directive (CEC, 1995) binding on member states and exerting influence on the rest of the world in respect of transactions involving the personal information of EU citizens. The most prominent effect of the Directive's external reach was the 'Safe Harbor' agreement, hammered out between the EU and the US. Safe Harbor provides that, in the absence of general data protection legislation, US companies subscribing to a set of rules under the enforcement of the Federal Trade Commission (FTC) are deemed to provide adequate protection. Yet the harmonisation and international effects of the Directive may prove to be short lived and less powerful than was desired, testifying to the difficulty of overcoming legal, cultural, administrative and practical diversity above a certain, and possibly low, level. An important question for the future is whether this level can be raised through processes of transnational regime formation and of normative and practical standardisation, and whether it could be enforceable (Bennett and Raab, 2003).

Instruments of privacy protection

Despite important cross-national divergences in the extent and efficacy of the implementation of information-privacy principles and rules, a great deal has already been achieved through a variety of instruments. The most important international documents of this kind have already been mentioned. For the rest, among the most prominent means of privacy protection are laws, codes of practice and technological solutions, but there is increasing recognition of the important role played by consumer and citizen education as well as social, organisational and political processes, including the activity of privacy-advocates as well as groups devoted to civil liberties and consumers' rights.

Legislation and regulatory agencies

At the level of individual states, comprehensive data protection laws have been regarded as essential, starting with Sweden in 1973 (Bennett and Raab, 2003, Table 5.1). By the turn of the 21st century, legislation could be found in some 40 countries, although not necessarily with the same coverage of types of data processing: for example, there is no general legislation for the private sector in the US, and Canada and Australia have only recently legislated for that sector. In recent years, EU member states, including the UK with its 1998 DPA, have adopted new laws in the light of the Directive, with Greece and Italy legislating for the first time. Countries that entered the EU in 2004 have passed laws based on the Directive. South America as well as the Asia-Pacific region have experienced the spreading adoption of general legislation as well.

Particularly in the US, many have argued that sectoral, rather than general, legislation is a preferable route to follow, as and when necessary. There are, indeed, a great many sectoral laws both in the US and in Europe. However, in the absence of comprehensive legislation, US consumers and citizens are left with a patchwork of protection (Gellman, 1993) that places many kinds of information systems and processes outside the reach of statutory privacy protection unless and until there happens to be a political or populist impetus to create a law to cover a specific situation. This explains the origin of, for example, the sectoral US privacy laws in respect of children using the Internet, video rental records, healthcare, and financial services.

To say that this leaves privacy protection more open to the vagaries of politics and crisis management, rather than establishing it more generally and with deeper roots, is not to be sanguine about the way in which privacy is protected in the host of countries that have followed the route of comprehensive legislation. Specific laws covering sectors or particular information practices, such as data matching and data sharing, could indeed offer a flexible and focused means of protection, but ideally underpinned by general data protection law, and especially by machinery to enforce it. But as with comprehensive laws, oversight and implementation are essential for effectiveness, and thus the role of public supervisory agencies is central, for laws are not self-enforcing and the fostering of a privacy culture needs an authoritative champion (Flaherty, 1989).

In the UK, the Office of the Information Commissioner was created by the 1998 DPA, succeeding the Data Protection Registrar established under the 1984 DPA. The Commissioner performs a range of functions: as ombudsman, investigator, consultant, educator, negotiator, policy adviser and enforcer (Bennett and Raab, 2003, ch 5; Raab, 1993, 1996). The Commissioner is also an interpreter of the law and a giver of guidance on its meaning, as well as on best practice. This is a formidable challenge, for it is generally acknowledged that one of the main drawbacks to effective UK data protection is that the 1998 DPA is complicated, unclear and ambiguous in crucial respects; the Commissioner himself has lamented its unwieldiness and has aimed to simplify its implementation (Information Commissioner, 2004a, pp 9, 24-8). Data protection officers in companies as well as public sector bodies look to the Commissioner for a lead, but this is sometimes not – or cannot be – forthcoming, owing to resource difficulties or to the genuine uncertainty that surrounds many provisions, such that decisions have to be left to the judgement of these practitioners. A lively and sometimes anguished and inconclusive discourse has developed among them in many sectors, as they seek greater certainty about, for example: when to disclose information about students or patients to other organisations seeking it; how to handle confidential references; when and how consent should be obtained from individuals; and how to implement individuals' rights as granted by the Act.

The Commissioner's Office is not the only organisation involved in guidance and interpretation: legal and business consultants, and now the Department for Constitutional Affairs (DCA, 2003), are also sources of advice on best practice and on the meaning of arcane legal provisions. Ultimately, it may fall to the law courts to give definitive rulings, case by case. *Michael John Durant v Financial Services Authority*, heard in the Court of Appeal in 2003, has narrowed the definition of 'personal data' significantly, with potentially deep implications for practice (Information Commissioner, 2004a, pp 43-5, 2004b). The Durant case may serve to relax restrictions on the processing of personal data that is inherent in transactions with customers or citizens, and thus arguably weaken the protection of their privacy by removing, by definition, large amounts of what was hitherto regarded as 'personal data' from regulation, and particularly from access by the individual where the data are not deemed to be held in a 'relevant filing system' owing to the way in which manual files are, or are not, 'structured'.

Varieties of self-regulation

Another major set of instruments can be described as the means by which organisations regulate themselves, rather than following the mandate of legislation. 'Self-regulation' is a general term that covers mainly voluntary practices, including privacy commitments, codes of practice, adherence to standards, and online tokens or 'seals'. It is normally the private sector that is the site of self-regulation, although codes, commitments, and so on are also found in the public sector, where they cover practices such as video surveillance and the online delivery of public services; the government's 'Trust Charter' (PIU, 2002; DCA, 2003), which became the 'Public Service Guarantee' in 2004 concerning data sharing by official agencies, is a UK example of the latter.

Self-regulation can be an adjunct to statutory measures, implementing or supplementing legislation. The voluntary adherence to a code of practice, for example, does not release an organisation or industry from the obligation to comply with applicable laws or free it from external enforcement. However, in other contexts, codes of practice have been promoted in order to avoid or to anticipate legislation. The Safe Harbor illustrates this: a US company may voluntarily subscribe to it, although if it does so, it does not escape possible enforcement by the FTC – although, in the event, this has been a rather weak threat.

Many companies and agencies, online or offline, commit themselves to protect customers' or citizens' personal information. These pledges are often perfunctory, public relations exercises without independent means of verification or sanction. 'Privacy policies' shown on merchants' websites are often of this nature. Yet privacy commitments are arguably a necessary first step, especially if they mean that a company has taken some trouble to become aware of privacy principles and of how the information processing activities used on customers' data may impinge on their privacy. Privacy codes of practice are a step up from this and are the most complex and varied of the range of self-regulatory instruments, with many strong proponents in the business world. Codes enjoin adherence to a set of rules and provide important guidance about good practice based on some version of 'fair information principles'.

Five kinds of privacy code can be identified (Bennett and Raab, 2003, ch 6). The *organisational code* applies to one firm or agency (say, Reader's Digest) that is bounded by a clear organisational structure. Perhaps a more prevalent category is that of the *sectoral code* developed by an industry (say, the British Banking Association) for adoption by their member firms, tailoring general rules to the industry's circumstances. Internationally, sectoral codes have begun to be developed within industries that operate on a global scale (say, the International Airline Transport Association). One drawback is that trade associations do not necessarily represent the whole sector, and may be dominated by one or two large players. Moreover, while some associations apply serious sanctions for non-compliance, others do not, and the public may not be able to tell which is which.

Then there are *functional* codes, which are defined less by the practice in which the organisation is engaged. Direct marketing associations in the UK and in other countries have responded to long-standing concerns about direct marketing by developing privacy codes of practice; such codes have now moved onto the international level. Telephone, mail, and email Preference Services run by these associations allow consumers to remove their names from the members' marketing lists – assuming that consumers know whom to contact to put this into effect. A fourth type, *technological codes*, has developed as new and potentially intrusive technologies have some into view. These codes typically apply to new applications, such as electronic funds transfers, the issuance of debit cards and personal identification numbers. Smart-card technology also lends itself to specific codes. Finally, *professional codes* pertain to information processing professionals, for market and survey researchers (for example, the Market Research Society), and for a range of health- and welfare-related professionals. Professional associations create them, and they can be reinforced by disciplinary measures that could entail a loss of professional reputation. These codes may also be incorporated into larger sets of ethical guidelines and codes of conduct. The National Health Service provides an important illustration of these developments (DH, 2003).

For many organisations and industries, privacy codes have become a favoured method of internal discipline and public reassurance. The EU Directive (Article 27) provides a mechanism for the promulgation of international codes. In the UK, the 1998 DPA empowers the Commissioner to encourage the adoption of codes and allows him to develop them where he thinks fit, although the slow and controverted progress towards a code governing privacy in the workplace, and its elaborateness and complexity, perhaps indicates that codes of practice are not necessarily an easy or quick option.

Privacy codes the world over are variable devices: they have been formulated with different amounts of care and analysis, follow no consistent format, and differ in their procedures for implementation, complaints resolution and communication. In addition, codes operate within complicated and varied sets of incentives in and between sectors, professions and the like. Without an external regulatory framework to impose sanctions for non-compliance, they generally suffer from the reasonable, if not necessarily accurate, public perception that self-regulation may mean little more than self-serving regulation, to the detriment of individual rights. Whether this perception outweighs the value of codes in fostering and maintaining public trust is a question that cannot be answered in general terms.

The adoption of specific privacy standards is relevant here. Many have envisaged the formal development of standards as playing a constructive role in privacy protection, not least in international commerce where required registration to a standard, obliging independent and regular auditing, would provide greater certainty that 'adequate' data protection is being practised by the data-receiving organisation. An information security standard has operated in privacy protection for some years; the International Organization for Standardization Standard (ISO) 17799 was adopted in 2000, preceded by the British Standard BS 7799. In the 1990s, the idea of a more general management standard for the complete set of privacy principles gained in prominence within standards organisations following the emergence of Canada's 'Model Code for the Protection of Personal Information' under the auspices of the Canadian Standards Association (CSA, 1996; Bennett and Raab, 2003, ch 6). It was thought that there could be a threefold strategy: a general data protection standard setting out practical steps to be taken by an organisation for legal compliance; sector-specific initiatives in areas such as health information and human resources management; and task-specific initiatives mainly related to the Internet (Dumortier and Goemans, 2000). But influential multinational firms have been apprehensive about regulatory burdens affecting international trade, and have resisted further development.

Turning more specifically to the online environment, the proliferation of privacy seals as a further means of self-regulation reflects the growing salience of online commercial transactions. Notable schemes have been developed by the TRUSTe organisation (www.truste.org), by the Better Business Bureau Online (www.bbbonline.org), and by WebTrust (www.webstrust.org). By displaying one of these symbols, websites indicate that they have been certified or registered as adhering to certain privacy protection practices and policies, thus enabling customers' informed choice. Once again, customers need to be aware that schemes vary in their stringency, in the nature of any audits, in their dispute resolution provisions, and in their helpfulness to consumer choice. There is as yet no market leader among schemes, and their proliferation may leave consumers confused.

Technological instruments

'Technological determinism' is a largely discredited theoretical assumption. However, if some part of the 'privacy problem' can be shown to be caused by properties inherent in technological design, then technologies could be configured to protect privacy, rather than to invade it; for instance, by designing a piece of equipment to collect no personal information in the transaction process (Chaum, 1992). 'Public-key' or 'asymmetric' cryptography builds anonymity into an information system without reducing its ability to allow identity to be verified (Diffie and Landau, 1998). Thus, technologies themselves are becoming an important privacy instrument, considered by many to be particularly well suited to the global online environment.

These 'privacy-enhancing technologies' (PETs) exist in several forms (as is further discussed by Borking, Chapter Three, in this volume). *Systemic instruments* are produced by the decisions of the engineers who design networks, equipment or computer code, and from technical standards and protocols. These instruments illustrate Reidenberg's (1998) conception of 'Lex informatica' and Lessig's (1999) thesis about the regulatory power of computer code. *Collective instruments* result from government policy; they are policy applications in which government or business builds privacy protection into the technical systems that provide goods and services. Attempts to develop public-key encryption infrastructures for government service delivery, and certain configurations of smart cards, provide examples; another is the 'Privacy Incorporated Software Agent' (PISA), which converts identities into pseudo-identities (Borking and Raab, 2001).

In contrast, *instruments of individual empowerment* require explicit choices by individuals, who activate the PET by choosing to enhance privacy in their online transactions. Proprietary encryption instruments, devices for anonymity and pseudonymity, filtering instruments and privacy management protocols are some examples. The Platform for Privacy Preferences (P3P), constructed by the World Wide Web Consortium (W3C), is the best-known initiative. When individuals use their browsers (enabled with P3P readers) to read the site's privacy policy, they are automatically notified whether the privacy policy matches their preferences, and can decide if they want to transact with the website merchant. One implication of devices of this kind is that, if they were to predominate as the means of online privacy protection, those who can afford to take advantage of PETs, or who are sophisticated users of ICTs, may be better able than others to protect their privacy. In terms of public policy concerning who gets what privacy, how, and the nature of privacy as a value, there is room for debate about the place of individual self-help in a comprehensive privacy regime.

The wide variety of available applications and their variable quality make it difficult to generalise about PETs' effectiveness. It is not sensible to regard PETs as a 'magic bullet' solving the privacy problem, for PETs may be more useful as complements of regulatory or self-regulatory instruments (Bennett and Raab, 2003, pp 153-6). An influential report by the Organisation for Economic Co-Operation and Development (OECD, 2001, p 6) on PETs saw them as helpful, but as "necessarily complementary to other tools (educational, contractual, regulatory, etc)". The OECD (2001, p 25) also took the view that proactive consumers and national law provided some of the necessary conditions for PETs to be effective. PETs may also act as a condition or standard for service delivery, and they may be an alternative to legislation or other forms of regulation, different from them but not necessarily better. They may be necessary, but insufficient, for certain kinds and media of transaction because legal, organisational and cultural conditions cannot be ignored in PET approaches to privacy protection.

Putting the instruments together

A view that prevails is that laws and other instruments, taken singly, are insufficient to protect privacy, and that something other than a monotechnic approach should be the aim. Data processing is complex, dynamic and diverse (Raab, 1993; Kooiman, 2003), thus suggesting the need for 'requisite variety' and the importance of establishing new relationships between state regulation and societal and other forms of privacy protection. Good privacy protection has therefore been seen in terms of several instruments comprising a 'privacy toolkit', a 'mosaic of solutions', or a 'regulatory mix' (for example, Industry Canada, 1994; Cavoukian and Tapscott, 1995).

These are fashionable, but somewhat different, metaphors for combined approaches to data protection. However, they are misleading because they fail to describe the actual or desirable *relationship* among the instruments in practice. These metaphors tend to see each policy instrument as a supplement, complement or substitute for the others, ignoring the question of clashes and compatibilities. In fact, each country's system of data protection relies on a rather more integrated combination of instruments, one that has, however, rarely been rationalised because the instruments emerged empirically and then became incorporated as adjuncts, to one degree or another. In Australia, practical discourse has recently emphasised a 'co-regulatory' approach, involving a statutory context for flexible industry codes of practice, developed in association with the Privacy Commissioner. In the EU, a side effect of the 1995 Directive has been to establish a somewhat clearer way in which each country's supervisory authority can enhance the integration of instruments. The evolution of regulatory practice has also moved towards recognising complex relationships within privacy protection regimes. For example, the UK Information Commissioner, as we saw, has powers in regard to the promotion and promulgation of codes of practice, but is also involved in the processes of governmental policy – and statute formation on proposals where the protection of personal data is at stake. The Commissioner's various roles bring his Office into important, and sometimes mutually supportive, relationships with the media, pressure groups, technology designers and others whose activities, in various ways, affect privacy outcomes; on the other hand, criticism often emanates from these quarters, especially concerning the quality, quantity, and accessibility of guidance to practitioners who have difficult decisions to make.

Reidenberg (1997) describes comprehensive privacy regimes by noting specific interactions among state, business, technical and citizen mechanisms. When writing about 'co-production' (Raab,

1997b), I have observed that the combination of instruments is more than incidental to their effectiveness. This is because, to varying extents, these instruments are interdependent, as their wielders often know and emphasise. Privacy commissioners, for example, are very ready to recognise how important it is to their own work to have a public that is knowledgeable about data protection and willing to bring complaints for investigation. For their part, many privacy advocates want laws that punish those who breach self-regulatory codes. When they resist legislation, self-regulating organisations often profess that the market and customer-controlled PETs will work effectively alongside codes or commitments to give people the privacy they want. These interdependent relations, as well as others that could be explored, suggest that attempts to analyse, and to design, a privacy protection regime must be alert to the synergy that may be achieved in broader and multiple relations within and across jurisdictions, organisations and instruments; but equally, conflicts need to be addressed.

In this context, the role of groups and movements that champion the privacy claims and rights of citizens or consumers is significant in various ways. These include the constant questioning of the adequacy of the panoply of instruments; investigations of what is actually happening in, say, the world of financial services or electronic commerce; surveys of public opinion; intervention in policy and governmental processes and enquiries; consultation with regulatory bodies and standards organisations; publicising abuses; bringing technological expertise to bear; and in a host of other responsive or proactive activities. These are often undertaken in a confrontational spirit, and are not necessarily less (or more) effective for that; but there is also a more collaborative mode in which these roles are played in relation to other participants in the processes of policy making and implementation. Being 'inside the tent' poses dangers, but also has its advantages.

The perception of interdependence among actors and instruments opens the way to crafting more comprehensive policy approaches that transcend both action at the single-country levels – potentially reaching a global dimension – and actions undertaken by only one type of participant or 'stakeholder'. This suggests a holistic conception of regulatory policy and practice (Bennett and Raab,

2003, ch 8), an approach that makes it possible to construe the governance of data protection in terms of complex regimes, thus helping us to understand the intricate pathways along which privacy protection is provided. This does not mean that there is, or should be, orchestration from a central point; nor does it imply automatic harmony, for there are many clashes among these diverse actors and their divergent interests, especially where groups act adversarially on behalf of consumers or citizens. However, to consider them more explicitly as interactive agents is to make possible a richer, and more realistic, conceptualisation of privacy protection as something more than, and perhaps other than, the mechanical application of a set of 'tools'.

Moreover, the nature of current and future information flows means that it is by now well understood that privacy cannot be adequately protected at the level of the single national jurisdiction. Consumers and citizens in the UK transact with organisations based abroad, and their personal information flows through myriad channels and jurisdictions in which the application of privacy protection varies, or is non-existent. In addition, especially in the post-'9/11' climate, they may not be able to have any say in who accesses their data if, for instance, they fly in airplanes or converse through mobile telephones. As indicated earlier, international instruments have guided information privacy from an early date, and the EU Directive has powerfully influenced national laws and other provisions, such as the Safe Harbor, towards greater consonance, at least on many essential elements, and encourages transnational codes of practice. Beyond the adoption in 2000 of ISO 17799 as the privacy security standard, an initiative to establish a global management standard for privacy through the ISO has been met with strong obstacles. PETs can operate globally, as do online commitments and privacy seals. Transnational groupings have taken shape in some important regions, of which the (expanding) EU and Asia-Pacific have been among the most evident. Official regulators – supervisory authorities – come together, learn from each other, compare experiences, fulfil obligations for mutual assistance, and co-participate in supervisory activities.

Conclusion

Despite several decades of regulatory activity, the efficacy of data protection for consumers and citizens is far from certain, as the tools employed appear to be outstripped by the dynamics, complexity and diversity of the world they were meant to regulate. Members of the public, individually and even collectively, are less powerful and less well informed than they would need to be in order to present a countervailing influence comparable to the public or private sector appetite for personal data. Rights of complaint and avenues for redress are difficult, time-consuming and costly to put in motion, and are only sometimes met with success. The protective instruments that are supposed to improve the practices of the data-processing world, thus reducing the occasion for complaint and redress, are far from efficient and are not yet well articulated with each other. A new, and more joined-up, 'governance of privacy' has yet to take shape, whether domestically or globally, and the current climate of anxiety over terrorist threats to national and global security is not propitious for moving forward on this front.

After years of experience with 'computer age' laws and their implementation, there is a growing concern about the implications that these developments hold, not only for the value of privacy, but for existing and future regulatory policy and practice both in terms of national action and international harmonisation. The 'death of privacy' has often been pronounced, although many would argue that rumours of its demise are exaggerated. The 'failure of privacy protection' has often been heralded; but are the criteria for making that judgement well established, and is privacy protection best seen as a single, readily identifiable technique or, instead, as a multi-faceted social, cultural and political movement, in which the manipulation of 'instruments' plays an integral part?

In the current period of transition in the field of privacy and data protection, both nationally and globally, the robustness of established assumptions that have been built into the many laws and international instruments of regulation since the 1970s are increasingly in question. To some extent, it is the individual-rights assumption about privacy, underpinning the conventional privacy paradigm, and sustaining legal approaches, which may now be questioned, as we have seen, by societal-value approaches that do not begin and end with the individual (Regan, 1995; Bennett and Raab, 2003, chs 1, 2). Laws may be passed, but their implementation is often in grave doubt, in part owing to their dauntingly opaque and cumbersome provisions. It is also attributable to the weakness of the institutions charged with enforcement, and to the labyrinthine processes involved in, say, redressing consumers' grievances or changing the practices of offending organisations, which can too easily evade or avoid the effective reach of the law. Yet hope seems to spring eternal, or else there is – or rather, was, before '9/11' – the cachet of political correctness about legislating for privacy. Thus, the number of countries joining the 'club' of data-protecting states proceeds apace, with new members in Latin America, the Asia–Pacific region and Central and Eastern Europe taking out memberships. Older members have refurbished their domestic statutes, and new codifications of privacy principles and rules continue to be devised at regional and sectoral levels. They cover industries or processes that pose specific threats to the privacy of persons in their roles as workers (for example, codes governing privacy in employment), customers (for example, website privacy statements), or members of the public (for example, codes for the use of video surveillance systems).

But the globalisation of flows of personal data in the era of Internet commerce, employee mobility, and movements of immigrants and asylum-seekers makes it difficult for single states to regulate transactions in the interest of protecting their citizens and residents, and perhaps especially online consumers or those transacting business with multinational firms. It places a premium on the harmonisation or standardisation of rules, practices and controls, and even of basic definitions such as 'personal data', 'sensitive data', 'identifiability', and 'consent'. It therefore challenges countries, international organisations, and pressure groups to develop new institutions, fora and procedures for achieving these aims and for settling disputes between countries, or between individuals and the firms or governments whose processing of personal data invades privacy.

However, as this chapter has argued, such solutions, whether they involve legislation and the regulatory agencies to enforce it, organisational self-regulation through codes of practice and the like, technological tools for privacy protection, or citizen and consumer education in the ways of information technology and in the uses of personal data in market situations affording choice, are no longer sufficient each by itself, and perhaps never were. If the outlines of a new, more integrated strategic conception can be discerned, consumer and other civil society groups could play a major role in the articulation of problems and solutions.

References

Bennett, C.J. (1992) *Regulating privacy: Data protection and public policy in Europe and the United States*, Ithaca, NY: Cornell University Press.

Bennett, C.J. and Raab, C.D. (2003) *The governance of privacy: Policy instruments in global perspective*, Aldershot: Ashgate.

Borking, J. and Raab, C. (2001) 'Laws, PETs and other technologies for privacy protection', *Journal of Information Law and Technology*, vol 1, no 1 (http://elj.warwick.ac.uk/jilt/01-1/borking.html).

Cavoukian, A. and Tapscott, D. (1995) *Who knows? Safeguarding your privacy in a networked world*, Toronto: Random House.

CEC (Commission of the European Communities) (1995) *Directive 95/46/EC of the European Parliament and of the Council on the Protection of Individuals with regard to the Processing of Personal Data and on the Free Movement of Such Data*, OJ L281, 23.11.1995, Brussels: Official Journal of the European Communities.

Chaum, D. (1992) 'Achieving electronic privacy', *Scientific American*, vol 267, pp 96-101.

CoE (Council of Europe) (1981) *Convention for the protection of individuals with regard to automatic processing of personal data (Convention 108)*, Strasbourg: CoE.

CSA (Canadian Standards Association) (1996) *Model code for the protection of personal information*, CAN/CSA-Q830-96, Rexdale: CSA.

DCA (Department for Constitutional Affairs) (2003) *Public sector data sharing: Guidance on the law*, London: DCA.

DH (Department of Health) (2003) *Confidentiality: NHS Code of Practice*, London: DH.

Diffie, W. and Landau, S. (1998) *Privacy on the line: The politics of wiretapping and encryption*, Cambridge, MA: MIT Press.

Dumortier, J. and Goemans, C. (2000) 'Data privacy and standardization', Discussion paper prepared for the CEN/ISSS Open Seminar on Data Protection, Brussels, 23/24 March (www.law.kuleuven.ac.be/icri/).

Flaherty, D. (1989) *Protecting privacy in surveillance societies: The Federal Republic of Germany, Sweden, France, Canada, and the United States*, Chapel Hill, NC: University of North Carolina Press.

Gandy, O.H. Jr (1993) *The panoptic sort: A political economy of personal information*, Boulder, CO: Westview Press.

Gellman, R. (1993) 'Fragmented, incomplete and discontinuous: the failure of federal privacy regulatory proposals and institutions', *Software Law Journal*, vol 6, no 2, pp 199-231.

Harvey, F. (2003) 'Your private life seen through a lens', *Financial Times*, 29 December, p 8.

Industry Canada (1994) *Privacy and the Canadian information highway: Building Canada's information and communications infrastructure*, Ottawa: Information Highway Advisory Council, Industry Canada.

Information Commissioner (2004a) *Annual report and accounts for the year ending 31 March 2004*, HC669, London: The Stationery Office.

Information Commissioner (2004b) 'The "Durant" case and its impact on the interpretation of the Data Protection Act 1998' (www.informationcommissioner.gov.uk).

Kooiman, J. (2003) *Governing as governance*, London: Sage Publications.

Lessig, L. (1999) *Code and other laws of cyberspace*, New York, NY: Basic Books.

Lyon, D. (2001) *Surveillance society: Monitoring everyday life*, Buckingham: Open University Press.

Lyon, D. (2003) *Surveillance after September 11*, Cambridge: Polity Press.

MORI (2003) *Privacy and data-sharing: Survey of public awareness and perceptions*, Research study conducted for the the Department for Constitutional Affairs, London: MORI.

OECD (Organisation for Economic Co-operation and Development) (1981) *Guidelines on the protection of privacy and transborder flows of personal data*, Paris: OECD.

OECD (2001) Directorate for Science, Technology and Industry, Committee for Information, Computer and Communications Policy, Working Party on Information Security and Privacy, 'Report on the OECD forum session on privacy-enhancing technologies (PETs)', Paris: OECD (www.olis.oecd.org/olis/2001doc.nsf/LinkTo/dsti-iccp-reg(2001)6-final).

OECD (2002) Directorate for Science, Technology and Industry, Committee for Information, Computer and Communications Policy, Working Party on Information Security and Privacy, 'Inventory of privacy-enhancing technologies (PETs)', Paris: OECD (www.olis.oecd.org/olis/2001doc.nsf/LinkTo/dsti-iccp-reg(2001)1-final).

PIU (Performance and Innovation Unit) (2002) *Privacy and data-sharing: The way forward for public services*, London: PIU, Cabinet Office.

Raab, C. (1993) 'Data protection in Britain: governance and learning', *Governance*, vol 6, no 1, pp 43-66.

Raab, C. (1996) 'Implementing data protection in Britain', *International Review of Administrative Sciences*, vol 62, no 4, pp 493-511.

Raab, C. (1997a) 'Privacy, democracy, information', in B. Loader (ed) *The governance of cyberspace*, London: Routledge.

Raab, C. (1997b) 'Co-producing data protection', *International Review of Law, Computers and Technology*, vol 11, no 1, pp 11-42.

Raab, C. (1998) 'Electronic confidence: trust, information and public administration', in I. Snellen and W. van de Donk (eds) *Public administration in an information age: A handbook*, Amsterdam: IOS Press.

Raab, C. (2001) 'Electronic service delivery in the UK: proaction and privacy protection', in J.E.J. Prins (ed) *Designing e-government: On the crossroads of technological innovation and institutional change*, Boston, MA, and The Hague: Kluwer Law International.

Regan, P. (1995) *Legislating privacy: Technology, social values and public policy*, Chapel Hill, NC: University of North Carolina Press.

Regan, P. (2002) 'Privacy as a common good in the digital world', *Information, Communication and Society*, vol 5, no 3, pp 382-405.

Reidenberg, J. (1997) 'Governing networks and rule-making in cyberspace', in B. Kahin and C. Nesson (eds) *Borders in cyberspace*, Cambridge, MA: MIT Press.

Reidenberg, J. (1998) 'Lex informatica: the formulation of information policy rules through technology', *Texas Law Review*, vol 76, no 3, pp 552-93.

Schoeman, F. (1992) *Privacy and social freedom*, Cambridge: Cambridge University Press.

Westin, A. (1967) *Privacy and freedom*, New York, NY: Athenaeum.

3

The use and value of privacy-enhancing technologies

John Borking

Introduction

As legislation to protect personal data has become increasingly complex, technology has provided ever more sophisticated solutions for complying with that legislation. But this is not technology's only role. Moving beyond minimum compliance, technology can provide applications that positively enhance consumer privacy and provide consumers with greater control over their data. This chapter will consider the role of technology in this context. It will begin by examining briefly the importance of privacy, before moving on to outline the content and significance of the Data Protection Directive. The chapter will discuss how systems of privacy-enhancing technologies (PETs) can be built, before assessing their benefits, costs and limitations. Finally, what might the future hold for this technology? And do PETs have a future?

The need for privacy: trust and autonomy

At the outset, it is important to recognise why privacy is so important. Perri 6's opening chapter to this volume has categorised some of the risks involved in information use. Many other commentators have also written extensively on the meaning and importance of privacy. For the purpose of this chapter, however, I would like to focus on two concepts inextricably linked with privacy – trust (see Patrick, 2003)[1] and autonomy.

Many organisations are striving towards a more individualised, faster and more efficient provision of goods and services. Yet individualised marketing and service provision (by both the public and private sectors) can only succeed if there is a high level of trust between providers and consumers. Without trust, virtually all of our economic and social relationships would fail. Trust enables communication and cooperation; privacy and data protection can help build trust. For instance, research continues to show that the biggest factors behind consumers' failure to shop online are concerns about privacy and security.

One of the moral reasons for informational privacy protection is to guard against information wrongdoing (using personal data outside the sphere where these data may legitimately be used). Privacy protection helps to plot and maintain the boundaries (Walzer, 1995) of the different relatively autonomous domains of social reality, or, as Jeroen van den Hoven (1998) puts it, 'spheres of access'. Several moral philosophers and sociologists have written about the existence of and need for social differentiation, using the notions of social 'spheres', 'domains' or 'fields' with their own autonomy and integrity. Information management is practised in order to maintain the integrity and functional unity of these social domains in which we all live and feel at home. Violation of privacy occurs when there is a morally inappropriate transfer of data across the boundaries of these domains.

In effect, creating constraints on access to personal information helps prevent the unauthorised intrusion into areas of our lives not normally open to others, preventing individual loss of autonomy (the capacity to live one's life as one chooses) and promoting the societal acceptance of the incomplete description of our self (biography, thoughts, desires and aspirations). This means that it is impossible to describe an individual totally as this is (if ever achievable) a static and never a dynamic picture. Consequently, the claim that you want to know everything about a person is morally disrespectful towards that individual. Such an act encroaches on one's moral autonomy, or, as the Council of Europe (1989) puts it, "respect for human dignity relates to the need to avoid statistical dehumanisation by undermining the identity ... through data-processing techniques allowing profiling, or the taking of decisions based on automatic processing".

This chapter aims to show how PET can be regarded as a tool to promote social justice and to diminish tensions among societal spheres, by accepting that all human beings must be able to develop in an autonomous way without unwanted intrusion.

First, however, the later discussion of technology will be put into context by outlining Europe's major piece of data protection legislation, the Data Protection Directive.

The content and importance of the Data Protection Directive

Within Europe, the Data Protection Directive (DPD) (95/46/EC) remains the key piece of legislation protecting personal information. Its provisions are incorporated in the UK's 1998 Data Protection Act. The DPD sets out a number of basic requirements, under nine privacy principles, for the lawful processing[2] (from capture to destruction) and acceptable use of personal data. Within organisations, 'data controllers' are responsible for making sure that this legislation is complied with; they are liable for any unlawful processing of data. 'Data processors' (who process data on the controller's behalf) are separately liable for shortcomings in the way the process is organised within their organisations. Data subjects are those who bear personal data.

The Directive's nine privacy principles may be summarised as follows:

1. *Intention and notification:* the processing of personal data must be reported in advance to a country's Data Protection Authority or an organisation's privacy officer, unless the processing system in question has been exempted from notification.
2. *Transparency:* data subjects must be aware of who is processing their personal data and for what purpose.
3. *Finality:* personal data may only be collected for specific, explicit and legitimate purposes and not further processed in a way that is incompatible with those purposes.
4. *Legitimate ground for processing:* the processing of personal data must be based on a foundation permitted by national legislation, such

as consent, contract or some other legal obligation. For sensitive data, such as health data, stricter limits apply.

5. *Quality:* the personal data must be accurate and not excessive in relation to the purpose in question.

6. *Data subjects' rights:* data subjects have the right to access and correct their data. (See also *Transparency.*)

7. *Security:* providing appropriate security for personal data held within IT systems is one of the cornerstones of the DPD.

8. *Processing by a processor:* if processing is outsourced, it must be ensured that the processor observes the instructions of the controller.

9. *Transfer of personal data outside the EU:* in principle, the transfer of personal data to a country outside the EU is permitted only if that country offers adequate (that is, similar to EU-level) protection.

Within the DPD, the definition of personal data is crucially important. Personal data are identified as any information regarding an identified or identifiable natural person. According to Article 2, a natural person may be directly or indirectly identifiable. A person may be directly identifiable from his/her name, address, personal reference number, a generally known pseudo-identity or a biometric characteristic (such as a fingerprint). Indirect identification depends on (a combination of) other unique characteristics or attributes, from which it is possible to extract sufficient information for identification. If, for example, one has a postcode and a house number, it may be possible to identify the occupant of a house using a telephone directory (see Borking and Raab, 2001).

Non-identification is assumed if the amount and the nature of the indirectly identifiable data are such that identification of the individual is only possible with the application of disproportionate effort. Whether we can assume the existence of disproportionate effort depends on the nature of the data, the size of the population and the resources of time and money one is willing to spend in order to be able to identify the person (Raab, 1999)[3]. Internet identifiers such as an Internet provider (IP) address, the browsing activities of a user, session login data and the listing of websites visited by an Internet user are classified as personal data.

If personal data are to be processed appropriately and consumer privacy is to be taken seriously, data processing policy must be given an important position within organisations' systems of operational management. According to the law, technical means should be used for the protection of consumer privacy. For example, Article 17 of the DPD makes clear that, before collecting personal data, a controller must consider appropriate security measures. Data controllers must implement appropriate technical and organisational measures to protect personal data, especially in network transmissions. Recital 46 highlights the requirement that these measures should be taken "both at the time of the design of the processing system and at the time of the processing itself", thus indicating that security cannot simply be bolted on to data systems, but must be built into them.

PETs can help ensure that personal data are handled correctly and that consumer privacy is respected. This chapter will look at how these technologies can be built and used, starting at the beginning with privacy threat analysis.

Privacy threat analysis

Privacy-proof information systems[4] cannot be built without an upfront analysis of risks. Privacy is closely related to information security, although security is just part of the story. Nonetheless, privacy threat analyses can be based on a risk assessment for information security (as in British Standards BS 7799: 'The Code of Practice for the Risk Analysis and Management Method'; the *Information security handbook* of the Central Computers and Telecommunications Agency [CCTA]; or *Information Technology Security Evaluation Criteria* [ITSEC], as published by the European Communities in 1991). These approaches have to be modified as security is just part of the problem; privacy threats will also emanate from the sloppy behaviour of data subjects or controllers, which may provoke phenomena like bin raiding and, in the end, identity theft.

Figure 3.1 highlights the way privacy protection can be handled[5].

Figure 3.1: Privacy threat analysis[6]

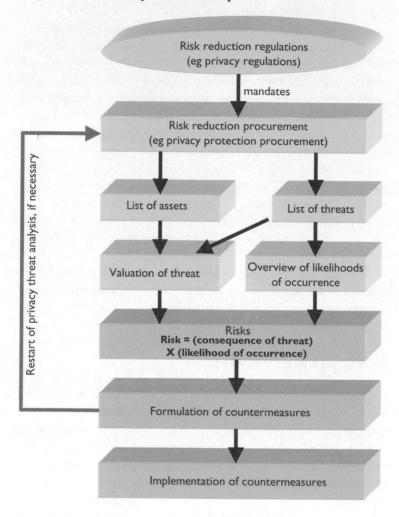

In effect:

- At the first level of analysis, 'assets' and 'threats' are evaluated. Assets represent the objects or subjects that bear personal data and hence are vulnerable to privacy threats. These assets are then evaluated (to determine how important it is that they are protected) and ranked in value. Value may be expressed in an arbitrary unit such as, if possible, a monetary unit or in some other unit. Risk assessment experts carry this out[7].

- Threats are then identified[8] and the potential severity of those threats is assessed. This is determined by expert judgement or, preferably, by statistical analysis (Borking and Giezen, 2001).
- The next stage of analysis is risk assessment. A risk is the product of the consequences of the threat times the likelihood of the occurrence of the threat. This should at least give some insight into where and how to invest effort and money.
- Next, responses ('countermeasures') to these risks are formulated. However, if the countermeasures, of themselves, create secondary threats, the whole threat analysis has to be repeated, until no further threats are identified.
- Finally, the countermeasures are implemented.

Privacy threat analysis has to be tied in with standard system development procedures, which primarily deal with the functionality of systems. The reconciliation of these two sides is considered next.

Building a compliant system

As we have seen, the requirements of the DPD must be implemented efficiently in organisations in order to give proper support to the consumer's right to privacy with respect to personal data. It is therefore important to devise systems that protect the processing of personal data.

The design of these systems is key. For example, a system may contain an inescapable 'date of birth' field, but an analysis of the company's processes may show that recording the birth date of all persons is excessive. System design can tackle this and ensure that users correctly observe the law. As a rule, privacy protection will constitute a supplementary system of measures and procedures (in addition to usual processing and security measures), but it should be assigned a significant place in these management processes.

When organisations are asked what they have done to protect privacy, they tend to talk about the use of safeguards to prevent unauthorised access to personal data. However, while this is an important aspect of privacy protection, it is not sufficient in its own right. This is because, irrespective of this form of security, personal data do tend to leak out of organisations in an uncontrolled way, often due to negligence of the data processors, and stored data are rarely encrypted and are thus easy to read. Consequently, effective protection depends entirely on the security measures being correctly implemented and functioning properly.

It is therefore vital to protect the individual's privacy at the point of data collection. Such measures may do away with the need to generate or record any personal data at all. Alternatively, they may minimise or even obviate the need to use or store personally identifiable data.

PETs

Information and communication technologies (ICTs) have, in fact, been used to produce what have become widely known as PETs. PETs are a coherent system of ICT measures that protect privacy by eliminating or reducing personal data or by preventing the unnecessary and/or undesirable processing of personal data; all without losing the functionality of the information system (Borking, 1996). As discussed before, the driving legal principles behind the concept of PET are embodied in Articles 6.1c and 6.1e (data minimisation) and 17 (data security), and Recital 46 (design of the information system) of the DPD.

Several forms of PET exist and each has its specific function (that is, anonymity, pseudonymity, unlinkability, or unobservability) for protecting privacy by preventing identification. Some forms offer more protection than others. Anonymisation, for example, creates the highest level of protection as personal data are not processed or stored. Deletion of personal data directly after the necessary processing and successful closure of a transaction also protects the individual well. Another type of PET involves preventing processing of personal data that are not anonymised. In this type of PET, privacy principles have to be implemented in information systems to achieve compliant data processing.

The next sections will consider two types of PET – identity protectors and encryption.

The identity protector

The use of an information system involves a number of processes[9]: authorisation, identification and authentication, access control, auditing and accounting. After analysing processes within a system, it still may be necessary in certain cases to know the user's or consumer's identity for accounting and authorisation purposes.

For the processes of identification and authentication, access control and auditing, knowledge of the user's identity has been proven to be unnecessary (Hes and Borking, 1998)[10]. This opens up the possibility of using ICT to protect the privacy of users, consumers and citizens.

From a functional point of view, the application of PET in this context is not difficult. Two key elements are decisive in the capture, storage and processing of personal data: the use of an 'identity protector' within the data system to convert the identity of the data subject into one or more pseudo-identities (Clarke, 1996)[11] and the use of identity domains in data processing. An identity protector is comprised of at least two different domains: one where the identity of the person involved is known or accessible (the identity domain) and at least one domain where this is not the case (the pseudo-identity domain)[12]. The pseudo-identity domain serves partly to ensure that the data subject cannot be traced from previously obtained personal data, and partly to ensure that personal data cannot be consulted on the basis of a known identity (see Figure 3.2).

The identity protector can be incorporated at any point in the information system (see Figure 3.3). A simple guideline for the designer of a new information system is to minimise the identity domain.

The identity protector in a data system can take several forms, for example:

- a separate function implemented in the data system, such as a functional access profile for entering a database[13];
- a separate data system supervised by the individual (for instance, a smart card for biometrics identification);
- a data system supervised by a third party who is trusted by both the service provider and consumer.

Figure 3.2: The identity protector

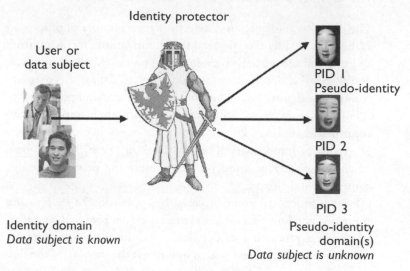

Identity protector

User or
data subject

PID I
Pseudo-identity

PID 2

PID 3

Identity domain
Data subject is known

Pseudo-identity
domain(s)
Data subject is unknown

Figure 3.3: The working of the identity protector

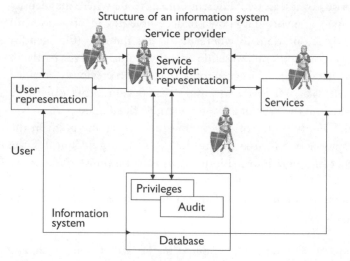

Structure of an information system

Service provider

Service
provider
representation

User
representation

Services

User

Privileges

Audit

Information
system

Database

The controller can ensure that access to data and the ability to obtain non-anonymised data is dependent on the user's rights within the information system. A user engaged in medical research, for example, would have access only to data from which identification was not possible. On the other hand, identification data would be available in a hospital on the basis of functional authorisation and the relationship between the care provider and the patient.

Ideally, the identity protector enables consumers to manage their own personal data. They determine when and to whom their real identities will be revealed. However, in many cases when the law requires that the real identity always has to be revealed (as in criminal investigations, opening a bank account, getting a passport or in a hospital registration system for patients) this is not possible and the identity protector has to be managed by another party (preferably by an independent third party).

When there is no need to identify consumers, but one legitimately would like to process their data (usually for statistical reasons), then the use of a pseudo-identity is sufficient and consumers can manage their identity protectors themselves. One of the classic examples of an identity protector is when one votes anonymously in parliamentary elections. In shops, anonymous loyalty cards[14] for discounts can be used or when a certain amount of prepaid cash is stored on a card, one can buy goods and services (such as food in canteens) anonymously. Prepaid telephone cards can be loaded into a mobile telephone; the money is deducted from the card and there is no link to the user's identity. Prepaid cards are also used for road-pricing systems.

Cryptography

One technology that is almost indispensable for ensuring the reliability of information and transactions in an open electronic environment is cryptography. An increasingly popular option in this field is public-key cryptography. Multinational corporations, like banks and petroleum companies, already use this technology. In e-government, citizens will start to use it in their dealings with central and local administrations.

This technique can be used in two ways. One can have a public encryption key, which anyone can use to write an encrypted message that can be read only by the person with the corresponding private decryption key. Or one can have a public decryption key, so that users can authenticate the source of an encrypted message, which can only have come from the owner of the corresponding private encryption key. The second arrangement is known as a digital signature system.

Public-key cryptography is only effective if one has a reliable method of linking the key to the identity or another attribute of the owner. To make this possible, a public-key infrastructure (PKI) is required. Within the PKI, a trusted third party (TTP) provides the necessary link, making use of its own electronic signature. A digital certificate is a digitally signed electronic document issued by a TTP, linking the public key to attributes of the certificate holder.

The use of MIX nodes[15] and Onion Routing[16] in telecommunications and other networks is a promising way of protecting data in transit between the sender and recipient. By installing a series of nodes and using certain encryption/decryption techniques, it is possible to modify and regroup data in transit so as to make it almost impossible for an unauthorised party to tell whether a message is 'incoming' or 'outgoing', or therefore to analyse or track the data[17] (see Figure 3.4).

Case study: a hospital information system with PET

To put the previous discussion into context, the following case study provides a practical example of a system that has used both encryption and identity protectors.

The PET hospital information system now in use at dozens of

Figure 3.4: MIXes

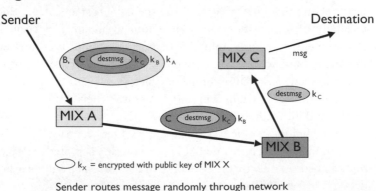

k_x = encrypted with public key of MIX X

Sender routes message randomly through network of MIXes using layered public-key encryption

Note: destmsg = destination message

hospitals in the Netherlands uses an identity protector, which was installed in 1997 by an international software developer. The system is divided into various domains. In some of these domains, data subjects are identified; in others they are anonymous. Furthermore, only authorised users are able to make data in pseudo–identity domains identifiable.

The project began with a privacy audit conducted by the Data Protection Authority. The contractor was then asked to develop practical measures to hide the true identity of patients and physicians as well as related information held in the database (including the electronic patient record system).

Data relating to patients were divided into three sets. The first set consisted of direct identification items, such as the patient's name, address, date of birth and insurance details (the identity domain). The second set was made up of all diagnostic and treatment data (the pseudo–identity domain).

In both domains, a patient number identified the patient. A number encryption protocol was applied, however, and different numbers were used in each domain. No link could therefore be made between an item of information in one domain, and an item in the other. This made it impossible for anyone to obtain an overview of a patient's data without going through the authorised channels.

In the identity domain, a system of serial numbers was used to identify patients. The patient numbers used in the pseudo–identity domain were obtained by encrypting the serial numbers. The encryption protocol allowed the original patient numbers to be obtained by decryption, with encryption and decryption performed by the application software. The encryption keys used by the protocol were made available only once the identity of the application user had been confirmed.

A third domain was created for statistical and medical research, containing aggregated data only.

Nobody without a functional authorisation in this PET system could process any data in it. Even if privacy protection was not at stake, using PETs provided for significant data security. In fact, the effect of PETs on the performance of the hospital's database has been tested and performance efficacy and response time has not been affected by the application of the functionalities of PETs. The cost of building in these functions was only 1% more than without, as the functionalities of PETs had been incorporated into the design (data model) from the beginning. Had PETs been applied to old, existing systems, the cost may have been much greater – PETs work best when incorporated into the design of new systems. So far (since 1998), no complaints have been received about this hospital information system either from the patients or the medical staff and management.

The other face of PET: privacy management systems

In situations where it is not possible to use the PET strategies[18] described above – for example, when the law requires the processing of personal data – a mix of other technologies can be employed to protect privacy more effectively.

Several international software developers have, in fact, marketed privacy management systems that enable organisations to define, implement and manage corporate privacy policies and practices.

These privacy policies and practices are defined and captured in an electronic privacy language. This language has been designed to capture the complex relationship between business operations and personal information in an executable format[19]. The monitoring and processing of personal information can be automated, so that when transactions conflict with an organisation's privacy policy[20], a warning signal is displayed on the user's computer and the organisation's privacy compliance officer may be alerted.

With privacy management systems, privacy compliance officers and organisations can take control of privacy-related risks and can keep all relevant information for privacy management up to date. Privacy audits can be executed effectively and efficiently, as privacy rules and policies are well defined. Privacy management systems can also easily generate reports on compliance[21]. Yet privacy management systems would not exist if P3P and privacy ontologies had not been developed. This is considered next.

P3P

Key to privacy management systems is the implementation of a privacy policy that can be matched with the privacy preferences of the consumer and citizen.

The world-wide-web consortium, better known as W3C, had developed P3P before there was any privacy management system available. P3P[22] is a tool enabling easy communication about one's own privacy preferences in a standard machine-readable format. The vocabulary of P3P shows:

- who is collecting data;
- what data are collected and for what purpose/s;
- the opt-in and opt-out alternatives for some data uses;
- who the data recipients are;
- the information the data controller provides access to;
- the data retention period;
- how disputes related to the organisation's privacy policy would be resolved; and
- where the human-readable privacy policy is.

A form of P3P has been implemented in Microsoft Explorer[23]. With this tool, transparency can be improved if an appropriate default setting is chosen. The default should be set so that not all data are automatically publicised.

Privacy knowledge engineering (PYKE) and privacy ontologies

In order to achieve a PET strategy where the processing of personal data is in accordance with data protection legislation, the law has to be translated into machine-readable code.

In 1999, research staff at the Dutch Data Protection Authority began to develop a third type of PET, now known as privacy knowledge engineering (PYKE). They were interested in whether privacy law could be translated into machine-readable code, so that the law could be built automatically into information systems.

As it was impossible to stabilise the dynamics of legislation, the researchers chose to build into an information system the nine privacy principles described above. A method has since been developed to realise privacy knowledge engineering (Kenny and Borking, 2002). The procedure works as follows:

- First, and as privacy law is usually complex, privacy principles are determined and the law is simplified by linking relevant DPD articles with their corresponding privacy principles. In effect, this clusters the DPD articles into generic principles.
- The next step is splitting the privacy principles into 'elements' (pieces of text that are structured subsets of the privacy principles). Thus, the principles are deconstructed into a set of elements that relate to the principles they are derived from. This emphasises the context of the privacy protection regime and what has to be achieved.
- This will lead to the formulation of the ontology. This ontology provides a conceptual model of the data protection principles on which the DPD has been based. It may then be implemented into information systems (online and offline). It can be used as a backbone in conversations about privacy preferences, for the matching of privacy policies and exchanging personally identifiable information (PII) and for the automatic treatment of personal data in databases according to the data subject's privacy preferences.

In order to exchange automatically personal data within the boundaries of the data protection law, transfer rules have to be formulated and embedded in the information system to decide when PII can be transferred to other information systems[24]. Ontologies are also needed about the domains in which the privacy ontologies are applied. Thus, privacy protection built into information systems in a healthcare environment not only need generic privacy ontologies, but also ontologies referring to the healthcare environment. In fact, we need a worldwide accepted library of privacy ontologies and the domains in which they will be used. European research is in progress in order to realise this[25]. In the communication between software agents (personal digital butlers) that will hit our society during the next five years, privacy ontologies are a *sine qua non* if we want to keep our privacy protected on the Internet.

Why should organisations use PET?

We have seen how PET can be built and used. The discussion has highlighted the strengths of PET on numerous occasions. Nevertheless, there may be some value in summarising the costs and benefits of PET, particularly within an organisational context, to highlight the 'business case'.

Benefits

As we have seen, PET can be used as a tool of compliance with privacy/data protection law. PET might lead to a reduction in data processing costs as it can streamline organisational procedures and reduce 'red tape'. It should help link databases and ensure that data are processed legally.

PET and related privacy management systems enable organisations to better control privacy risks and intrusions and thus reduce potential liabilities. It can also reduce privacy auditing and privacy policing expenses. PET should decrease the need to ask for the same data over and over again because of anonymisation and pseudonymisation techniques. And, above all, the quality of information held should be improved.

Last, but not least, PET can increase consumer/citizen satisfaction and trust. It can empower citizens and consumers by allowing them access to control their data. Furthermore, when PET-based access has been provided for consumers, it can reduce the expenses related to formal legally granted data access.

Costs

Apart from the standard costs that are applicable for every ICT project (such as the costs of the feasibility study and technical and functional design costs), the following non-recurring expenses can be listed – the costs of:

- a privacy-threat analysis;
- an analysis of the need to process what (if any) personal data;
- designing the data models;
- the functional and technical design of the PET;
- any adjustment of the existing infrastructure;
- developing the chosen form of PET or the procurement of PET products; and
- the technology.

Other expenses include the costs of:

- training users and administrators;
- introducing authentication tools, if necessary;
- communicating about the PET-specific way of working; and
- maintaining the PET-proof system.

Costs are also dependent on the chosen form of PET. For example, the costs of anonymising personal data are often one-off. Anonymisation should also minimise expensive information security measures. When identity domains and pseudo-identities are used, the costs are higher as software has to be tailor-made in order to fit the environment in which the information system operates. In the future, software packages will be marketed to do the same. The data models will also be more complex. However, and as we have seen, the Dutch example of the PET hospital information system proved that the total system building costs were only 1% higher as PET had been built in from scratch (see Dutch Ministry of the Interior, 2004).

PET challenges

One might think that an identity protector creating anonymity or pseudonymity would facilitate fraud or improper use. However, detection and correction tools can be built into PET information systems. One possibility for the identity protector is to prevent users from being able to use their anonymity to commit fraud. If, for example, people might take improper advantage of their anonymity with regard to healthcare insurance, hospital insurance cards could require as a form of access control verification of the biometric data of the bearer with the actual holder, rendering it impossible for someone else to use such a health insurance card. This kind of access control takes place within the information system without revealing the user's identity (for more information, see Hes et al, 1998). The identity protector can also be constructed, so that misuse will be detected and corrected. In such circumstances the identity protector could warn the user and even take measures against him or her, such as revealing his or her identity to the service provider or to the authorities. However, users should always be given the chance to prove they have been falsely accused of misconduct before their identity is revealed.

PET and combating terrorism

In the state of fear and anxiety relating to combating terrorism and transnational crime in the post '9/11' era, people have accepted many new incursions into their personal privacy (Susser et al, 2002). In the pre-'9/11' period, such incursions often would have been quickly called 'Orwellian' or seen as telltale symbols of a hi-tech police state. Now one hears often that for public policy reasons, the use of anonymity and even the right to privacy protection should be lifted and surveillance should be increased.

As I have pointed out in this chapter, different life domains deserve protection from various kinds of intrusion in order to keep people and society sane. The importance of respecting the value of individuality and private life has been acknowledged since the Second World War by international human rights treaties, European Directives and national legislation. However, that does not mean that under strictly regulated circumstances, such as a criminal court order, that the protection of our legal order may not require giving up one's privacy and anonymity. But this should be allowed only when there are concrete and verifiable safeguards against misuse of this power by the authorities. As we have seen, PET applications have been developed that enhance security while simultaneously safeguarding privacy. PET systems can be constructed to be fraud-proof. Without developing and implementing PET, we would become more vulnerable than ever, as privacy legislation alone does not eliminate the risk of personal data abuse and lags behind technological developments.

Conclusion

Developments in ICT are constantly broadening the scope for the collection, storage, processing and distribution of personal data online and offline. This constitutes a growing threat to the privacy of consumers and citizens. However, other developments in ICT offer ways of protecting the rights and interests of users and those to whom data relates.

PET is an excellent and promising means of satisfying the basic privacy requirement that all data processing should have a legal basis. In spite of the challenges, its future should remain bright. Naturally, further investigation and research remain necessary, and continuing efforts will have to be made to promote the use of PET in information systems – as, for example, through the EU-subsidised Privacy Incorporated Software Agent (PISA) project (2000). This project is developing a guaranteed privacy environment for Internet users.

In addition, criteria to test the claim that a system is PET-proof have to be further developed, as is occurring in PETTEP, a joint research project of the Schleswig-Holstein (Kiel) and Ontario (Toronto) data protection authorities. Furthermore, privacy audits are essential when checking for compliance with privacy legislation. Special tools that can scan quickly to determine whether PET-equipped systems actually comply with the DPD must be further developed. Certification in the context of a privacy audit can be helpful in this regard, and can serve to reassure consumers and members of the public that information systems and controllers adequately protect their privacy.

Certainly, data protection authorities can stimulate the deployment of PET by actively promoting PET in information systems and through PET research (Bennett and Raab, 2003). The law alone cannot protect privacy, as it is not self-executing. Lawyers and technologists should proactively try to solve privacy problems instead of reactively responding to complaints when harm has already been done.

I strongly believe that owners and controllers of information systems do have a moral obligation to protect consumers and citizens against privacy intrusion. PET provides a rigorous structural way of achieving this goal.

Notes

[1] Trust can be defined as consumers' thoughts, feelings, emotions, or behaviours that occur when they feel that an organisation or individual can be relied on to act in their best interest when they give up direct control. See Patrick (2003). See also www.pet-pisa.nl

[2] 'Processing' is construed broadly and so would include the obtaining, recording, holding, organising, retrieval, use of, disclosure of or destruction of personal data.

[3] Concepts of 'identification' and 'identity' are essentially contested in theory and often arbitrary and ambiguous in practice.

[4] Information systems (transaction processing, programmed decision making and decision support systems) provide people with the information required for performing goal-oriented activities.

[5] Other risk analyses (that have been developed in Canada) are the Privacy Impact Assessment (PIA) and the Privacy Diagnostic Tool (see the Privacy Diagnostic Tool Workbook version 1.0 developed by the Office of the Information Commissioner of Ontario: www.ipc.on.ca/). A PIA seeks to set forth the essential components of any personal information system. See, Flaherty (2000).

[6] For the analysis of threats to privacy, a five-pronged approach is chosen:

1. *Privacy regulations*, as defined in a certain country or region: these regulations inherently list a number of privacy threats, if these regulations are not adhered to.

2. *Purpose of the system,* which creates its own threats: because the user (private person) wants to achieve something, that person creates privacy threats.
3. *Solution adopted,* which may or may not create threats of its own.
4. *Technology used:* because of the way a certain system is implemented, certain threats may emanate that are not necessarily consequences of the intended purpose. Meanwhile, the technology will harbour some of the privacy enhancement measures.
5. *Situation in which the ultimate system will be used,* which, although not necessarily creating threats of its own, may or may not aggravate (or alleviate) the previously identified threats and hence may necessitate more demanding technological measures.

[7] For more information about how this is done, see Fischhoff et al (1981). When an expert is not available, see, for guidance, van Blarkom and Borking (2001).

[8] The following basic threats can be discerned:

- *Secret possession of (control over) personal data files:* the data subject and the authorities are unaware of the existence of the personal data.
- *Secret processing of personal data:* processing out of sight or knowledge of the data subject.
- *Out of bounds processing by controller:* processing of personal data that is not within the bounds stipulated in the 'personal data constraints'. These are restrictions on the processing of personal data, as they are defined by the data subject or by an external authority, or can be expected to be outside the scope and intention of the collection.
- *Illegal processing:* processing of personal data that is in violation of national or international law.
- *Personal data deterioration:* personal data that are out of date, due to external changes or incorrect/incomplete insertion or collection.
- *Failure to respond to complaints:* the controller does not respond (or responds incorrectly, incompletely or late) to requests for changes to the personal data.
- *Out of jurisdiction processing:* personal data are transferred to a controller who has no legal obligation to respect the law of the

data subject's country or where the law is weaker than in the data subject's own jurisdiction.

- *Personal data and personal data constraints validity violation:* the controller and processor disobey the obligations concerning the retention and safeguarding of data, including the obligation to take precautions against loss or corruption of the personal data or the personal data constraints. This reflects the obligation of the controller to terminate possession if the retention date is surpassed and to maintain proper measures against loss or corruption.

[9] A process is an exchange of information between two or more elements within an information system.

[10] For example, identity is not necessary when privileges in an information system are given on the basis of a group characteristic (being a member of a club), or personal characteristics, for instance age (all people older than 65 years can travel half price), or authentication can be based on a biometric characteristic (iris scan) in lieu of an identity.

[11] Pseudonymity as well as anonymity are key concepts in the design of information systems and privacy-protecting tools, and have received considerable attention in recent years.

[12] "The notion with privacy enhancing technologies is that … the individual's true identity can be protected when it is not necessary to use it" (France, 2000, p 215).

[13] The Dutch Burns Information System uses:

1. biometrics to authenticate users (fingerprint and voice templates stored on a smart card);
2. a trusted third party to verify identity;
3. firewalls to prevent intrusion by unwanted third parties;
4. a virtual private network;
5. database encryption;
6. a balanced (not holding more data than strictly necessary) dataset.

[14] The Dutch Data Protection Authority has negotiated with and required from the supermarket consortia that there has to be a choice between personal and anonymous loyalty cards. At the time of writing, there are approximately 80,000 anonymous loyalty cards issued by the biggest supermarket company out of a total of more than 2.5 million loyalty cards. However, anonymous loyalty cards are not the default position; that is, you have to ask for an anonymous card from a cashier.

[15] A MIX is a store-and-forward device that accepts a number of fixed-length messages from different sources, performs cryptographic transformations on the messages, and then forwards them to the next destination in an order not predictable from the order of inputs.

[16] An Onion is a recursively layered data structure that specifies the properties of the connection at each point along the route. The union has multiple layers of cryptography around the data that have to be protected. For more information see Federath (2001).

[17] There are many ways to protect your privacy on the Internet: **Anonymity and pseudonymity tools:** (1) Anonymising proxies; (2) MIX networks and similar web anonymity tools; (3) Onion Routing; (4) Crowds; (5) Freedom; (6) Anonymous e-mail. **Encryption tools:** (1) File encryption; (2) E-mail encryption; (3) Encrypted network connections. **Filters:** (1) Cookie cutters; (2) Child protection software. **'Agents of choice':** (1) Personal information managers; (2) P3P.

[18] In applying PET, the controller can choose two strategies: either focusing on preventing or reducing identification, or focusing on preventing unlawful processing of personal data, thus complying with the DPD. A combination of both is also possible.

[19] The privacy language works with key privacy parameters such as actors, data, actions, purpose and conditions. Using these parameters, an organisation can model and design its privacy policy and data-handling processes according to privacy law. Take, for example, 'consent'. This can be modelled with a 'condition' parameter, such as:

ABC Bank [actor] may disclose [action] a customer telephone number [data] to *ABC Marketing Department* [actor] for offering new services [purpose] if a customer has consented to *ABC Bank* offering new services by telephone [condition].

[20] A privacy policy is a critical mechanism for soliciting and winning consumer trust, particularly as it fosters transparency. However, many organisations do not have privacy policies on their web pages, and so fail to reassure consumers about their information policy. See, for example, the findings of Privacy@web by Consumers International (www.consumersinternational.org).

[21] In Canada in the Government of Alberta Enterprise Architecture (GAEA), an organisation-wide privacy management system, was implemented in 2003.

[22] See www.w3.org/P#P/; also P3P and Privacy – Center for Democracy and Technology/IPC Ontario; also www.cdt.org/privacy/ pet/p3pprivacy.shtml. However, there are doubts about the efficacy of P3P: see Catlett (2000).

[23] Apart from a cookie management tool (deletion and refusal to accept cookies), Internet Explorer and Netscape have an eye in the status bar of Netscape and Internet Explorer browsers as a warning symbol for the website's level of privacy. AT&T have as a warning symbol a privacy bird that chirps. When using 'privacy settings' tools, users can express their personal privacy preferences. Users are able to indicate whether they want to download background information on media they are watching or reject marketing emails. In the German version of Microsoft office 2003, several Internet-enabled features have been implemented that empower users to exercise their right to control data that they send from their computer by default (as required by German data protection law). In other non-German versions, the default level can be turned on; for many users, however, this can be troublesome as it is not clear how this should be done.

[24] For more information on the use of ontologies, see www.pet-pisa.nl

[25] For example, in the EU-funded PRIME (privacy and identity management) research project.

References

Bennett, C.J. and Raab, C.D. (2003) *The governance of privacy: Policy instruments in global perspective*, Aldershot: Ashgate.

Borking J.J. (1996) 'Der identity protector', *Datenschutz und Datensicherheit*, vol 11, pp 654-8.

Borking, J.J. and Giezen, J. (2001) 'Privacy threat analysis', EU–PISA project, The Hague (deliverable D 7, at www.pet-pisa.nl).

Borking, J.J. and Raab, C.D. (2001) 'Laws, PETs and other technologies for privacy protection', *Journal of Information, Law and Technology*, January, vol 1, no 1 (http://elj.warwick.ac.uk/jilt/01-1/borking.html).

Catlett, J. (2000) 'Open letter to P3P developers and replies', *CFP2000: Challenging the assumptions, proceedings of the tenth conference on computers, freedom and privacy*, New York, NY: Association for Computing Machinery, pp 155-64 (www.junkbusters.com/ht/en/standards.html).

Clarke, R. (1996) 'Identification, anonymity and pseudonymity in consumer transactions: a vital systems design and public policy issue', Conference on 'Smart Cards: The Issues', Sydney, 18 October (available at www.anu.edu.au/people/Roger.Clarke/DV/AnonPsPol.html).

CoE (Council of Europe) (1989) *Protection of personal data used for employment purposes*, Recommendation No R (89) 2, adopted by the Committee of Ministers, 18 January.

Dutch Ministry of the Interior (2004) *Privacy enhancing technologies: White book for decision makers*, December.

Federath, H. (ed) (2001) *Designing privacy enhancing technologies: Design issues in anonymity and unobservability*, Heidelberg/New York, NY: Springer Verlag, pp 96-129.

Fischhoff, B., Lichtenstein, S., Slovic, P., Derby, S.L. and Keeney, R.L. (1981) *Acceptable risk*, Cambridge: Cambridge University Press.

Flaherty, D.H. (2000) *Privacy impact assessments: An essential tool for data protection, in one world, one privacy*, Roma: Garante per la Protezione dei Dati Personali.

France (2000) *One world, one privacy*, Roma.

Hes, R. and Borking, J. (1998) *Privacy-enhancing technologies: The path to anonymity*, The Hague: Registatiekamer, pp 15-22.

Hes, R., Borking, J.J. and Hooghiemstra, T.F.M. (1998) *At face value: On biometrical identification and privacy*, Background Studies and Surveys No 15 of the Dutch Data Protection Authority, The Hague.

Kenny, S. and Borking, J. (2002) 'The value of privacy engineering', *Journal of Information, Law and Technology*, vol 1, pp 1-14 (http://elj.warwick.ac.uk/jilt/02-1/kenny.html).

Patrick, A. (2003) 'Privacy, trust, agents and users: a review of human-factors issues associated with building trustworthy software agents', in G.W. van Blarkom, J.J. Borking and J.G.E. Olk (eds) *Handbook of privacy and privacy-enhancing technologies: The case of intelligent software agents*, The Hague: Dutch Data Protection Authority, pp 153-68.

Raab, C.D. (1999) 'Identity checks – and balances', in E. Bort and R. Keat (eds) *The boundaries of understanding: Essays in honour of Malcolm Anderson*, Edinburgh: International Social Sciences Institute, pp 87-95.

Susser, E.S., Herman, S.B. and Aaron, B. (2002) 'Combating the terror of terrorism', *Scientific American*, August, vol 287, no 2, pp 56-61.

van Blarkom, G.W. and Borking, J.J. (2001) *Security measures for personal data*, Background Studies and Surveys No 23, Dutch Data Protection Authority, The Hague (www.cbpweb.nl).

van den Hoven, J. (1998) 'Privacy and the varieties of informational wrongdoing', *Australian Journal of Professional and Applied Ethics*, vol 1, no 1, pp 30-43.

Walzer, M. (1995) 'The art of separation, the communitarian critique of liberalism', in A. Etzioni (ed) *New communitarian thinking: Persons, virtues, institutions and communities*, Charlottesville, VA/London: University of Virginia Press.

Part Two: Contexts

4

The data-informed marketing model and its social responsibility

Martin Evans

Introduction

The blend of tracking customers' transactions, their financial status, profile characteristics and financial value to the company has now become the bedrock marketing model for many businesses and is being extended by the use of many more sources of personal data. Furthermore, the last 20 years or so have seen a number of significant developments that have fuelled this even further. This chapter explores some of these together with possible social implications arising from their implementation.

More specifically, the chapter is structured around four themes. First, the positive contribution of the data-informed marketing model to both business and consumers. Second, the increasing range of sources of data for this model together with their nature and uses in marketing. Then there is discussion of possible implications for business, individuals and society of the ways in which the model is – and might – be operationalised. Finally, recommendations are made with regard to how emerging issues of concern might be addressed.

The contribution of the data-informed marketing model to business (and consumers)

First, the nature of the data–informed marketing model is briefly outlined. The model represents a major shift from relatively anonymised targeting via mass media communications, to the identification and targeting of named individuals. This is based, in part, on the rationale that there can be fewer 'missed targets' if marketers concentrate on those who are either known to have an interest in their products and services or possess characteristics that match those who do. There are also potential advantages to consumers, some of whom might want to be treated as individuals, so the data-informed model can result in more individualised direct forms of customer–organisation interaction. It also affords convenience advantages for many consumers because they can save the time that would otherwise be spent searching bricks and mortar stores.

Contribution to 'the bottom line'

Consider the following: a TV advertising campaign for a gardening product might use primetime slots between 7pm and 9pm for which the audience might be five million households. The 30-second advertisement might cost £50,000 for nationwide coverage, and if there are three repeated exposures per evening for a month, costs would be around £4.5 million plus production and payment of celebrity opinion formers, of, say, £½ million. Total costs for the campaign would therefore be around £5 million.

Now, consider the purchase of a list of 500,000 names and addresses of consumers who subscribe to gardening magazines and who have responded to gardening competitions. This would be a 'warm list' of those who have expressed interest in gardening. The cost of renting the list might be around £80 per thousand names, which would be £40,000 plus production and mailing costs of, say, £300 per thousand (£150,000). This would total £190,000 for the campaign. If the response is, say, 8%, the 40,000 responders would have cost the company £4.75 each (£190,000/40,000). However, the TV campaign would normally produce nothing like this response rate and there might only be, say, a 0.5% response (25,000 people). The £5 million campaign would have cost £200 per response (£5,000,000/25,000).

Clearly this approach wins in this example because, although it oversimplifies reality, it shows how more focused targeting, based on having contact details of specific individuals, can help marketers demonstrate the cost effectiveness of their campaigns. This is increasingly necessary, as pressures on marketing budgets require marketing managers to be more accountable to their budget holders.

It is no surprise, then, that many companies have become relatively disillusioned with traditional mass media communications over recent years partly because of the high costs of media advertising. But there are other reasons why marketers have been searching for alternatives.

Contribution to targeting and individualism

Market fragmentation

At the same time as the cost effectiveness of media campaigns has been queried, there has been an explosion in the number of communications channels. Consider the number of specialist magazines that marketers could select to promote their wares. Only ten years ago there were far fewer teenage, computer, or money-management magazines than adorn newsagents' shelves today. Before 1980 there was only one commercial TV channel in the UK; now, courtesy of cable and satellite technology, there are hundreds. This has created a 'clutter' of marketing messages for the consumer and the marketer has to find ways of cutting through it to reach target prospects. The divorce rate has risen and with it the number of small and single households of both sexes, so again marketers need to target the increasing number of smaller, fragmented market segments.

Fragmentation of markets has also resulted in diminishing audiences for individual media and this has resulted in mass communication being seen as less effective. The Henley Centre (1978) predicted this trend as far back as the 1970s when they discussed household behaviour as being 'cellular' rather than 'nuclear' – households were beginning to do things together less and less and beginning to behave more independently: families were not eating together as often and were having TV and sound systems in their 'own' rooms.

Individualism

One reason for such fragmentation of markets is consumers' desire to be treated more as individuals. Evidence of the trend toward individualism was uncovered during the 1970s and led, among other things, to the Regan and Thatcher election campaigns from the late 1970s and into the 1980s based on 'self-reliance' (BBC2, 2002). 'Standing on one's own feet' and 'freeing the individual from the state' were the sorts of mantras of those elections and were manifestations of research that revealed individualism (McNulty, 2002).

Individualism is manifested in greater pluralism within society, evident in the high street where pluralism in clothing styles is observable. The logical extension of this is that if more consumers want to express individuality, then it provides marketers with opportunities to treat them individually and not only offer more self-expressive products but also to target them as individuals.

Contribution to relational interaction

Relational marketing is not concerned simply with a one-time sale but aims to build long-term relationships with customers as a way of realising their life-time value. The connections are based on the mutuality of interaction between equal partners and characterised by trust, commitment, communication and sharing, which result in the mutual achievement of goals. This is probably somewhat idealistic but the principles might be regarded as normative objectives. The successful implementation of relational marketing would also make marketing more efficient because (wasteful) expenditure on advertising and promotion could be reduced because of the more relevant targeting.

Taking these points further, marketers have grasped opportunities to extend individualised interaction beyond mere transactions and into 'relationships'. They see significant competitive advantage through this because the knowledge of individual customers and potential customers can be used to predict what they might want to buy, thus interacting with them as if they were in a relationship. Analysis of customer data can also lead to the identification of those who contribute most (financially) to the company and those who contribute little. The former can be the focus of targeting and the latter 'deselected' or excluded (a point discussed later).

In effect, data–informed targeting is seen to have the potential to overcome many of the difficulties of advertising clutter and market fragmentation as well as contributing to marketing being more cost effective. It can also satisfy consumers' desire for easier and more direct ways of dealing with companies at the same time as allowing marketers to exploit the desires of some customers to be treated as individuals. Repeated interaction between the 'direct customer' and the 'direct marketer' can, potentially, lead to relationship marketing which, in theory, can enhance the treatment of customers as individuals at the same time as gaining competitive advantage for companies, especially in markets where retention of existing customers is much cheaper than acquiring new ones.

Whereas this section has briefly analysed some of the 'demand' drivers within the context of the contribution of data–informed direct marketing to marketers and consumers, the following section explores some of the 'supply' catalysts in explaining the growth of this phenomenon, within the context of an expanding range of sources of personalised data for marketing.

Sources, types and uses of personal data

One effect of modern business is that consumers and companies are generally not as close to each other as was sometimes the case in the past. Retailers, in particular, used to know their customers well. In earlier decades, for example, the 'corner shop' catchment area was relatively small and customers would shop several times every week. Shopkeepers would be able to get to know them, their families and their purchase patterns. Now, of course, so many of us shop at more anonymised superstores that have adopted self-service (and in some cases self-scanning) approaches. In the absence of intimate knowledge of individual customers based on real interpersonal contact, the database promises to be a surrogate for the type of knowledge of customers referred to above. This section focuses on how different sorts of data can perform this function. Figure 4.1 summarises some of these sources and types of data available to

Figure 4.1: Data 'layers'

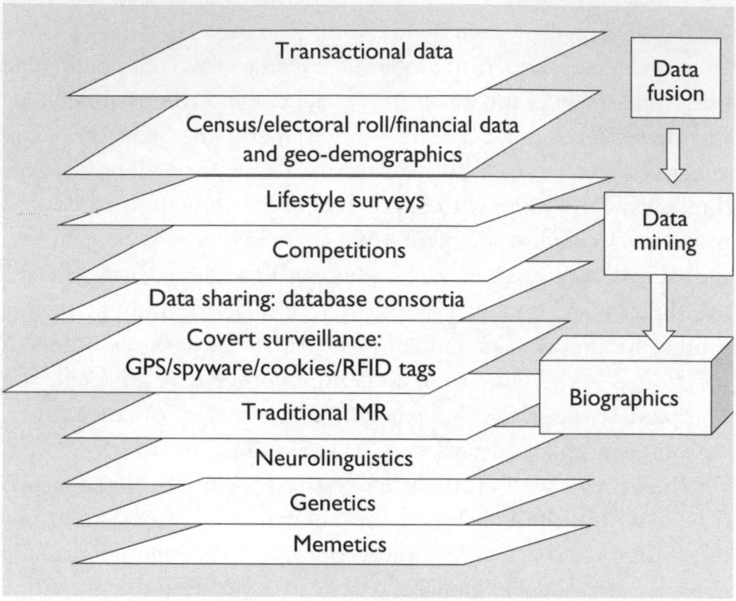

Note: GPS = global positioning satellites; RFID = radio frequency
identification; MR = market research.

companies. For many, the starting point would be their own internal
data on customer transactions.

Transactional data

Transactional data can easily be collected via the barcode scanning
systems linked with individual shoppers' loyalty cards. For example,
for a certain Mrs Brown, an inspection of a retail loyalty scheme
database would reveal her address and a variety of behavioural
information: that she shops once per week, usually on a Friday, has
a baby (because she buys nappies), spends £90 per week on average
and usually buys two bottles of gin every week (Mitchell, 1996).
By knowing what individual consumers buy and the value of their
average shopping basket, the retailer might be able to target them
with relevant offers while the consumers save money in the process.
Targeting is likely to be increasingly at point-of-sale rather than

time-lagged via mailshots. Various supermarkets, for example, are experimenting with 'smart-trolleys' which, once customers have swiped their loyalty card, will be able to access their transactional profiles in order to target relevant offers in real-time and indeed in the right location within the store. The use of radio frequency identification (RFID) tags (as will be discussed later) will be able to track where the customers are in store, relative to the aisles that are relevant to these personalised offers. If customers see this as a convenient and timely benefit, then probably there will be few problems. However, there can be concerns over the wider implications of the collection and use of personal data as later sections explore.

The collection of transactional data is increasingly facilitated via loyalty card schemes. We are beginning to see the introduction of 'smart' cards, which look like an ordinary credit or loyalty card but which incorporate a small memory chip, which can also store large amounts of cardholder information, from age and date of birth to previous purchases and even medical records (Evans et al, 1996).

Transactional data are analysed by marketers to identify patterns of buying, so that relevant offers can be made to appropriate consumers at appropriate times. The method of communicating offers could be via mail, telephone, e-mail, fax or, as suggested earlier, at point-of-sale. All of this could be of great value to consumers as well, as long as such communication is timely, accurate and relevant. If not, consumers will apply the 'junk' label to such communication.

Another major component of transactional data analysis concerns a range of 'metrics' that are used to identify the 'better' customers in terms of the recency, frequency and monetary value (RFMV) of their purchase patterns and the extent of individual customers' long-time value (LTV) to the organisation (this is a sort of profit and loss account for each customer based on projecting purchase patterns over future years). There are some implications of this, such as the possible exclusion of some customers on the grounds of relatively low financial contributions, and this issue is explored later.

Transactional data are 'behavioural', that is, they identify what consumers have actually purchased. This is increasingly being overlaid by other data that aims to profile individuals even further: in terms of their characteristics, lifestyles, financial standing, their housing neighbourhood, and so on.

Profile data

Census/electoral roll/financial data/geo-demographics

The use of the national Census for marketing purposes in the UK led to the development of geo-demographic systems and was a major catalyst in providing alternatives to anonymised market research samples. The 1981 Census was the first to be so analysed and, although names and addresses cannot be revealed from the Census, a link via the postcode system with the electoral roll means that it is possible to identify individual households and their characteristics.

There are several geo-demographic products, but two leading ones are ACORN and MOSAIC from the companies CACI and Experian respectively. These companies now overlay analyses of Census data with a variety of other data sources including financial data such as county court judgements (CCJs) for bad debt and lifestyle survey data (see below). The result is a profile of neighbourhoods, often at full postcode level of around 15 households. The basic rationale behind geo-demographics is that 'birds of a feather flock together', making neighbourhoods relatively homogenous. An easy criticism in repost, however, is that 'I am not like my neighbour'.

Marketers can easily profile the area around a postcode in terms of geo-demographic categories. This could be the catchment area of an existing retail outlet, bank, pub, and so on, or it could be the profiling of a 'drive time' distance around one of several possible locations to site a new branch of a multiple retailer. It is likely that the retailer would know the geo-demographic profile of existing best customers and from this use the geo-demographic profiles of potential areas to select the most promising site.

In other circumstances a marketer might be able to profile their 'best' customers in geo-demographic terms and, in order to acquire 'more of the same' (in an acquisition strategy), could purchase (from Experian or CACI, for example) the names and addresses of others who match this profile, for potential direct mail or telemarketing contact.

One issue concerning geo-demographics that has raised data protection concerns is the use of the electoral roll. In November 2001 a member of the public won his case against Wakefield Council, which had not been able to confirm that his electoral roll data (name and address) would not be supplied to third parties (such as marketers) without his consent (Acland, 2001). This had been a worry of the Information Commissioner who had been concerned that the electoral roll, which is compiled for voting purposes, should not be used for another purpose (one of the principles of the data protection legislation). The result has been the inclusion of opt-out options for electoral roll submissions and this should help to alleviate privacy concerns. But this means that only a smaller and, by definition, an incomplete electoral roll can now be used. Even within months of the electoral roll 'opt-out' being introduced, over 10 million people had opted out (Larkins, 2003) and by 2004 this had risen to 26% of the population (McElhatton, 2004). So there are problems for marketers in the database's lack of geographical coverage. For about 8% of local authorities, in excess of 40% of citizens opted out, but for about 16% of authorities, the proportion doing so was less than 10%, so there is tremendous variation in the completeness of the electoral roll around the country. One reason why the industry wants access to the electoral roll is to check the accuracy of names and addresses, for geo-demographic systems and for targeting purposes but also for credit referencing. In terms of the former, the reduced completeness of the electoral roll could lead to an increase in poor (junk) targeting. In terms of the latter, industry has been 'jubilant' over the outcome of a court case that would have contested the legitimate use of the electoral roll for credit referencing. The case collapsed due to the failure of the complainant to secure legal aid (Rubach, 2003).

Lifestyle surveys

The contemporary 'lifestyle survey' asks respondents to tick those responses that apply in terms of the products and services for which they claim an interest or actually purchase. Many questions are included, covering (claimed) buying behaviour across many different product and service categories. In the mid-1990s several companies operated these surveys. They were sent to the majority of UK households either via addressed or unaddressed mail, leaflet drops or as inserts in newspapers and magazines. More recently there has been some consolidation in the industry and most are run by the same companies that operate geo-demographic products, such as Experian and CACI. Some questions are sponsored by specific companies – for example a car insurance company might sponsor a question asking for the month in which the car insurance is renewed. Because these surveys are not anonymised (the data will be filed in a database by name and address of respondent and used to compile mailing lists), it is likely that the month prior to respondents' renewal date, they will receive direct mailings soliciting defection to the sponsoring company.

One topical application is the use of lifestyle data as a sort of surrogate for the missing millions from the electoral roll as a result of the new opt-out facility discussed earlier. But there are likely to be accuracy and reliability concerns unless lifestyle surveys become more precise and useful. It is well known that lifestyle surveys are prone to a degree of respondent bias, sometimes of a cynical nature (to deliberately undermine the quality of the data collected). There is a degree of concern among marketers that lifestyle surveys are not entirely accurate and can sometimes lead to poor targeting. However, their coverage is extensive, with the industry claiming that over 16 million individuals have completed a lifestyle survey.

There is a concern that as more 'surveys' are used to populate marketing databases with personalised data, consumers are tiring not only of them but also of traditional anonymised market research as well, the former tarnishing the image of the latter.

Competitions

Competitions have long been used not only as a form of sales promotion but also to gather personalised data. It is obvious that those entering a competition could be existing customers but equally they might never have had any contact with the organisation concerned. As a result, the competition is a good way to gather data from prospects as well as to upgrade existing data on customers, depending on the sorts of questions asked. Indeed these questions are often the main purpose of the competition, even if, to the entrant, the competition itself is more clearly *their* intent.

Data sharing

There is clear evidence of a trend toward the creation of strategic alliance *consortia* between companies based on sharing data (Marsh, 1998). For example, an insurance company could have an agreement with motor companies, a vehicle breakdown service and a satellite TV company. There is clearly synergy to be had between these if data are shared, with respect to complementary business via 'cross-selling'. Indeed, Unilever, Kimberley Clark, and Cadbury have formed the Consumer Needs Consortium (called JIGSAW), which aims to reduce research and database costs.

Another significant consortium operating in the financial services sector (called TANK!), involves the Royal Bank of Scotland and is backed by the Direct Marketing Association (DMA) and Institute of Direct Marketing (IDM). Forty other financial services organisations have pledged support (Kemeny, 1998a). Although initially the intention was to pool general relational marketing statistics, it soon progressed to sharing data on responses to different types of direct marketing campaign (Kemeny, 1998b) in order to identify general approaches that work more effectively.

At the time of writing, the Nectar Consortium included BP, Debenhams, Barclaycard, Sainsbury's, First Quench (whose brands include Thresher Wine Shop, Victoria Wine, Wine Rack, Bottoms Up, Drinks Cabin, Haddows and Huttons), Adams, Ford, Vodafone and EDF Energy (whose brands include London Energy, Seeboard Energy and SWEB Energy), with more likely to join (especially from the banking, pharmaceutical and dry-cleaning sectors). By the end of the scheme's first year of operation, Loyalty Management UK (the operating company) claimed that over 12 million households (50% of UK households) held at least one card (Bennion, 2003). The 'small print' of this scheme states: "Information regarding the specific goods or services you buy from a particular participating company will not be passed to us or any other participating company except where required to do so to operate the Nectar programme" (Nectar loyalty programme application form, 2002). The implication is that consumers may not be fully aware of which companies will see their personal data (this is another issue explored later).

In the UK, 216 catalogue companies are signed up to the Abacus data-sharing consortium. Its databases have been combined into one, holding information on around 215 million catalogue transactions from 26 million individual consumers. These data are further enhanced by Claritas' Lifestyle Universe, which overlays income, lifestyle and lifestage data at an individual level for every UK household. Updated weekly, it gives users access to every mail order buyer in the UK (May, 2002).

Surveillance

Global positioning satellites (GPS) can track the location of mobile phones to within several metres without the owner knowing. The extent of public awareness of this is not clear. In the UK an aerial photographic census also is being created (Anon, 1999) by Simmons Aerofilms and the National Remote Sensing Centre. This census will be married with other data sets such as the national Census (Stannard, 1999). The value of this is that actual photographs of properties can reveal further details of households – whether there are solar panels on the roof, swimming pools in the back garden or caravans in the drive.

There is also the surveillance of web traffic, via technology such as 'cookies': the 'surfing' behaviour of those visiting websites can provide valuable information about how people navigate the Internet. But some consumers might resent this. DoubleClick is a company that specialises in Internet advertising and was sued in California because it was claimed that it obtained and sold personal data unlawfully. The company acquired Abacus (see above) and this "enabled it to combine anonymous internet usage data with personal consumer information ... amass a range of detailed information on consumers visiting certain sites, including their names, addresses, age, shopping patterns and financial information" (Dixon, 2000, p 10).

What some see as the replacement for the bar code, RFID technology is an interesting development. These are small tags, some so small as a grain of sand, which are embedded within products or their packaging. They emit radio signals that can be collected by handheld or static scanners. Their main current use is to track goods as they move through supply chains and help in the stock control and ordering processes. However, they are being used in experiments by various retailers, such as Marks & Spencer, House of Fraser and Tesco, to track items in store. Not only can this lead to more accurate shelf stacking, but as mentioned earlier with respect to the 'smart trolley', the tags potentially can trigger offers of complementary products (cross-selling) in real time, as the consumer moves through the store.

Another application is in tackling theft. As items are taken off the shelves, they can be tracked through (and out of) the store and matched with what was actually paid for. Some tags could even incorporate a miniature camera that can help identify thieves (BBC Radio 4, 2003). The future use of such tags might be much broader, however, and could include tracking post purchase (or theft) and even through to disposal: GPS tracking of the tags can even be used. RFID tags also could become an alternative to biometric recognition because the tagged clothes of a consumer could help a retailer, as the consumer enters the store, to identify from where the clothes were purchased and the personal details of the consumer.

The film *Minority Report* demonstrated real time recognition of customers as they entered a store or even just walked around a shopping mall. Recognition was via automatic retina identification (biometrics) and on this basis customer transactional and profile records were accessed and relevant promotions and offers delivered at the same time. This might have been futuristic at the time of the film's release (2002) but the technology is certainly available and perhaps RFID will even replace this. A London department store and a casino have already introduced biometric recognition (facial recognition software) so that their 'special' customers can be recognised as they enter and then quickly greeted personally by a manager (Steiner, 2002); and, again, RFID could be an alternative way of identifying customers – as long as they didn't swap clothes!

Does the prospect of being tracked every minute of the day via the items we carry or wear, represent an invasion of personal privacy?

Some clearly think so, as reported elsewhere (for example, London, 2003; Shabi, 2003). Again, those not contributing as much financially to the company are not likely to be targeted with such attractive offers and this 'exclusion' issue is addressed later.

Market research

Another type of data is that generated by market research; this is not attributed to named individuals, yet it performs a very significant role. It is reassuring that traditional market research data are not being totally ignored by industry, because it is important to understand 'why' consumer 'behaviour' is as found via response rates to personalised targeting. This only comes from more qualitative research. But there is also evidence that companies are concentrating on transactional and profile data because they see this as *the* surrogate for insightful understanding. For example, Mitchell (2001, p 14) quotes a director of one of the largest retailers in UK:

> We've given up trying to understand our customers ... helping us cut a lot of complexity from our business. The academic's instinct is to gather a large amount of information, formulate a theory, and apply it to a situation ... [this] creates waste in the form of the wrong information at the wrong time, leading to the wrong decisions ... or ... fruitless attempts to predict or alter customer behaviour.

The favoured approach by this company, 'sense and respond' (Haeckel, 2001), is to react quickly on the basis of customer contact via call centres, the Internet and interactive digital TV. This is understandable in the current context of pressure to achieve short-term profit in order to provide shareholder value. However, it can lead to a relegation of more affective customer understanding in favour of behavioural and tracking transactional data.

Neurolinguistics

Different people process information differently, *neurolinguistically*. Indeed it has been found that male and female brains process information differently (Evans et al, 2000), with the female brain taking more notice of more cues within a piece of communication and using colour, imagery and graphics much more to interpret meaning compared with the typical male brain. Neurolinguistic Programming (NLP), as it is termed, uses knowledge of how information processing styles differ and is being used in practice to target consumers. Tunney (1999) explains its use by one company in identifying 14 different types of information processing styles. Ford is also using brain scans to detect which car designs prompt different responses and the Open University with London Business School are using them to evaluate TV commercials. As Steven Rose, director of brain and behaviour research at the Open University, states, "What would be worrying would be if marketers, governments or police felt they could control people's thoughts by manipulating brain processes in this way.... I am not sure marketing are going to be looking at this ... but I would be surprised if they don't" (Leighton, 2004). It is interesting to revisit Packard at this point, who wrote: "Eventually – say by A.D. 2000 – perhaps all this depth manipulation of the psychological variety will seem amusingly old-fashioned. By then perhaps the biophysicists will take over 'biocontrol', which is depth persuasion carried to its ultimate" (Packard, 1957).

Genetics

There are concerns over the use of genetic data for assessing insurance risk (Specter, 1999). Clearly, for financial services companies, it would be useful to be able to assess risks on the basis that genes patterns can indicate individuals' future potential susceptibility to illness or disease (Borna and Avila, 1999). In a survey of 3,000 UK households, three quarters were against genetic tests for insurance underwriting, 85% against insurance companies rejecting applicants on this basis and 78% against them charging higher premiums on the basis of genetic tests. Indeed, 68% of the sample thought that this use of genetic data should be prohibited by law (Borna and Avila, 1999). Introna and Powlouda (1999) report that medics have expressed concern over this trend. The logical extension of the scenario is that those who do not need insuring will be insured and the rest will be excluded. This issue is considered in more detail in Chapter Six of this volume.

Memetics

Another type of data that might raise some ethical concerns is the science of *memetics*. This has recently attracted significant attention (Dawkins, 1989; Marsden, 1998, 1999; Blackmore, 1999; Williams, 2002). Whereas a 'gene' passes forms of behaviour down (vertically) through the generations, a meme acts as a sort of 'horizontal' communicator of how to behave. The difference, however, is that memes work more like a viral contagion. A good example of the principle is how it is often difficult not to start yawning if others are yawning (Marsden, 1998). Could memes go some way to explaining the spread of extreme xenophobia, Nazism or ethnic cleansing? It might be an unconscious communication and one that might be most enduring if instilled at an early age. Will it become possible to 'create' a meme that marketers can use to communicate through societies, with consumers becoming infected with a mind virus that is not recognised consciously, but which results in them suddenly joining the next fad or fashion? Some say this is nearly possible and research is being conducted to "design and engineer highly infectious memes that could be used in marketing campaigns" (Marsden, 1998).

To summarise this section so far, there is a range of personalised data sources that marketers are using, experimenting with or considering using. The vast majority of personalised data for marketing purposes lies within the first four 'layers' in Figure 4.1. Indeed these sources are now considered to be mainstream underpinning of the data-informed marketing model. Many marketers are exploring the use of the fifth, sixth and seventh 'layers' and others might see the last three as the next phase. It is a pity that more do not use traditional market research to inform the more behavioural data with affective insights.

Having explored some of the data sources available to companies, it is worth extending the discussion of how this information is used. The 'metrics' of RFMV and LTV, introduced earlier, can be used to select different market segments for differential targeting and new interactive media can facilitate two-way communication, as discussed below.

Technological facilitators

New technological media (for example, the Internet, interactive TV, mobile telephony, kiosks, and so on) have opened up new channels of interactive dialogue, which can be customer initiated as well as organisation initiated. As much of society continues to be 'time poor' due to long working hours, many seek timesaving purchasing methods, such as direct mail and telemarketing. The continuing trend away from cash as the means of payment to credit, debit and smart cards, through the post and over telephone and Internet cables, has enabled purchasing behaviour to take place when the customer wants it – 24 hours per day and from the armchair, office, travelling laptop computer and even a mobile phone that can also access the Internet. There can therefore be clear advantages to being a 'direct consumer' and 'direct marketing' is its reciprocal.

Telephonic technology now facilitates the real time targeting of potential customers via, for example, GPS analysis so that consumers walking past a store can be contacted at that moment via their mobile phone, with offers that might be based on their transaction or profile characteristics. Biometric recognition has already been mentioned and this is the likely technology for the UK's proposed identity card scheme.

Digital printing technology allows personalised mail-based targeting to a high degree: "You can personalise page by page, it's easy to put a name anywhere throughout the copy" (Arnold, 2002, p 12). A development of this in the US was what appeared to be a handwritten mailing targeted at members of a particular healthcare segment. So convincing was this that over 150 people complained on the basis that it looked like a friend writing to them telling them they needed to lose weight (Rubach, 2002).

Mobile telephony is also a major new medium. In the Indian government election of 2004, wireless short message service (SMS) messaging was a major communications vehicle for the political parties. The film company Twentieth Century Fox has a 'home entertainment' unit and for the launch of the DVD version of the film *Minority Report*, they used a sound clip from the film. Receivers of this telephone message were surprised to hear a man drawing breath and then saying: "Where's my Minority Report?" and then screaming: "Do I even have one?". The voice was Tom Cruise, the star of the film. The message ended: "Don't miss out on your Minority Report. Buy it now on DVD and video". This led to complaints to the Advertising Standards Authority (ASA) based on the telephone message being offensive and that it could have caused distress and, indeed, that it did not make clear it was an advertisement. Some people who received the message had to pay to call their answer phone to retrieve the message if they had not been able to answer their phone when it was initially sent. Twentieth Century Fox Home Entertainment justified this by saying that it was only sent to those who had registered their details on the company's website (30,000 of them) and had actually asked for communications concerning films and DVDs. So the company considered it appropriate to communicate with those who had 'opted in' for relational interaction. The company also thought that most people who had expressed this sort of interest would be familiar with Tom Cruise's voice. However, the ASA upheld the complaints on the basis that when consumers are out of the film context and going about their daily routine they would not necessarily be thinking of receiving a message from Tom Cruise and the nature of the message could indeed be seen to be somewhat menacing and could therefore cause offence (Rosser, 2003).

Technology will continue to facilitate more examples of personalised targeting of selected market segments. It may be possible to target an individualised TV message, analogous to personalised mailing, to a unique address via fibre optic cable (Channel 4, 1990). However, this technology is still only in experimental form.

The significant point about personalised two-way interactive media is that it affords a very different approach from traditional mass media one-way communications media.

Relational use: do consumers want it?

Such mutual interaction, at least according to marketers, can lead to the development of relationships, but do all customers really want a 'relationship' with their bank or supermarket? Some will certainly develop affective attachment to various brands through the normal image-building process of mass media advertising and product use, but there is little evidence that the majority of consumers see personalised marketing facilitating a positive relationship, based on the constructs of relationship marketing (mutual respect, commitment, cooperation and trust).

Many of the data sources outlined earlier are being fused within (and between) data-informed companies with a view to developing a clearer understanding of their customers for closer relational interaction. This fusion leads to 'biographics', which are a detailed description of individuals' purchasing behaviour and profile characteristics. However, although companies can collect personalised data and fuse and mine them to form biographical profiles, this, also, should be used in a true relational way, according to the above components of relationship theory. There is a degree of theory–practice mismatch here because companies are not overly concerned with inviting customers to establish mutual relationships based on information exchange. Consider the following: "Relationship marketing ... requires a two-way flow of information. This does not mean that the customer has to give you this information willingly, or even knowingly. You can use scanners to capture information, you can gather telephone numbers, conduct surveys, supply warranty cards, and use a data overlay from outside databases to combine factors about lifestyle, demographics, geographics, psychograhics, and customer purchases" (Schultz et al, 1993).

This, possibly commonplace view, would define relational interaction between companies and consumers as an oxymoron. The implications of this will be considered in the next section.

The social and business implications of the data-informed marketing model

Consumer reactions

For customers, personalised direct interaction may indeed offer a number of substantial benefits. For example, the consumer can interact with organisations more conveniently (Lavin, 1993) via the Internet or telephony and organisations will be able to treat them as known individuals via their biographical databases. Because they can explore a range of different suppliers of products and services from the relative comfort of home (or office), they can access a more extensive product assortment (Gehrt and Carter, 1992). Some, however, will prefer face-to-face contact and the social dimension of 'shopping'.

Also, Perri 6 (1998) and Evans et al (2001) found that the situation is complex. At the same time as participating in direct interaction, consumers also express various concerns. They are, for example, simultaneously, streetwise and cynical. Although direct personalised targeting is clearly a convenience to the time-constrained contemporary consumer, it can also be its own worst enemy because the consumer can be bombarded by unwanted or untimely (junk) information.

There is also a 'privacy paradox' in that some consumers are somewhat cynical about 'relational' interaction and concerned about divulging personal information, but are participants nevertheless. There might be a desire on the part of organisations to develop relationships with customers but customers do not always want to reciprocate. Consumers are increasingly cynical about companies in general, so companies using the rhetoric of relational interaction are often likely to be met with disbelief and distrust (Evans et al, 2001). It is likely that this cynicism is predicated upon a lack of trust resulting from business scams, unfulfilled promises and marketing hype.

There are further problems with the data-informed model, in terms of 'who else' has access to personal consumer data. This raises issues of the security of data exchange and privacy.

Data used for other purposes

State data for marketing databases

Whereas the Census was originally, and indeed for many decades, used for social planning (transport, housing, and so on) from 1981, as we have seen, it has also been used commercially. The 2001 Census was the first to be announced to citizens as being for business planning as well as social planning. New questions potentially relevant to companies were added as a result of their lobbying. In fact the 2001 Census included a clever question revealing the sexuality of the respondent's partner (Exon, 1998; Brindle, 1999). The question wording asked for names of partners in the household and presumably marketers will assume same or different sex partners to indicate sexuality (the gay market being an important one for many companies to target, and possibly for some insurance companies to exclude). But are all consumers aware of these developments and in any case would they be comfortable with them?

The main proposition here is whether 'social'/'state' data ending up in company databases is a wider societal concern. Perhaps it is *not*, at a simple and innocent level, but the creeping commitment of what individuals are required to divulge to the state and then the incremental nature of what companies can access from the state is a legitimate concern because it is not always clear that information divulged for one purpose will actually be used for others.

Research data for marketing databases

Sometimes information is collected without there being clear commercial reasons but because it is thought it might be useful at some later stage of more sophisticated data mining (the analysis and modelling of data). Data protection legislation actually states that the data collected should be adequate and not excessive, but marketers can easily declare the importance of all that is collected. So again there is the issue of data collection for dubious purposes. In not all instances are consumers aware that their information will be used to update personalised records.

Marketing data for state databases

Consumer data held by companies are being used by government departments. CACI, for example, has an entire department dealing exclusively with government contracts for its ACORN geo-demographic and related products. As discussed earlier, geo-demographic systems use an increasing range of financial data sources to overlay Census, housing and demographic data. The resulting 'financial' ACORN and MOSAIC products can easily be seen to be of potential value to the Inland Revenue (for example) to check financial details and trends against tax returns from those they want to investigate further (Key, 2000).

Could it be that the state has been content to provide companies with the space to collect, fuse and mine data from a variety of sources and then for various departments to buy or take what they can use for reducing fraud and for other instances of social (individualised) monitoring? Chapter Five in this volume discusses this further.

Company databases to other companies

This includes the 'data consortia' phenomenon discussed above. The sharing of data is also an issue in terms of new legislation. Mail Marketing (a direct and database marketing company), for example, shared some of its lists with Infocore, a US list company (Wood, 1998). The online retailer Amazon has been accused of transferring data on UK consumers to the US (Walker, 2002). However, the 1998 Data Protection Act prevents companies from exporting personal information to countries that do not have adequate data protection – and this clearly includes the US.

There is a 'treaty' between the EU and the US identifying certain US companies seen as implementing adequate data protection ('Safe Harbor') as discussed by Charles Raab in Chapter Two, this volume. However, even the US president weighed into the debate in 2001 and threatened to withdraw from this because it could hamper US multinational companies that are not part of the treaty. Indeed, it is thought that only a handful of US companies have sufficient data protection to be covered by the treaty (Walker, 2001).

If personalised data are being transferred to unsafe countries, this raises concerns over data security.

So, there are a number of potential concerns over the exchange of personal data beyond the immediate consumer–organisation level. These security dimensions lead us to a brief exploration of the wider privacy issues that can help us form a more contextualised view of the data-informed business model.

Privacy issues

The discussion here aims to explore the constructs of privacy so we can more easily identify what might be privacy concerns.

Information privacy

Information privacy refers to the extent to which individuals can *control* who holds their data, and what is done with those data (Westin, 1967). In the US, many consumers already believe that they have lost all control over how information about them is used, with some even suggesting that, if they could, they would add privacy to their constitutional rights to life, liberty and the pursuit of happiness (Schroeder, 1992). Indeed, there has been a plethora of books written on this issue in the US in recent years (Rothfeder, 1992; Larson, 1994; Charrett, 1999; Chesbro, 1999; Rosen, 2001).

On the other hand, many organisations argue that they should have the right to access consumer information for business purposes. Many marketers believe that because they have committed valuable resources to the development of databases, the information these hold is their property to do with as they see fit (Cespedes and Smith, 1993). Taking this further, it is worth considering the attitudes toward this issue that are held by some in the industry. In 2001 the UK Information Commissioner's Office ran a hard-hitting advertising campaign to warn consumers of the dangers of parting with their personal details. There was an outcry from many direct marketers, as reported in an industry journal: "These ads have angered many industry figures and have been labelled excessive, shocking, inaccurate and, crucially damaging to direct marketers" (Mutel, 2001, p 11). Some went even further: "just what in God's name does the IC [Information Commissioner] think it's doing … the current radio commercial extolling the public to be wary of giving either written or verbal details does nothing but instil fear into the public's mind" (Ramsden, 2001, p 11).

As a result of these privacy conflicts between consumers and organisations, Westin (1992) envisages a rise in what he calls 'consensual databases', where consumers consent to information surrender in return for some type of reward such as coupons, samples or money. However, as Mitchell (2002, p 14) states, "Permission isn't enough ... is ticking a box once, permission to spam me for the rest of my life ... there's only one way out: to put consumers in the driving seat, empowering them to specify what sort of messages they are looking for by time, place and category". In reality there may be no easy solution. Specifying which data for which purposes could be too cumbersome to administer and police.

Physical privacy

Physical privacy relates to the physical intrusion of marketing communications (for example, direct mail, telesales, e-mails) into the daily lives of consumers. The 'hottest' prospects are, somewhat obviously, targeted most heavily, such as those with the highest spending power. Ungoed-Thomas and Nuki (1998) reported their uncovering of a 'Midas' list of those aged between 25 and 45, earning more than £50,000 per annum, who own lots of electronic products and engage in relatively expensive leisure activities. They "are being sent 250 mailshots a year, five times the national average". If these people enjoy receiving information about even more things they can spend their money on, then there probably isn't a problem, as long as they can sustain such expenditure levels. However, many will feel this is just too much – as one consumer reported: "every day it comes through the door ... it's relentless ... I don't read it on principle because Britain is turning into a huge buying experience and I hate it" (Rule, 1998).

Consumers often perceive that they have little or no control over the prospecting efforts of companies (Waldrop, 1994), although the mail, telephone, fax and e-mail 'Preference Services' run by the DMA have started to impact this. It is illegal to telephone a consumer who has withdrawn permission to receive such communications from a company, however the personal data were collected, and databases must be cleaned against the Telephone Preference Services (TPS) list. Although the mail preference service operates on a similar basis, it is not at present legally binding. Level of awareness of these services is not particularly high, so the opportunity exists to raise it.

Accuracy

Accuracy is another privacy construct because incomplete or inaccurate personal details can lead to a different sort of privacy invasion, for example the discourtesy and disrespect that could undermine relationships. Companies clearly do not intend to use personal data inaccurately but "with the amount of data in use by direct marketers it is not surprising that mistakes happen" (Fletcher, 1995, p 58). When the recipient's name and address are incorrect, this can lead to distrust and annoyance.

Concerns over the accuracy of data held might be heightened in certain circumstances, as when inaccurate information about creditworthiness results in exclusion or where there is a failure to clean databases against bereavement registers and Preference Services databases. There are, unfortunately, plenty of examples of inaccurate names and names of deceased people remaining on lists (Reed, 2001).

A related issue is not so much inaccurate targeting but no targeting at all. The following is a brief discussion of 'deselecting' customers.

Social exclusion

As we have seen, an outcome of data mining is the identification of specific customers' contribution to profit because data mining can identify consumers' RFMV and LTV and this in turn can identify not just the 'better' customers but also those who do not contribute as much to profit as the company might wish. This might lead to some disaffection among the 'less attractive' segments of the population when they realise that others are being presented with the 'better' offers. It has been suggested, even from within the industry, that alienated customers might even see this as somewhat 'Orwellian in nature' (Wright, 1999). There are some signs that this has been recognised by government. It set up the Social Exclusion Unit, which is concerned about low-income neighbourhoods becoming devoid of physical stores and financial premises because of company disintermediation strategies. In the US the 1977 Community Reinvestment Act aims to promote responsible lending in poor neighbourhoods.

In summary, we have seen that consumers are increasingly

streetwise yet cynical towards marketing's relationship rhetoric. Their personal data are not always kept within the exchange transaction they expect: there are security issues of data moving to and from the state, to organisations beyond those of the immediate exchange, and their data can even exclude them from any further exchange. The final section now explores some possible recommendations for addressing the emerging concerns.

The way forward

Looking to the future, the data-informed marketing model is going to have to do a better job of facing its responsibilities, if the industry is to achieve its potential. With this in mind there are a number of ways that industry can tackle these difficult issues. This section discusses how permission marketing, self-regulation, consumer education and legislation might help.

Control and permission

Awareness campaigns, for example, for the Preference Services and opt-outs, can show consumers how they can reduce the amount of direct marketing if they so wish. Other media might allow for a shift in the balance of control from marketer to consumer. Such media include the Internet, or other direct response media (Patterson, 1998), which allow consumers to 'go looking' for their interests. Personal details may also become the subject of a different sort of marketing transaction – one in which the consumer is the marketer. By perceiving 'property rights' (Davies, 1998) to apply to personal details, consumers may become vendors of their own details to selected organisations for specified purposes. This shift in the ownership of information might see the rise of intermediaries, or infomediaries, who would act as brokers on behalf of consumers. It might mean something more radical – such as making contracts with consumers whereby they are paid – or rewarded in another way – for revealing certain personal details to named organisations for specific purposes, as proposed by Westin (1992). Mitchell (2001, p 14) thinks that tangible payment could be the answer: "Treat your customer's data as you would his home ... don't enter without permission … once inside, respect his wishes and if you want to use his property/information for your own purposes to make money from it … then pay him rent". There are potential hurdles here as well, though, as 6 has discussed in Chapter One, this volume: will consumers really know the true value of their data? Would payment devalue trust if this were its only measure? Would there be so many opting out altogether that marketing might be forced back to mass marketing, or is this actually *the* solution?

Self-regulation

Privacy and social responsibility issues, for companies, customers and legislators, may be alleviated by increased attempts by the industry to police itself. Self-regulation "goes beyond the minimum requirements of legislation and has to be adhered to in spirit as well as to the letter" (Titford, 1994, p 341). A number of authorities and codes of practice have been introduced by the industry over the last decade:

- The British Code of Advertising Practice (ASA) endorses several more specialised codes, such as that of the DMA.
- The DMA requires its member organisations to adhere to the spirit, not merely the letter, of its Code of Conduct. The DMA also provides more specialised codes for e-Commerce, SMS and e-mail campaigns and for direct marketing to children.
- The Advertising Standards Authority has the 'British Code of Advertising, Sales Promotion and Direct Marketing' Code.
- There is also the Mail Order Protection Scheme (MOPS), which provides financial recompense to consumers after off-the-page selling companies fail.
- The Preference Services reflect a recognition of consumers' rights and concerns.

The problem with all of these codes is that they are not legally binding. Unfortunately, some companies refuse to abide by decisions made by regulatory bodies.

Education

Given that consumer knowledge of data-informed practice is a factor in how they perceive the industry, companies need to allow the consumer greater access to information. Consumers should be made aware of what is collected and for what purpose, to avoid susceptibility to scaremongering by the media. Additionally, they need to know how to protect their information, how to query information held on a company's database, and how to remove their information if they so desire. The Information Commissioner is the most likely sponsor and originator of such education campaigns, but it would not be surprising if consumers would rebel even more if they know the extent of data use, misuse and potential privacy invasion. Or might this be the ultimate solution, to force marketing back to more traditional approaches?

Legislation

It is interesting to check the level of compliance with the 1998 Data Protection Act. In a study of UK-based websites, the University of Manchester Institute of Science and Technology (UMIST) and the Information Commissioner (Macaulay and Bourne, 2002) found a rather mixed picture. The larger companies and those in regulated industries exhibited high levels of compliance but smaller companies and those in unregulated sectors did not. Specific issues included the following:

- There were low levels of internal data security in some small companies.
- Many companies collected and used data even if they did not ask for it (for example, information entered into e-mails or discussion groups/communities). Legally they cannot use such data for which they have not been granted permission by the data subject (consumer).
- Only 60% of children's sites had a privacy policy.

In another study, three quarters of the sample of 200 companies was not prepared for the new data protection legislation of 1998

(GB Information Management, 1999). The lack of awareness among companies is a concern because it suggests they are more concerned with today's campaigns and, perhaps, feel the new legislation is not particularly important. Privacy issues should really be considered as opportunities: if seriously addressed, they could pave the way for a move closer to the (mutual) relational ideal.

Legislation is a partial solution but it needs to be adhered to; indeed, companies might do well to go beyond compliance, if a mutually beneficial relationship with their consumers is their real, not just rhetorical, intention.

Conclusion

We have seen that it has become increasingly possible to develop more personalised, even biographical, understandings of individual customers. This has fuelled the paradigm shift from company–customer *transactional* interaction to the notion of retention and loyalty strategies within *relational* company–customer interaction.

But the dangers expressed in this chapter revolve around 'data' becoming a surrogate for consumer insight. It is clear that both consumers and companies are cynical these days. Consumers engage with personalised interactive targeting, so have a degree of 'personalisation pragmatism', but some are concerned about many of the implications of their personal data being available to many people. At the same time, some companies react against privacy legislation and think of it as a solution looking for a problem.

There are wider implications of personalised targeting in that acceptable relationships between State, companies and consumers could be shifted out of equilibrium when consumer data collected by companies are used by the State and vice versa and when personalised data are abused, albeit mostly inadvertently.

Permission marketing should be deployed and real adherence to (and the exceeding of) voluntary and legal controls is necessary. Maybe even companies should admit the real post-modern agenda: to separate consumers from as much money as is mutually sustainable for reasonably long repeat purchase periods. This can still be mutually beneficial, is realistic and pragmatic (as long as the materialistic consumer society is itself sustainable). If this does not happen then we are in danger of seeing consumer cynicism turning into real discontent, which could lead to even greater distrust of companies. If organisations continue to disregard the moral expectations of society, they are putting themselves on a collision course with consumer dissatisfaction and alienation. This can lead to an increase in the already cynical view that the claim of 'relationships' is mere rhetoric.

References

6, P. (1998) *The future of privacy, volume 1: Private life and public policy*, London: Demos.

Acland, H. (2001) 'Ruling puts DM industry firmly on back foot', *Marketing Direct*, December, p 2.

Anon (1999) 'UK perspectives airs photographic census', *Precision Marketing*, 24 May.

Arnold, C. (2002) reported by Rubach, E. (2002) 'Up close and too personal', *Precision Marketing*, 1 February, p 12.

BBC2 (TV) (2002) *Century of the self*, November.

BBC Radio 4 (2003) 'Beyond the bar code', Radio 4 *In Business* series, 2 October.

Bennion, J. (2003) 'Business awards briefing notes', London: Loyalty Management UK.

Blackmore, S. (1999) *The meme machine*, Oxford: Oxford University Press.

Borna, S. and Avila, S. (1999) 'Genetic information: consumers' right to privacy versus insurance companies, Right to know: a public opinion survey', *Journal of Business Ethics*, vol 19, pp 355-62.

Brindle, D. (1999) 'Census check on partners', *The Guardian*, 5 March, p 12.

Cespedes, F.V. and Smith, H.J. (1993) 'Database marketing: new rules for policy and practice', *Sloan Management Review*, Summer, pp 7-22.

Channel 4 (1990) 'Direct marketing', *Equinox* series.

Charrett, T.S. (1999) *Identity, privacy and personal freedom: Big Brother v new resistance*, Boulder, CO: Paladin Press.

Chesbro, M. (1999) *Privacy for sale: How Big Brother and others are selling your private secrets for profit*, Boulder, CO: Paladin Press.

Davies, S. (1998) 'New data privacy storm threatens global trade war', *Financial Mail on Sunday*, 29 March, p 3.

Dawkins, R. (1989) *The selfish gene*, Buckingham: Open University Press.

Dixon, L. (2000) 'DoubleClick sued over data scandal', *Precision Marketing*, 7 February, p 10.

Evans, M., O'Malley, L. and Patterson, M. (1996) 'Direct marketing communications in the UK: a study of growth, past, present and future', *Journal of Marketing Communications*, vol 2, no 1, pp 51–65.

Evans, M., Nairn, A. and Maltby, A. (2000) 'The hidden sex life of the male and female shot', *International Journal of Advertising*, vol 19, no 1, February, pp 43–65.

Evans, M., O'Malley, L. and Patterson, M. (2001) 'Bridging the direct marketing-direct consumer gap: some solutions from qualitative research', *Qualitative Market Research: An International Journal*, vol 4, no 1, pp 17–24.

Exon, M. (1998) 'The moral marketing maze', *Precision Marketing*, 28 September, p 12.

Fletcher, K. (1995) 'Dear Mr Bastard...', *Marketing Direct*, July/August, vol 58, p 58.

GB Information Management (1999) reported in Anon (1999) 'Most firms ignorant of new data rules', *Marketing*, 20 May, p 10.

Gehrt, K.C. and Carter, K. (1992) 'An exploratory assessment of catalog shopping orientations', *Journal of Direct Marketing*, vol 6, Winter, pp 29–39.

Haeckel, S. (2001) reported in Mitchell, A. (2001) 'Playing cat and mouse games with marketing', *Precision Marketing*, 16 March, p 14.

Henley Centre, The (1978) *Planning consumer markets*, London: The Henley Centre.

Introna, L. and Powlouda, A. (1999) 'Privacy in the information age: stakeholders, interests and values', *Journal of Business Ethics*, vol 22, pp 27–38.

Kemeny, L. (1998a) 'Data "tank" for bank practices', *Precision Marketing*, 16 November, p 1.

Kemeny, L. (1998b) 'Financial services think [tank] for common pool', *Precision Marketing*, 14 December, p 5.

Key, A. (2000) 'The taxman: snooper or helper?', *Marketing Direct*, January, p 7.

Larkins, V. (2003) '10 million tick electoral roll opt-out box', *Marketing Business*, February, p 6.

Larson, E. (1994) *The naked consumer: How our private lives become public commodities*, New York, NY: Penguin.

Lavin, M. (1993) 'Wives' employment, time pressure, and mail/phone order shopping', *Journal of Direct Marketing*, vol 7, no 1, pp 42-9.

Leighton, N. (2004) 'They're reading our minds', *The Sunday Times*, 25 January.

London, S. (2003) 'Radio ID tags spread waves of anger among privacy activists', *Financial Times*, 1 March, p 1.

Macaulay, L.A. and Bourne, I. (2002) 'Study of compliance with the Data Protection Act 1998 by UK based websites', Report, Information Commissioner/UMIST.

McElhatton, N. (2004) 'Opt-out voter rates rising', *Direct Response*, February, p 5.

McNulty, C. (2002) Interview in BBC2, *Century of the self*, November.

Marsden, P.S. (1998) 'Memetics: a new paradigm for understanding customer behaviour and influence', *Marketing Intelligence and Planning*, vol 16, no 6, pp 363-8.

Marsden, P.S. (1999) 'Help advertising evolve: clone consumer thought-patterns', *Admap*, March, pp 37-9.

Marsh, H. (1998) 'What's in store?', *Marketing*, 15 October, pp 37-8.

May, M. (2002) 'DIY data', *Marketing Direct*, July/August, pp 43-4.

Mitchell, A. (1996) Interview in BBC Radio 4 series *You and Yours*, January.

Mitchell, A. (2001) 'New consumer expectations, new way of life', *Precision Marketing*, 12 April, p 14.

Mitchell, A. (2002) 'Permission to target is not a licence to spam', *Precision Marketing*, 12 July, p 14.

Mutel, G. (2001) 'Too much information – a damaging prospect', *Precision Marketing*, 31 August, p 11.

Packard, V. (1957) *The hidden persuaders*, Harmondsworth: Penguin, p 195.

Patterson, M. (1998) 'Direct marketing in postmodernity', *Marketing Intelligence and Planning*, vol 16, no 1, pp 56–67.

Ramsden, I. (2001) reported in Mutel, G. (2001) 'Too much information – a damaging prospect', *Precision Marketing*, 31 August, p 11.

Reed, D. (2001) 'New life for suppression', *Precision Marketing*, 6 July.

Rosen, J. (2001) *The unwanted gaze: The destruction of privacy in America*, New York, NY: Vintage Books.

Rosser, M. (2003) '20th century to persist with voicemail ads', *Precision Marketing*, 14 February, p 1.

Rothfeder, J. (1992) *Privacy for sale: How computerisation has made everyone's private life an open secret*, New York, NY: Simon and Schuster.

Rubach, E. (2002) 'Up close and too personal', *Precision Marketing*, 1 February, p 12.

Rubach, E. (2003) 'Industry hail Robertson defeat', *Precision Marketing*, 23 May, p 1.

Rule, J. (1998) reported in Ungoed-Thomas, J. and Nuki, P. (1998) 'Mailshot firms blitz "Midas" consumers', *The Sunday Times*, 17 May.

Schroeder, D. (1992) 'Life, liberty and the pursuit of privacy', *American Demographics*, June, p 20.

Schultz, D.E., Tannenaum, S.I. and Lauterborn, R.F. (1993) *The new marketing paradigm*, Lincolnwood, IL: NTC Books.

Shabi, R. (2003) 'The card up their sleeve', *Guardian Weekend Magazine*, 19 July, pp 14–19.

Specter, M. (1999) 'Cracking the Norse code', *The Sunday Times Magazine*, 21 March, pp 45–52.

Stannard, H. (1999) reported in Anon (1999) 'UK perspectives airs photographic census', *Precision Marketing*, 24 May, p 5.

Steiner, R. (2002) 'Watch out, big spenders, Big Brother is watching you', *The Sunday Times Business*, 11 August, p 1.

Titford, P. (1994) 'Self-regulation in direct marketing', *Journal of Database Marketing*, vol 2, no 2, p 341.

Tunney, D. (1999) 'Harnessing the subconscious to bolster sales', *Marketing*, 13 May, p 20.

Ungoed-Thomas, J. and Nuki, P. (1998) 'Mailshot firms blitz "Midas" consumers', *The Sunday Times*, 17 May.

Waldrop, J. (1994) 'The business of privacy', *American Demographics*, October, pp 46-54.

Walker, C. (2001) 'US threat to axe data treaty puts multinationals on alert', *Precision Marketing*, 6 April, p 1.

Walker, C. (2002) 'Amazon accused of data law "flout"', *Precision Marketing*, 25 September, p 1.

Westin, A. (1967) *Privacy and freedom*, New York, NY: Athenaeum.

Westin, A. (1992) 'Consumer privacy protection: ten predictions', *Mobius*, February, pp 5-11.

Williams, R. (2002) 'Memetics: a new paradigm for understanding customer behaviour', *Marketing Intelligence and Planning*, vol 20, no 3, pp 162-7.

Wood, J. (1998) 'Mail marketing group to share leads with US firm', *Precision Marketing*, 15 June, p 6.

Wright, B. (1999) as reported in Beenstock S (1999) 'Supermarkets entice the "ultra" consumer', *Marketing*, 15 April, p 15.

5

Personal data in the public sector: reconciling necessary sharing with confidentiality?

Christine Bellamy, Perri 6 and Charles Raab

Introduction

In order to carry out their work, public services collect, process and store vast quantities of data relating to every man, woman and child in the UK. Yet public officials and data subjects alike are confused about the powers that government agencies possess to exploit those data and the safeguards that have been put in place to protect the privacy of the individuals to whom they belong. On the one hand, the impact of the poll tax in reducing rates of returns for the 1991 Census apparently revealed a widespread assumption that different government departments routinely pool personal data. On the other hand, successive reports on child deaths following neglect or abuse – such as the Laming report (2003) into the death of Victoria Climbié – or reports into homicides by people with paranoid schizophrenia who have lost touch with services – for example, Christopher Clunis who in the 1990s killed Jonathan Zito – regularly criticise public services for failing to share data, even about high-risk cases.

Government ministers and public servants often speak of a 'balance' to be struck between data privacy, on the one side, and the advantages to the public interest from greater sharing of personal data, on the other. In the last few years, however, imperatives on government agencies to share more personal data have become much greater, as a result of fundamental shifts in social policy, as well as wider policy pressures for the 'modernisation' and 'joining up' of public services

(6 et al, 2002). At the same time, too, the British government has domesticated into British law the European Directive on data protection in the 1998 Data Protection Act, and also the European Convention of Human Rights, in the 1998 Human Rights Act, which now acknowledges privacy as a fundamental right. The question of the 'balance' between these two imperatives has therefore risen much higher up the public policy agenda than was previously the case, but the question of where and how such a balance should be drawn is still far from being satisfactorily addressed.

In late 2003, the government issued legal guidance on data sharing, arguing that where departments are carrying out functions for which there are proper legal powers, the sharing of personal data for such purposes requires no special authorisation, so long as the principles of data protection law and confidentiality law are followed (DCA, 2003). However, this guidance may be challengeable, turning as it does on definitions that some lawyers continue to regard as contestable. Many public services remain unsure about their exact legal position, not least because they have low confidence in making judgements about who 'needs to know' what information for what purposes, to meet the requirements of confidentiality law and data protection principles.

Data sharing in contemporary British government

The most obvious reason for the growing interest in data sharing in public services, and the associated issue of privacy, is that the Labour government first elected in 1997 has committed itself to a programme for 'modernising' public services. In pursuit of such consumerist values as convenience, comprehensibility and accessibility, there has been a sustained drive towards a massive extension of e-government services, including a target for 100% availability of online services by 2005. In prospect is a growing choice of electronic one-stop channels offering an ever wider range of government services, 24 hours a day, seven days a week, all drawing on increased capacities for pooling basic 'tombstone' and possibly other data, too, about service users. Second, under the slogan 'joined-up government' a more integrated approach to public service delivery sits at the very heart of the present administration's interest in public services reform, especially for those with multiple problems dealt with by closely related services. A case in point is the growing interest in breaking down barriers between the NHS and social care agencies.

Emphasis on improving horizontal coordination does not by itself lead to tensions with privacy and confidentiality. To understand why such tensions have arisen under the present government, we need to understand why its approach to social policy now involves much more use of the kind of risk assessment, data matching and social sorting techniques that are often associated with the strengthening of capacity for surveillance in the so-called 'information age' (Gandy, 1993; Lyon, 2001, 2003). To do so, we identify five important drivers of Labour's social policy, all with major implications for government's information management and data sharing practices (6 and Peck, 2004).

Joined-up working at the area level

By contrast with previous attempts to strengthen administrative coordination, Labour's approach focuses on joining up service delivery at the level of the individual client or the (very) small neighbourhood, because the underlying belief is that the most pressing social problems are highly concentrated, geographically and socially (SEU, 2000). In its first term, the Labour government developed such key policy instruments as multi-agency zone structures in health, education and employment, and the National Neighbourhood Renewal Strategy (SEU, 1998). Subsequently in its second term, the National Action Plan for Social Inclusion for 2001-03 drew this work together. This plan places much emphasis on inter-agency data sharing, in order to identify communities, minorities and groups of individuals 'requiring tailored and targeted interventions' that are to be both intelligence led and supported by multi-agency working (DWP, 2001).

Citizen obligations

Contemporary social policy also attaches greater priority to the definition of duties than has previously been the case. The growing willingness to impose sanctions on those who fail to meet them reflects the 'communitarian' strand that many commentators perceive to run through so much of the present government's approach (Driver and Martell, 1997, 2002; Levitas, 1998; Dwyer, 2000; White, 2001). This strand encourages policy makers to believe that individual antisocial behaviour, unwillingness to seek work, abuse of entitlements programmes and failure to comply with obligations for effective and disciplinary parenting (for example) are at the root of many social ills, and that the public services should therefore identify those who are either failing in these ways or are at risk of doing so. Indeed, it is a reflection of Labour's emphasis on rights and duties as reciprocal elements in citizens' relations with the state that subjecting individuals' data to tests for risk is now regarded as a reasonable quid pro quo for receiving help from public funds (DSS, 1999a, 2000a, 2000b).

Prevention and risk management

The impetus towards information-intensive government has also been fuelled by the growing emphasis on prophylaxis rather than post hoc remedy. For example, the increasing emphasis on intelligence-led, 'problem-oriented policing' (POP), in contrast to 'fire brigade' responses to crime and disorder, reflects the more general shift from 'resilience' to 'anticipation' (Wildavsky, 1988; Hood and Jones, 1996) in the criminal justice system. Public health has also become heavily oriented to the identification of communities, and even individuals, at high risk in order that they can be offered early intervention services. Policy initiatives that focus on micro-level, pre-emptive interventions are, however, intensely demanding of data about individuals, nowhere more so than in the field of social security fraud, crime and disorder, youth offending and 'early years' initiatives such as the Sure Start programme. Risk-based approaches, using actuarial-type assessments of individuals, families and small neighbourhoods, are now used in child protection, mental health, public protection against high-risk offenders, social security and many other fields.

Combating social exclusion

Labour's social policy prioritises combating social exclusion over combating poverty, on the basis that a wide range of factors explain heightened risks of poverty to a greater degree than poverty explains the presence of those other factors (DSS, 1999b). A wide range of street-level professionals have increasingly been expected to build more comprehensive data sets on their clients, in order to develop multi-agency interventions to address the full range of their needs. In practice, most data sharing around social exclusion has been concentrated on the very worst-off communities and groups, but the government hopes that the programme might eventually be extended to identify all those at risk of social exclusion and to develop early preventive intervention, for example school-based programmes for combating substance misuse.

Rationing

A highly interventionist social policy created obvious tensions with public expenditure policies, especially during Labour's first term when it sought to comply with inherited restrictions on public expenditure. But even in subsequent years, resource constraints have led to pressures for innovative methods of rationing. Being explicit about rationing criteria is politically risky, but keeping rationing implicit requires high levels of trust by politicians in, and a measure of public deference to, administrators and professionals. As a politically cautious government that had come to power by raising public expectations at a time of falling public deference, Labour had a problem in this regard. The use of information systems – often drawing on data from a number of agencies – has proved politically attractive for allocating policing resources between competing geographical areas, for allocating social workers' attentions to young people at risk, and for prioritising individuals in the context of community care, all on the basis of clear procedures and 'objective' data, even if those data are necessarily selective.

Three illustrations of data sharing in contemporary street-level services

It is the interaction of the five factors discussed above, rather than any of them singly, which explains the current preoccupation of policy makers with expanding the sharing of personal data in the administration of social policy. In the following section we illustrate this point by considering three particular examples where the various rationales outlined above are being deployed to create new imperatives for the sharing and exploiting of personal data by public services.

Social security fraud

The Labour government has made 'the war on fraud' a core element in its New Contract for Welfare (DSS, 1998a, 1999a). This war is driven not only by the desire to save public funds, but also by a strong belief that a system so wide open to fraud as is the British social security administration creates unacceptable moral hazards and erodes popular support for the welfare state. Investigating fraud is, however, a labour-intensive and expensive business, unless resources can be effectively targeted. Since the mid-1990s, the Department of Social Security (DSS, now the Department for Work and Pensions, DWP) has developed increasingly sophisticated data matching techniques that enable it to identify people most likely to be committing fraud by comparing data held in social security records with records held by other government departments, especially those used for tax administration. DWP's legal powers to use such techniques, and also to access such private sector records as payrolls and bank accounts to investigate cases thus identified, were explicitly sanctioned in the 1997 and 2001 Social Security Fraud Acts, both of which aroused considerable disquiet in Parliament when they were first introduced. By contrast, the bi-annual National Fraud Initiative of the Audit Commission, an exercise that cross-matches large swathes of personal data in files relating to such matters as housing benefits, local authority and health service payrolls, local authority tenancies and student maintenance grants, to identify possible cases of fraud, relies on no legal sanction other than the

Commission's general powers of audit. The NFI is nevertheless growing steadily in scope and is now proudly claimed to be 'the UK's premier public sector fraud detection and deterrence service' (Audit Commission, 2002).

The upshot of this growing use of data matching to detect fraud is that the files relating to anyone who pays national insurance contributions or personal taxes, receives a state pension, claims social security or housing benefits, is employed by a local or health authority, occupies certain kinds of social housing or applies for a student maintenance grant are liable to be included in data matching exercises conducted by government. Customer data are also requisitioned for the purpose of detecting housing benefit fraud from gas, electricity and telephone companies. This wholesale use of customer data has been commented on adversely from time to time by the Information Commissioner (formerly the Data Protection Registrar), but pressure for a statutory framework to govern such practices has been strongly resisted by ministers, along with proposals for judicial review. Instead, DWP, the Audit Commission and most other public agencies routinely draw up and publish voluntary codes of practice (for example, DSS, 1998b). All DWP claim forms carry a prominent notice warning its 'customers' that their data may be used in such ways, but proposals to require claimants to give consent to the free use of the data for any anti-fraud measures the government may wish to introduce were rejected by ministers during the passage of the social security fraud Bills, on the grounds that this would amount to consent under financial duress.

'Actuarial justice'

The growing pressure for data sharing in the field of crime and disorder reflects an important shift to what is known as 'risk-based penology' or 'actuarial justice' (Feeley and Simon, 1994; O'Malley, 1998; Kemshall, 2003). This approach is characterised by a preoccupation with reducing and managing risk, and with averting danger, through the use of increasingly sophisticated risk assessment and surveillance techniques. The targeting and control of particularly prolific or dangerous offenders according to their threat to the public comes to take precedence over traditional values of due process and individual rehabilitation. Nowhere is this more evident than in the reorientation of the National Probation Service, whose primary responsibility is now conceived to be the protection of the public rather than the rehabilitation of their clients (Raynor and Vanstone, 2002). Probation officers are now required to apply formal risk assessment tools to determine the treatment of individual offenders as well as to allocate resources to cases with the highest priority (National Probation Service, 2001). It is increasingly recognised, too, that the most useful risk assessments make use not only of 'static' socioeconomic data, but also of 'dynamic' information about the offender's current circumstances, which has often to be sourced from a range of agencies. The management of risk is increasingly undertaken through multi-agency arrangements such as the Youth Offending Teams set up under the 1998 Crime and Disorder Act and the Multi-Agency Public Protection Arrangements set up under the 2000 Criminal Justice and Courts Act to deal with particularly dangerous offenders, especially paedophiles. It is well recognised that the effectiveness of these kinds of multi-agency partnerships depend, in large part, on the vigour with which partner agencies establish systematic arrangements for sharing information about their clients (for example, National Probation Service, 2001).

Data sharing in health and social care

Much of the NHS still has weak electronic information systems. In many areas, the systems of family doctors (GPs) and local hospital trusts are not integrated, and integration between health and social care is poorer still. For this reason, it is now a priority that all (but only) relevant information from patient records should be able to follow patients through their particular 'pathway of care'. The aspiration is for an electronic Integrated Social Care Records Service to provide a national digital 'spine' of essential health and healthcare information about each patient. A programme of Electronic Record Development and Implementation Pilot projects has now been completed, many of which experimented locally with inter-agency integrated patient record systems. However, the results were mixed and only a minority have been able to attract continuing local funding: in much of the country, trusts are awaiting investment from the NHS National Programme for Information Technology, contracts for which were let in December 2003. The largest current project in routine data sharing along pathways of care is in west London, continuing the work of the Lifehouse initiative.

However, patient data must also be shared for purposes other than the care of the individual patient. The mental health system in England has also been directed since the early 1990s to focus on risk assessment and control, and is expected to share data for this purpose under protocols defined in the Care Programme Approach. In many areas, these are still paper records and they are of varying quality: in the absence of what professionals regard as adequate information for assessment, there is anecdotal evidence that they tend to err on the side of assuming that, until evidence appears to the contrary, individuals present a high risk either to themselves or others. This can lead to more drastic interventions than might actually be warranted.

The 1997 Caldicott Committee Report (DH, 1997) on the management of patient data led to the creation in every NHS agency of officers called Caldicott Guardians, charged with the oversight of confidentiality protection. Successive Information Commissioners have nevertheless declared publicly that the NHS has not always been fully compliant with data protection principles. The NHS Information Authority has now issued, following extensive consultation, a confidentiality code (DH, 2003), as discussed by Jonathan Montgomery in Chapter Seven of this volume. In many ways, this is one of the most privacy-friendly codes in force in any British public service. For example, it provides that patients should have the right to ask that certain pieces of information should not be shared with particular agencies, and that these requests can only be overridden in emergency situations and where that decision can subsequently be challenged and held accountable. The code sets out the principle that patients should not be 'surprised' by any sharing of their personal information around the NHS system. However, it continues to rely heavily on 'implicit consent'– that is, clinicians taking it from a patient's behaviour or acquiescence in something, that they have or would have consented to data sharing, rather than requiring the patient's explicit authority.

The Caldicott Guardian system of oversight of confidentiality has been extended to social care, where similar aspirations for Electronic Social Care Records have been defined, and where another series of pilots have been undertaken. The programme of single needs assessments between health and social care is resulting in greater pooling of client information between these agencies, but there remain important sensitivities about the extent of access to medical records for social care assessment and case managers. Again, the guiding principle is that of the 'need to know', but it is often difficult to define in advance just who will need to know exactly what.

It is the field of children at risk and children under protection that, since the Laming report into the death of Victoria Climbié (Cowan, 2003; Laming, 2003), official guidance has gone into great detail in trying to list and codify just who should be sent and who should retain which pieces of information about which individuals. The White Paper, *Every child matters* (DES, 2003a) sets out proposals for new bodies, called Children's Trusts, that will combine social services, education and child health responsibilities. They are modelled on Care Trusts in mental health, and will use a single shared needs and risk assessment. Data sharing is to be based around single databases, called information hubs, detailing information from all agencies on all children in each area, each with a unique identifying number, and based on common national data standards. Fifteen local experiments called Information, Retrieval and Tracking pilots are taking this work forward, and there are new monies for all councils to improve data sharing. Despite the additional detailed prescription, however, the 'need to know' principle and the proportionality test about disclosures and needs remain at the heart of the judgment to be made in children's services. This leaves continuing scope for local and professional discretion (DES, 2003b, Annex 1).

Summary of the three examples

Taken together, these three cases reflect a mix of rationales for the expansion of data sharing involving personal records in contemporary public services. Some data sharing – for example in the NHS and the social care field – is being undertaken for the primary purpose of increasing the responsiveness and comprehensiveness of the services that are provided to the general population, or, more specifically, to defined client groups within that population. This kind of data sharing therefore sits four-square with the government's core aim of enhancing the quality of public services by joining them up at the point of delivery to users. Much of the expansion of data sharing is, however, heavily focused on the parallel problem of dealing in more cost-effective ways with moral hazards and more tangible dangers thought to be posed by specific individuals, or small groups of individuals, to the communities in which we live, or which threaten the values on which communities, and the public services that support them, are based. It follows, then, that the liability of those individuals to have their personal data exploited in such ways may be justified as the expression of their reciprocal social obligation to the communities to which they are deemed to constitute a threat.

The identity card debate

This uneasy mix of consumerist and communitarian imperatives for exploiting personal data held by public services can also be illustrated by current debates about the introduction of identity or entitlement cards. The project was first introduced as an 'entitlement card' (Home Secretary, 2002) to support easier access to public services, but it was later accepted that its main purpose was not to smooth the flow of benefits to public service customers but to assist in the targeting of sanctions on less favoured groups. In particular, the card was presented as a weapon in the struggle to combat identity fraud, illegal immigration and working, benefit fraud and even terrorism, although it is hard to see what the cards could add to existing measures. It now seems likely that full implementation will be delayed, perhaps until 2013, or even shelved completely. The government's White Paper

(Home Secretary, 2003) was studiously vague about the extent to which the central population register underpinning the card system would be built by matching data from other administrative sources. It was also vague about the protocols under which public and commercial services would be able to gain access to the citizens' records stored in the register. However, the Office for National Statistics (ONS, 2003) also proposed to construct a population register. An identity card system, once developed, would be one of several applications that could draw on such a data spine. If the identity card scheme begins, the project management imperatives to process as many applications as quickly as possible may actually increase the risk of fraudulent applications, because these pressures may in practice be more important than the need to ensure that each application is fully checked (6, 2003).

Debate about the identity card proposal has been highly polarised, and has drawn public and media attention afresh to the issues of privacy protection in the handling, and especially the sharing, of personal data by public services. It has also drawn attention to the tensions in the new agenda between measures designed to enhance consumer benefits and measures designed to protect communities from risk (6, 2005: forthcoming).

An emerging settlement?

Recognising the possibility of tensions – at least in the public mind – between inter-agency collaboration and client confidentiality, the Blair administration has made efforts to arrive at a settlement for governing 'joined-up' working in ways that are compatible with data protection and privacy principles. The prospect has been held out of creating joined-up, holistic privacy protection (Raab, 2003) to keep pace with possible incursions on privacy. This task has not proven straightforward. The aspiration was first set out in a report from the Performance and Innovation Unit (PIU) (now the Prime Minister's Strategy Unit) in 2002 (PIU, 2002). This report proposed that a new statutory framework would be needed, with a general power for public services to share data, and also specified 19 cases where specific legislative authorisation would be needed, most of them concerned with identifying and sanctioning wrongdoers of various kinds. As if by way of compensation, the report also offered new safeguards in the form of privacy impact assessments and a consumer's charter. Responsibility for implementation was given to (what later became) the Department for Constitutional Affairs (DCA). Its Data Sharing and Privacy Unit finally concluded that the PIU approach was inappropriate. No new general legal power was needed because it would add nothing to existing legal powers. The DCA's legal guidance set out the various provisions that might be included in any particular framework for data sharing, but left it to particular services to ensure that their own frameworks were in compliance with a complex and not fully codified body of law. The DCA proposed, however, to bring forward legislation empowering the government to remove specific prohibitions to data sharing in secondary legislation (DCA, 2003). It also presented a Public Service Trust Charter and a set of protocols for particular services on sharing and confidentiality. This approach amounts to no more than a general and overarching set of principles within which particular services must find their own settlements.

This also implies that settlements will vary considerably from service to service. There are striking differences in the service-level settlements struck between data sharing and privacy in those fields in which the community risk and sanctions agenda dominates and in those where the consumer benefit imperative is more important. In general, it is in the latter, exemplified by the new NHS confidentiality code, that the commitments to consent, consumer control and restrictions on professional powers are greatest. In both the benefit- and sanction-driven policy fields, however, there are two main principles used to justify and restrict incursions into the confidentiality of personal data. These are, first, the principle restricting the exchange of data to those organisations or professionals that 'need to know' in order to carry out their legitimate functions; and, second, the 'proportionality' principle, restricting data sharing to those purposes where the benefits – whether to the individual or to the public at large – are judged to outweigh the damage inflicted on confidentiality and privacy. However, the problem is that neither principle can be made sufficiently precise to define algorithms capable of yielding unambiguous decisions about the appropriateness of data sharing in any specific case, and those who make the judgments in the first instance may have a vested interest in sharing data. Detailed codification of permissions and prohibitions for sharing can never settle every case, and the issuing of legal guidance and model local protocols reflects a recognition that the PIU's high hopes for a fully codified settlement have had to be scaled back. The settlement now emerging builds on, constrains and provides guidance for carrying out data sharing, but does not seek to replace the need for case-by-case judgments based on the 'need to know' and proportionality principles.

An important consequence of this shift in policy is that attempts to set these case-by-case decisions within adequate frameworks of governance are being made, perforce, within each service or agency, rather than through the kind of overarching settlement envisaged by the PIU report. One implication is that consumers or users of public services have no single or easily comprehensible point of reference to understand the growing range of data sharing practices now employed by government, or the guidelines and protocols that govern those practices; a recent MORI (2003) survey revealed the extent of public ignorance about what happens to their data (see also 6, 2002). The question therefore arises as to how consumers can be confident about the degree to which the right to privacy enacted in recent human rights legislation is actually being respected.

As we have seen above, public service organisations vary considerably in the importance and priority they attach to consent and transparency, but even in the NHS and social care – the two service fields in which these values are relatively highly respected – consent to data sharing between agencies is, for most purposes, deemed to be implicit in taking up the service. The social security system makes no pretence of requesting consent to data sharing by claimants and the prominence given to warnings about data sharing offers no guarantee that those using the forms will understand the full scope of the DWP's current data matching exercises. It may likewise be doubted whether subjects of data held in local authority or health authority payrolls have more than the slightest glimmerings of the fact that such repositories are also exploited for these purposes. Nor is it clear that taxpayers fully understand the kinds of geographical mapping or risk assessment techniques currently used to prioritise interventions in certain neighbourhoods or on certain social groups or individuals, rather than others. Nor has there been much public discussion on the criteria underpinning these processes.

The selection of individuals, neighbourhoods or groups for special attention is not without important hazards for those who are selected. Even interventions designed to assist families or benefit neighbourhoods may have stigmatising effects, while the mistaken identification of a child at risk of abuse or a person who may be carrying out fraud as a result of data sharing or matching on the basis of mistaken identity may have long-term impacts on the well-being of the people involved. For this reason, the DWP, for example, has thus far resisted persistent calls to match data in social security records with those of the private financial services, for fear that the knowledge that a claimant has been identified as a possible fraudster would have disastrous consequences for that person's credit rating. The likely impact of the proposed ID cards scheme and its database (Home Secretary, 2003) on such problems is ambiguous at best. On the one hand, the establishment of an identity that is shared across the public services may reduce the risk of such mistakes; on the other hand, it may significantly and unwarrantedly increase government's confidence in the quality of personal data and thus in the robustness of its surveillance and risk assessment techniques.

Whether or not the approaches currently taken by government, both centrally through the initiatives of the DCA or within individual services, will be sufficient to secure public trust will depend on a number of factors. These include the extent to which they are subject to special demands from communities for disclosures about wrongdoers, whether the next wave of scandals and service failures turn out to be due to insufficient data sharing between agencies – for example, continuing failures by the new Children's Trusts or the Multi-Agency Public Protection Panels to preclude further child abuse or child murder cases – or whether the expansion of data sharing gives rise to new kinds of scandals arising from the pinpointing of individuals on the basis of false identity or rogue data matches.

Conclusion: directions for policy development

We conclude with some more prescriptive suggestions for future development that, we believe, follow in part from the argument of the previous sections.

Very few people would dispute that there must be sharing of some personal data in order effectively to protect children from abuse, to provide integrated care for children and adults alike spanning the health and social services functions, and to detect crime and fraud. Equally, few people would, on careful reflection, be content that agencies should be willing to share any information that they possess about any individual with any other agency involved in the provision of public services, on the generalised precautionary principle that it is impossible to know in advance what information might turn out to be of some legitimate use, even if it might also be misused, and even if it were not necessary for the other agency to know it. The confidence of the public in public services and the candour of clients with professionals rest on the belief that the sphere of circulation of personal information is limited appropriately, that those limitations may be overridden only in emergencies or special circumstances. Most people might also argue that that those overrides should be transparent and that those who override should be accountable.

These admonitions about the legitimacy of data sharing are, as we have noted, too vague and general to provide algorithms that could substitute for the exercise of professional judgment. But this is not an argument for seeking to substitute more precise and detailed rules, however much some frontline staff working in public services would welcome such rules in the hope of relieving them of the responsibility of making what are often difficult decisions. This is because any system of detailed rules that attempted to mandate, permit or prohibit sharing among prescribed and proscribed agencies of very specific categories of data, triggered by lists of key events, would fail in a whole variety of ways. We know that most frontline staff hardly read, and in particular cases often do not follow, for good as well as for bad reasons, the volumes of manuals that descend on them to guide many aspects of their work, from health and safety through to budget preparation. There is no reason to suppose that detailed data sharing guidance would enjoy a better reception. More importantly, such a set of rules could never be complete, because new problems emerge constantly, so that their strict application would soon lead to absurdities, both of excessive and of insufficient sharing. In this field, as in many others, accountable judgment based on concepts of necessity, relevance and reasonableness is both inescapable and sensible, even if it does leave some frontline professional staff feeling exposed. The data protection legislation could certainly have been better drafted, but there is no reason to suggest that an approach based on defining general principles could have been dispensed with.

However, in most cases, the standard of 'necessity' for fulfilling a vital public purpose or safeguarding interests of the users of the public service themselves – a standard that is embodied in the principles underlying data protection law – ought to mean just that. It ought not to be relaxed to the point of allowing sharing where it might merely be useful, convenient, precautionary or incidental. Many of the issues that are known to be of greatest concern to the public, as evidenced in qualitative research studies (for example, 6, 2002; Consumers' Association et al, 2002), relate to those very categories of information that service users themselves consider sensitive. Such information might be shared between agencies, but its sharing as a matter of routine would rarely be necessary to the work of the receiving agencies. The concern of women users of NHS services about the routine sharing of information about past pregnancy terminations is a well-documented case in point (Consumers' Association et al, 2002).

The same body of research, and also more recent surveys (MORI, 2003), has consistently found that the public, in general, and public service users, in particular, know very little about the extent to which, and under which conditions, their information is shared. One of the advantages of the development of online facilities for service users to exercise their right to know what is held about them might be that, at a trivial cost, they could be used to provide users with individualised information about the sharing of their personal data, on a routine and automatically generated basis. This would provide for what is known as 'subject access' in the jargon of data protection legislation, and is implied, for example, in the NHS intentions for 'My HealthSpace', a proposed online facility for service users to access their records and handle minor and routine transactions with primary care.

Second, the infrastructure for the application of data protection principles to data sharing practices within the public services remains very weak. The NHS, since 1997, and social services, since 2001, have both established the system of Caldicott Guardians specifically charged with protecting personal data, and such people have recently tended to be more senior and less likely to be information technology staff. Unfortunately, few other public services have followed this example. The Information Commissioner has no powers of unannounced inspection and no resources with which to exercise such powers, should they be given. These facts considerably weaken the credibility of the Commissioner as a regulator, and remedying this state of affairs should be one of the highest priorities for policy development. It may be that political reluctance to burden the private or public sector with regulatory constraints is denying the Commissioner powers and resources to develop a small inspectorate, some of which might be dedicated to public services work. As with inspectors in health and safety, environmental health or residential care, much of their work would no doubt be more advisory than adversarial in practice, but could nevertheless be at least as effective as these other inspectorates in cultivating commitment and supporting best practice.

Third, sanctions for the violation of the data protection principles are modest and little understood by people working in public services. This sends an implicit signal that reinforcing respect for privacy is a much lower priority than the many other demands on public services that are buttressed with effective sanctions.

Ultimately, however, the understanding of necessity and proportionality on which frontline professionals draw reflects the wider political climate that directs attention to some risks rather than others. It is inevitable that data protection principles will be interpreted according to the prevailing fear of blame from the media, from politicians and from public enquiries for tragedies deemed to have arisen either from failing to share or else from sharing too widely. We have argued here that recent governments have significantly shifted the emphasis towards the risks of failing to share.

It follows that effort put into defensive decision making is thereby being moved to lower standards of necessity and proportionality when making decisions about what information should be shared. For example, this shift is widely but anecdotally held to be putting downward pressure on the thresholds for referral in cases of child protection or the care of the elderly, and even for the compulsory admission into institutional care of people with mental health problems. Professionals have therefore to work harder to resist these pressures, even where they can argue that best-practice models support greater autonomy for clients. This example illustrates well how the framework of values governing data sharing and privacy in public services is intimately entwined with prevailing political attitudes toward risk (Cooper et al, 2003).

References

6, P. (2002) 'Strategies for reassurance: public concerns about privacy and data sharing in government', London: PIU, Cabinet Office, 166 pages (available at www.number-10.gov.uk/piu/privacy/papers/perri6.pdf).

6, P. (2003) *Entitlement cards: Benefits, privacy and data protection risks, costs and wider social implications*, Wilmslow: Office of the Information Commissioner.

6, P. and Peck, E.W. (2004) '"Modernisation": the ten commitments of New Labour's approach to public management?', *International Public Management Journal*, vol 7, no 1, pp 1-18.

6, P. (2005: forthcoming) 'Should we be compelled to have identity cards? Justifications for the enforcement of obligations', *Political Studies*, vol 53, no 2.

6, P., Leat, D., Seltzer, K. and Stoker, G. (2002) *Towards holistic governance: The new reform agenda*, London: Palgrave.

Audit Commission (2002) *Match winner: Report of the 2000 national fraud initiative*, London: Audit Commission.

Consumers' Association, NHS Information Authority and Health Which? (2002) *Share with care! People's views on consent and confidentiality of patient information – qualitative and quantitative research: final report*, London: Consumers' Association, in association with NHS Information Authority, Birmingham and Health Which?, London.

Cooper, A., Hetherington, R. and Katz, I. (2003) *The risk factor: Making the child protection system work for children*, London: Demos.

Cowan, J. (2003) 'Risk management, records and the Laming report', *Clinical Governance*, vol 8, no 3, pp 271-7.

Data Protection Registrar (1999) *15th Annual report of the Data Protection Registrar*, HC 575, London: The Stationery Office.

DCA (Department for Constitutional Affairs) (2003) *Public sector data sharing: Guidance on the law*, London: DCA.

DES (Department for Education and Skills) (2003a) *Every child matters*, Cm 5860, London: DES.

DES (2003b) *Children's trust pathfinders: Toolkit*, London: DES.

DH (Department of Health) (1997) *Report on the review of patient identifiable information* (Report of the Caldicott Committee) London: DH.

DH (2003) *Confidentiality: NHS Code of Practice*, London: DH.

Driver, S. and Martell, L. (1997) 'New Labour's communitarianisms', *Critical Social Policy*, vol 17, no 3, pp 27-46.

Driver, S. and Martell, L. (2002) *Blair's Britain*, Oxford: Polity Press.

DSS (Department of Social Security) (1998a) *New ambitions for our country: A new contract for welfare*, Cm 3805, London: The Stationery Office.

DSS (1998b) *Code of practice for data sharing*, London: DSS.

DSS (1999a) *A new contract for welfare: Safeguarding social security*, Cm 4276, London: The Stationery Office.

DSS (1999b) *Opportunity for all: Tackling poverty and social exclusion*, Cm 4445, London: The Stationery Office.

DSS (2000a) *Safeguarding social security: Getting the information we need*, London: DSS.

DSS (2000b) *Code of practice for data matching*, London: DSS.

DWP (Department for Work and Pensions) (2001) *United Kingdom national action plan on social exclusion 2001-2003*, London: DWP.

Dwyer, P. (2000) *Welfare rights and responsibilities: Contesting social citizenship*, Bristol: The Policy Press.

Feeley, M.M. and Simon, J. (1994) 'Actuarial justice', in D. Nelken (ed) *Futures of criminology*, London: Sage Publications.

Gandy, O.H. Jr (1993) *The panoptic sort: A political economy of personal information*, Boulder, CO: Westview Press.

Home Secretary (2002) *Entitlement cards and identity fraud: A consultation paper*, Cm 5557, London: The Stationery Office.

Home Secretary (2003) *Identity cards: The next steps*, Cm 6020, London: Home Office.

Hood, C.C. and Jones, D.K.C. (1996) *Accident and design: Contemporary debates in risk management*, London: UCL Press.

Kemshall, H. (2003) *Understanding risk in criminal justice*, Buckingham: Open University Press.

Laming, Lord (2003) *The Victoria Climbié Inquiry: Report of an enquiry by Lord Laming*, Cm 5730, London: The Stationery Office.

Levitas, R. (1998) *The inclusive society: Social inclusion and New Labour*, Basingstoke: Palgrave.

Lyon, D. (2001) *Surveillance society: Monitoring everyday life*, Buckingham: Open University Press.

Lyon, D. (ed) (2003) *Surveillance as social sorting: Privacy, risk and digital discrimination*, London: Routledge.

MORI (2003) *Privacy and data-sharing: Survey of public awareness and perceptions*, Research study conducted for the Department for Constitutional Affairs, London: MORI.

National Probation Service (2001) *The new choreography: An integrated strategy for the National Probation Service for England and Wales*, London: Home Office.

O'Malley, P. (ed) (1998) *Crime and the risk society*, Aldershot: Ashgate.

ONS (Office for National Statistics) (2003) *Discussion paper: Proposals for an integrated population statistics system*, London: ONS (at www.statistics.gov.uk/statbase/Product.asp?vlnk=10784).

PIU (Performance and Innovation Unit) (2002) *Privacy and data-sharing: The way forward for public services*, London: PIU, Cabinet Office.

Raab, C. (2003) 'Joined-up surveillance: the challenge to privacy', in K. Ball and F. Webster (eds) *The intensification of surveillance: Crime, terrorism and warfare in the information age*, London: Pluto Press.

Raynor, P. and Vanstone, M. (2002) *Understanding community penalties: Probation, policy and social change*, Buckingham: Open University Press.

SEU (Social Exclusion Unit) (1998) *Bringing Britain together: A national strategy for neighbourhood renewal*, London: SEU, Cabinet Office.

SEU (2000) *Report of policy action team 18 on better information*, London: SEU, Cabinet Office.

White, S. (2001) *New Labour: The progressive future*, Basingstoke: Palgrave.

Wildavsky, A. (1988) *Searching for safety*, New Brunswick, NJ: Transaction Publishers.

Part Three: Case studies

6

Data use in credit and insurance: controlling unfair outcomes

Harriet Hall

Introduction

This chapter considers how information on consumers is used in credit and insurance. It is not a chapter on privacy concerns, but on how data use can affect the availability of these services and how this may produce unfair outcomes.

Before considering the negative effects, it is worth pointing out that data manipulation is fundamental to modern, mass market credit and insurance. Credit and insurance share the fact that data are collected on millions of individuals to define the characteristics of those who are creditworthy or those who are an acceptable insurance risk. Data belonging to an individual are then set against these definitions, in order to decide whether and on what terms to grant credit or insurance. Before electronic collection and manipulation of data developed, many consumers were not able to buy credit or insurance at all (NCC, 2004).

Nevertheless, increasing sophistication in data manipulation means that lenders and insurers can segment their market and this may result in some consumers being excluded or only offered services on unfavourable terms[1].

This chapter examines categories of problems outlined by 6 and Jupp (2001). They point out that whereas in the past concern has been for people excluded from information, there is an additional concern that the use of information technology might itself be an engine of exclusion. They set out three categories of risk.

The first is that "organisational pressures ... may lead organisations to identify and focus on only the most profitable customers" (6 and Jupp, 2001, p 42), thus depriving less profitable customers of services that are essential to everyday life. They use geographical illustrations for this, citing the closure of bank branches in areas of deprivation and the use of data to site supermarkets where they will be accessible to more profitable customers. Discrimination may not be unjust in individual terms and may be based on significant characteristics of those excluded that are commercially justifiable. But it may have socially undesirable consequences. In some circumstances credit and insurance are seen as quasi 'essential services'. In these cases, consumers' lack of access can be seen as unfair in the context of needs. I call this *unfair exclusion*.

The second type of problem that 6 and Jupp identify is that "data systems will be accurate enough to enable companies to target the worst off customers and heavily market services to them that in fact worsen their position" (6 and Jupp, 2001, p 42). In a sense this is a variant of the first problem: it is a question of who the more profitable customers are. 6 and Jupp cite the example of the use of data sets on people in financial difficulty to sell them expensive forms of debt. The companies justify the high fees and rates of interest by pointing out the higher risk of default, claiming that they are actuarially fair. Nevertheless, the loans may increase the problems of those who take them, rather than solving them. I use the term *unfair targeting* for this type of problem.

Finally there is the concern "that information systems will not be accurate enough to enable this kind of focusing on the more profitable and that there will be problems of unjust discrimination based on crude categorical information" (6 and Jupp, 2001, p 42). In this case it is not the sophistication of the use of data that allows firms to target the more profitable, but the lack of sophistication that places people into undifferentiated or inaccurately differentiated categories. People are denied goods or services on the basis of belonging to a set that does not take into account other data that might make them profitable and suitable purchasers. I use the term *unfair discrimination* for this.

The chapter examines how data are used in credit and insurance, what problems relating to the categories identified by 6 and Jupp are evident, and what attempts have been made to tackle them. It then attempts to draw some conclusions.

Data collection and manipulation

This section sets out how information is collected to make decisions on the granting of credit and insurance.

Data and credit risk assessment

Credit reference agencies

Credit reference agencies collect information on loans to help lenders to assess the credit risk of an applicant. It should be noted that there is no obligation on a lender to consult a credit reference agency.

There are three credit reference agencies in the UK, which collect information on individuals and make it available to lenders for the purpose of deciding whether or not to grant credit to an applicant. I summarise here the information given by Experian (www.experian.co.uk). Experian collects information on individuals that is publicly available. The data come from the electoral roll, from county court judgements held by the Registry Trust[2], and from records of bankruptcies and individual voluntary arrangements.

In addition, it holds data in a closed membership group called Credit Account Information Sharing (CAIS). The other credit reference agencies have different closed groups. The group is closed in the sense that the information is only available to members. Members submit information to Experian on their customers' credit accounts, including debts repaid in the recent past and repayments made on current loans. The information includes credit given in the usual course of supplying services such as mobile phones and utilities. The information may be on failure to keep up with payments (negative information), loan repayments that may be delinquent (that is, three months or more in arrears) or in default (where the relationship has broken down and repayments are not being made) and may also include information on accounts where the consumer is keeping up with the payment according to the contract (positive information).

A lender that consults an agency is not obliged to submit data to the closed membership groups, but will not be able to consult the data submitted by the members of the closed groups if it does not. In addition, a member firm can choose the extent to which it contributes to the network of information, so it can choose whether to submit and take out only negative information or whether to include positive information.

This system of data sharing through credit reference agencies is governed by a scheme of self-regulation controlled by the Standing Committee on Reciprocity (SCOR), run by trade associations in the credit industry (British Bankers Association, Council of Mortgage Lenders, Finance and Leasing Association, and others) and the three credit reference agencies. The Principles of Reciprocity set out the conditions under which firms submit information on borrowers or credit applicants and take it out from credit reference agencies. The fundamental principle is that data may only be shared in order to promote responsible lending. It may not be shared for marketing purposes, although a firm may 'wash' its list of potential clients to exclude bad credit risks.

The following information is also shared under industry-wide schemes for data sharing by companies:

- Council of Mortgage Lenders' repossessions register;
- Credit Industry Fraud Avoidance System (CIFAS) – data on fraud committed or attempted by customers or by other persons on customers;
- Gone Away Information Network (GAIN) – information submitted on customers who have left an address while owing money without leaving a forwarding address.

When someone applies for credit from a lender that uses a credit reference agency, he or she must be told that a check with the agency will be made and asked to give consent to the data on the application form and future data on the management of the account, if credit is granted, being shared with a credit reference agency[3].

Credit scoring

Credit reference agencies are only one part of the decision to grant credit. A company may consult an agency but, as mentioned above, is under no obligation to do so. If it does so, it will have to interpret the information and almost certainly use additional information. The agency file, for example, will produce no data on age or employment, which may be relevant to a decision to grant credit. Firms use their own scoring systems, since they will have different approaches to risk: some may accept a higher level of risk of default and charge higher interest rates. Others may target good payers with low interest rates. Companies may also have different views on what risk factors are reliable predictors.

Some firms develop their own systems; others buy credit-scoring systems from credit reference agencies. All systems use historical data relating to the personal characteristics of existing customers, such as their age, salary, housing tenure, and analyses their risk potential against how they performed their obligations under loans granted to them. In addition, some companies may make inferences as to how rejected applicants would have performed if they had been granted a loan. This is called reject inference and is done by assuming characteristics that the accepted and rejected share or by using data from a credit reference agency as to how the rejected applicants performed with other lenders.

Scoring systems enable a scorecard to be developed with different weightings for the various distinguishing characteristics and potential customers are judged on the basis of their scores. If lenders are behaving rationally, credit-scoring systems should be tuned so that people are only excluded if there is statistical evidence that they are at risk of defaulting, the level of risk being set by the company's business model.

Data and insurance pools

Insurers collect data from a large number of events, and calculate the likelihood of the event occurring and the likely cost of it occurring if it does. Firms develop their own actuarial systems, using data to assess risk. For reasons of space, I do not propose to go into the details of data sharing used by insurers. As an example, Experian holds two relevant databases: the Perils Data Portfolio – postcode sector-level data on building stock, subsidence, flood, wind and crime; and the Claims and Underwriting Exchange (CUE) – comprising databases of Household Personal Lines Claims and Motor Personal Lines claims. The CIFAS register, referred to above under credit reference agencies, also contains information on insurance frauds[4].

Faced with an individual seeking insurance, insurers can apply the individual's profile to the model. This may be done without individual underwriting, that is, treating the consumer as if he or she had no particular characteristics that would make the risk greater than for the average person. This is how travel insurance is usually designed. Insurers will attempt to exclude people with such characteristics from cover altogether through the terms and conditions. This can cause problems if the exclusion clauses in the contract are not properly drawn to the consumer's attention.

Individually underwritten insurance involves looking at information belonging to the individual applicant and assessing the extent to which it deviates from a norm and then pricing the product accordingly, or in some cases writing in special terms or refusing to insure.

Difficulties can arise from the defining characteristics of the insured pool. Insurance works on the basis that although some people may suffer the loss insured against, others will not, so those who do not subsidise those who do. Insurers regard it as a matter of actuarial fairness that the level of risk of the event occurring should be about the same for those in the pool of insured. Most people would agree that fairness requires that, for example, a person with a conviction for dangerous driving should pay more in premiums than someone who has no convictions. There are two pools, one for those with convictions and one for those without.

Unfair exclusion

This section considers the first of the potential problems identified by 6 and Jupp (2001), that as companies find it profitable to use data to segment the market, they do so to such an extent that some people or groups of people may be excluded from goods or services.

To the extent that these services are essential to everyday life, this exclusion may be regarded as unfair. The behaviour of the company may not be unfair, but the outcome for the excluded individual is.

Unfair exclusion in credit

Datamonitor research (2003) shows that about 7.8 million adults are barred from mainstream credit because of credit scoring. The risk of their defaulting on a loan is too great for them to be accepted by mainstream lenders because of their income or credit histories. The sophisticated manipulation of data by mainstream companies excludes them, as it is designed to do. In a climate where companies are criticised for offering too much credit, it would be odd to argue that they should ignore the results of credit scoring to give credit to those who are at risk of defaulting.

Nevertheless, those who live on low incomes may need credit, not for luxuries but to tide them over or to cope with emergencies. To the extent that benefit levels or minimum wage levels are set so low that borrowing is necessary to deal with cashflow problems on a regular basis, it can be argued that access to credit is an essential service[5].

Responses to unfair exclusion in credit

What follows summarises a number of responses that have been made to the problem of exclusion from credit. They all have drawbacks, which make them less than ideal as solutions.

Door-to-door credit firms

There are firms that specialise in providing credit for consumers who otherwise would find it hard to get it, through door-to-door credit offerings. Borrowers who use them like them because they are the only kind of credit available to them, loans are available in small amounts and because those selling credit come to the borrower's home and there is a discipline in weekly collections of repayments (NCC, 2004). Customers for this type of loan appear to be targeted by the collectors, who have local knowledge of consumers and family connections between borrowers, rather than data manipulation. Kempson and Whyley (1999) point out that some targeting is done by getting round the prohibition in the 1974 Consumer Credit Act on selling credit door to door.

While home credit is an example of a response to exclusion from credit, firms that offer it are the subject of much criticism for high interest rates and for encouraging further borrowing before one loan has been paid off, although Kempson and Whyley make the point that not all loans are at extortionate rates of interest and these firms serve a particular market that would otherwise struggle to get credit. The companies say the interest rates are justified on the grounds of the expense of providing a service that suits the needs of their customers. The National Consumer Council (NCC) has recently been successful in a making a supercomplaint[6] to the Office of Fair Trading (OFT) on the uncompetitive aspects of this type of door-to-door service. In December 2004 it was announced that the Competition Commission would conduct an investigation which is expected to take over one year to complete.

Not-for-profit supply

Commercial firms may not be able or willing to grant credit to low-income consumers on other than very high interest rates and other restrictive terms. So, alternative sources of supply have been developed by not-for-profit organisations. Some success has been achieved in this field by organisations such as credit unions or housing associations that stand as surety for loans to their tenants made by local building societies, but by definition these are very local and advantage only a small number of people. The latest figure on the Financial Services Authority's website for credit union members was around 475,000 at June 2004.

The Social Fund

Another source of credit for those who are not served by mainstream credit companies is the Social Fund. The fund provides budgeting loans to those who have been on a number of income-related benefits for more than 26 weeks. The grant of a loan is discretionary.

Those who apply often do so because they know there is no other source of credit available to them. Users, while on the whole positive about it, complain that the scheme is a bit of a lottery (only 60% of applications are granted) (Kempson et al, 2000). Older users complain about the inflexibility of the repayments required and the length of the term of the loan (Kempson et al, 2002).

Unfair exclusion in insurance

In insurance, analysis of a consumer's data given on an application form in some cases results in refusal, or an offer to insure on terms that are too expensive for the consumer. The risk profile of the applicant does not match the insurer's risk pool. This is inevitable, given the use of data in the insurance industry. Again, as in credit, this is the purpose of the use of data. So, is insurance different from any other commercial product, which consumers may or may not be able to buy? Is there any way in which it can be regarded as an essential service, so that those refused can be seen as unfairly excluded?

I shall look at two cases in which insurance could be seen as a quasi-essential service, in property and home contents insurance. It is not possible to buy a house that is not insurable on a mortgage. If a home becomes uninsurable after purchase, it is arguable that there should be some response to make insurance available. In the case of home contents insurance, people living on low incomes in areas of high deprivation are more prone to burglary than those in other areas. Through low incomes they are likely to be less able to self-insure and their inability to replace stolen goods is compounded by the fact that they may not easily get credit.

Property insurance in areas liable to flooding

For property insurance, underwriting is generally done partly through assessment of the average risk applying to houses in the same postcode area, although insurers usually use multiple discriminators[7]. The data on loss from various causes in any area are aggregated to produce a way of predicting how many houses are likely to be affected in any year and at what cost. This has started to create problems in postcode areas where houses are so likely to suffer loss that it can no longer be regarded as a matter of uncertainty. Insurers are then unlikely to offer insurance, or may only do so at premium rates that consumers cannot afford. In some cases they would do better to self-insure.

Although I have included this as an example of unfair exclusion, it is not necessarily a matter of insurers concentrating on profitable business to the exclusion of the unprofitable. It is more that the model of insurance, which requires a certain degree of risk, does not match a situation where the risk of the insured-against event happening is too high.

Insurers who assess risk on postcode data are reluctant to provide cover for property in areas that are subject to frequent flooding. Flooding has become more frequent in recent years, perhaps because of global warming, perhaps because builders and local authorities have allowed development in river floodplains. An additional problem may have arisen because of policy decisions to reduce flood prevention barriers.

When this became evident as a problem, the government sought the help of the Association of British Insurers (ABI). The government sought to influence insurers to do what they, commercially, possibly could not justify. In January 2003 the ABI announced that:

- in urban areas where the risk of flooding is one year in 75 or better, insurers will continue to insure, although premiums will vary according to risk;
- where the risk is greater than one in 75, but improved flood defences to bring it to this level are planned for completion before 2008, insurers will maintain cover, including for purchasers from the current owner;
- where no such defences are planned, insurers will not guarantee to maintain cover, but will look at risk on a case-by-case basis;
- in return, the ABI expects the government to carry out planned expenditure on flood defences, to implement the findings of the review on flood defences, to give new planning guidelines to prevent building in areas of high risk and to improve early flood warnings (ABI, 2003).

In effect, what this solution does is to oblige insurers to widen the pool more than they might actuarially prefer. If they could exclude these properties that make frequent claims, they could reduce the premiums for everyone else. The owners of higher-risk properties are subsidised by the owners of lower risk properties. The reason why it works, in as much as it does, is because all insurers, through their trade association, agree to do the same. In theory, assuming all insurers are covering a selection of properties within the areas affected, they are all obliged to increase their premiums above what they could charge if they refused cover. There is no competitive advantage to be had. It does, however, leave out some householders with very high-risk properties. I deal with this more fully below.

Home contents insurance

A report for the Joseph Rowntree Foundation (Whyley et al, 1998) considered access to home contents insurance for low-income households. The lack of availability can be seen as an example of insurers failing to meet the interests of poorer neighbourhoods, finding more profitable business elsewhere. The research found that few were actually refused insurance, but many were uninsured because they could not afford the premiums, did not think their possessions worth insuring, found the minimum insured value too high or could not manage premiums collected in a lump sum once a year. The products of mainstream insurance companies were too inflexible or too expensive, or both.

The Rowntree project looked at a number of solutions to these problems, including offerings by commercial insurers that concentrate on the needs of low-income neighbourhoods and by partnerships between insurers and local authorities and sometimes housing associations, which collect premiums with rent. The latter solves some of the problems by pooling all local authority tenants together, whatever the risk level of the property, thus reducing premiums for those living in homes with a high risk of burglary, and allowing weekly collected premiums and a lower minimum value insured. Again, some subsidy of higher-risk tenants by lower-risk tenants is involved.

Adequacy of responses

If insurance in these cases is an essential service, then we need to examine whether the responses that have been developed meet the needs of those excluded. In the case of property insurance, if insurance against damage by flooding meets an essential need, what kind of protection will be provided for those who remain uninsurable, despite the ABI agreement? And if flooding is merely the first sign of problems arising from changing weather patterns due to global warming, what does a policy of intervening through self-regulation of insurance companies mean for damage caused by other natural causes? Recently, the ABI published a report on climate change and the need for insurers and government to act together to control damage (ABI, 2004). Is there an argument for a government fund for damage from these causes rather than seeking to make adaptations to normal insurance behaviour to meet the losses?

Unlike the problem with insurance and flooding, pressure to create a solution to a lack of home contents insurance has not come from central government – which felt no need to act to produce a countrywide solution – but solutions have been developed by authorities with a concern for their tenants or constituents. These solutions to a lack of access to an essential service are, consequently, patchy. They do not meet the needs of all those affected.

Unfair targeting

The second problem identified by 6 and Jupp (2001, p 42) is that "data systems will be accurate enough to enable companies to target the worst off customers and heavily market services to them that in fact worsen their position". Targeting with data use in insurance is likely to be a benefit to consumers. (Insurance companies, for example, use data to identify and target members of affinity groups who suffer a particular disease to offer them access to travel insurance, which might not be available on standard travel policies.) I shall, therefore, consider only credit in this section.

In credit, are firms deliberately using data to target those who are over indebted, whether or not the loans they offer are overpriced, identifying them by manipulating data? 6 and Jupp (2001) quote this as happening, without giving any hard evidence. A report on extortionate credit by the Personal Finance Institute at Bristol University (Kempson and Whyley, 1999) makes the statement that some sub-prime lenders buy lists of those refused credit by mainstream lenders, although no details are given[8]. Those who use door-to-door credit (see 'Unfair exclusion' above) are often thought of as unfairly targeted, although it is not clear whether borrowers are primarily targeted by use of their data.

There is a serious concern about those with multiple debts who are encouraged to consolidate their debts in one loan, sometimes secured on their home (Kempson and Whyley, 1999). The loans are sometimes at punitive rates of interest and often with severe penalties for late payment. It may, however, not be necessary to use data to target customers in difficulties for loans, as advertising produces applicants who choose to respond. Watching daytime television is instructive. Advertising credit at a non-peak time, when those out of work are likely to be watching, appears to pay off.

A scheme which involves targeting consumers using their data was set up in 2003 by Barclays Bank. Under this pilot scheme, the bank referred customers who had been refused loans on standard terms to Welcome Financial Services, a subsidiary of Cattles plc. Cattles is a company with the stated aims of serving the needs of those who cannot or do not want to access mainstream financial services. The loans given by Cattles were at rates from 20.9% to 35.9%, higher than mainstream loans by Barclays. If the loan was granted by Welcome, Cattles provided the processing, administration and monitoring, while Barclays provided the funds.

Recognising that it lacked the expertise in serving customers in this section of the market, Barclays used a different business model to give access to credit to those who were not creditworthy according to their usual scoring system. Was targeting these using data providing a service, albeit at a higher price to reflect the higher risk, or unscrupulously taking advantage? Barclays argued that it was allowing those with poor or limited credit ratings to show themselves worthy of a better score and thus more mainstream loans. Until there is further analysis of this experiment, including whether it was sustainable and profitable for Barclays, looking at any default by borrowers and at the terms of the loans to determine how easily borrowers could switch once they had shown themselves to be less risky, it is difficult to decide what, if any, control should be placed on firms seeking to identify borrowers by means of data on those refused 'mainstream' credit[9]. Targeting may not always be unfair. And as mentioned above, it may not always involve targeting using data.

Control of unfair targeting: credit

Statutory regulation

In theory at least, the 1998 Data Protection Act should provide some protection for those who find themselves on a list of the over-indebted, which might result in targeting. When applying for credit, applicants have to be told the purposes for which information is collected and consent to it. If it is to be collected to collate a list of those over-indebted so that additional loans can be marketed to them, they should know. However, even if the information is given in a sufficiently explicit form for them to understand, consumers are very unlikely to read that far, or to reject a loan on that basis. A database of those on publicly available lists, such as the list of county court judgements, would in any case be outside this notional protection.

The regulatory response to unfair targeting has tended to concentrate not on controlling the use of data but on examining the events around an application for a loan and seeking to prevent lenders granting a loan to those who will struggle to repay. This may reflect the fact that targeting using data is not seen to be the problem, or the main problem. However, some additional control on using data does exist.

The OFT has a code of conduct (1997) to which lenders who give secured credit to non-status borrowers (those with impaired credit histories or who find it difficult to borrow on 'normal' terms) should adhere, as a condition of their credit licence. Much of the code relates to lenders being open with borrowers and requiring them to assure themselves of the prospective borrowers' ability to repay. The only part of the code that might deal with questions of targeting using data collected from those with poor credit histories relates to cold calling. Lenders and brokers must avoid engaging in marketing credit by telephone to customers known to be or likely to be non-status, if the credit offered would be secured. There is no similar restriction on marketing secured credit to non-status borrowers using databases of those with poor credit histories by other means, for example by targeted mailshots.

The OFT announced in June 2003[10] that it would undertake a report on the debt consolidation industry, including advertising and marketing. It also announced a review of the 1997 non-status lending code. Both could offer an opportunity to control targeting through mailshots or other uses of databases consisting only of names of people who are known to be struggling with debt or who have been repeatedly refused credit. But the exact terms of the regulation would have to be carefully considered, since a company that offered reasonably priced credit on acceptable terms should not be prevented from identifying those who would benefit from transferring their debts.

The Department of Trade and Industry's (DTI) White Paper on consumer credit (2003) proposed to overhaul consumer credit legislation. There was, however, very little that related specifically to unfair targeting in the proposals, beyond a requirement to show annual percentage rates (APRs) in advertisements in circumstances where they would otherwise not be required, if the advertisements were targeted at those who might be credit restricted. Unless advertisements refer here to direct mailshots, this does not directly relate to data use.

The DTI paper states that 7% of the population fall within the criteria for those likely to be over-indebted, that is those who:

- have four or more current credit commitments;
- spend more than 25% of gross income on consumer credit; or
- spend 50% or more of gross income on consumer credit and a mortgage.

The DTI should consider some kind of codification of these triggers into regulation and self-regulation, to require firms to be able to justify either targeting for marketing or lending to consumers who are in any of these situations[11].

The role of SCOR

As described above, data sharing in credit is regulated under the Principles of Reciprocity by SCOR for those lenders who choose to join the closed member groups. While the self-regulatory system owes its existence to the fact that firms need to be able to trust each other and to prevent poaching of each other's customers, a fundamental principle is to promote responsible lending. The Principles of Reciprocity that govern data sharing should have an effect on unfair targeting.

Research carried out for the Financial Services Authority by B. & W. Deloitte in 2002, reported in the Financial Risk Outlook for 2003 by the Financial Services Authority, revealed that 6.1 million households found it moderately difficult or difficult to meet their debt obligations, with 1.8 million households falling in the difficult category − owing in aggregate £46 billion. This figure includes both secured and unsecured lending.

With such widespread difficulties reported, the emphasis in government circles has recently been on preventing further lending to those already over-indebted. This could, in theory, be achieved by a requirement for responsible lending, which in turn could be achieved by a requirement to consider data on existing debt and not lend to those who look as if they will struggle if granted further credit. This is the stated purpose of data sharing under SCOR. Unfair targeting should be prevented if the data are only used in accordance with Principles of Reciprocity. However, there are some difficulties:

• Membership is voluntary and firms can decide whether to contribute positive and negative data or negative data only.
• Data shared does not contain information on how well consumers keep up with payments other than loan repayments; thus rent, council tax and so on are not included. Arrears on these commitments will not show up in the credit reference agency file until a judgement has been obtained or in cases where consumers have given consent to the information being shared.

- While data concentrates on how borrowers keep up with payments, this does not take account of the fact that borrowers are not shown in default provided they are keeping up with minimum payments; sometimes these are very low and paying off a debt while meeting them would take a considerable time; but while they are met, borrowers can get another loan, as their credit status is unimpaired.

Arguments have been made that to encourage responsible lending, greater data sharing should be encouraged, or indeed required, to identify those who should not be offered additional credit. There are, however, arguments against this. It is disputed that information on consumers' commitments is predictive of the likelihood of default on loans (DTI, 2001). In addition, small, local not-for-profit or even commercial organisations, which wish to develop schemes for affordable credit, find the cost of checks at a credit reference agency expensive. Compulsion to share non-credit and positive credit data could make this worse. A requirement to consult a credit reference agency before offering a loan could have a significant effect on the availability of credit to some consumers.

The role of SCOR has wider ramifications than that of simple self-regulation to protect the interests of members. Some of the ways of improving credit risk assessment outlined above could only be definitively solved by a legal requirement to share data both positive and negative, and non-credit data. Whether this is desirable or not requires more detailed research into consumer behaviour once granted credit, the predictiveness of data on outgoings other than loan repayments and the effect on competition.

Given the interest of the government in promoting responsible lending, it is surprising that this aspect of data sharing remains in the hands of a self-regulatory body, particularly since there is little evidence of how the rule that requires data to be used only to ensure responsible lending is enforced. Unless it is enforced, companies can manipulate data on both good and bad payers to target consumers who will be a good risk (and thus make credit more expensive generally for bad payers) or target bad payers, who could be profitable because of the terms of the loan. The Principles of Reciprocity are not particularly transparent. There is no central secretariat and there is certainly no non-industry representative on the board. Enforcement is not open to scrutiny[12].

A report for the Centre for Studies in Economics and Finance at Salerno University (Jappelli and Pagano, 2000) shows that in all EU member states except the UK there is a public credit reference agency and in some countries there are no private agencies. The report also comments on the drift towards consolidation in the industry. A state-funded reference agency could ideally make an assessment of what is in the interests of consumers in relation to what kind of data are gathered and how much should be shared and at what cost. Whether state-funded bodies abroad do so was unfortunately not the subject of the report. The NCC might wish to consider whether any improvement in the sharing of data under SCOR should be made.

Unfair discrimination

Unfair discrimination: credit

The third and final problem indentified by 6 and Jupp (2001) is unjust discrimination based on crude categorical formation. In the area of credit, a number of differentiators are used that may exclude people from mainstream credit under the system of credit referencing and credit scoring. Many are excluded because of county court judgements or because they have no bank account. The self-employed, who number 3.2 million, are frequently refused mainstream terms for credit unless they can show three years' employment history and can produce records to be scrutinised by an accountant. In addition, one of the factors frequently taken into account is type of tenure of the home. Home ownership increases your score even if you are not seeking a secured loan.

I have no evidence to show that risk factors identified in this way are irrelevant. As I said above, if the market is working well there should be no incentive for a firm to refuse credit where there is no statistical evidence of the likelihood of default. Bridges and Disney (2001) quote research by Japelli in the US showing that the probability of a household being credit-constrained declines with an increase in family disposable income, age and savings. Crook, also quoted by Bridges and Disney, finds that the probability that a household is credit-constrained is negatively related to the number of years at the same address, ownership of the main residence, and the number of years of schooling of the head of the household. These seem fairly plausible risk factors. However, Bridges and Disney say that information on credit use in the UK is hard to come by, so that evidence of credit scoring producing unfair results for some would be difficult to find.

Some people may not get credit because of a personal history that is seen as a risk factor. Others are put in the category of being uncreditworthy because they have no financial record to show that they can keep up with repayments. They are discriminated against by the fact that they have not borrowed before, or have not borrowed from those who share data with other lenders, even though they may be able to keep up with repayments. As seen above, membership of closed interest groups in credit reference agencies is voluntary. The effect is that firms, such as pawnbrokers and home credit companies, which make a practice of lending to 'poor risks', do not have to share their data and no mainstream lender will be able to check on how well a consumer has kept up with a loan. Borrowers will not be able to improve their credit scores and so may have to rely on their existing lenders[13].

Bridges and Disney (2001) point out that there is also the potential for discrimination against low-income applicants based on something other than the obvious discriminators such as income, household tenure and age. This is because the credit-scoring card can be designed on a population of people who have been granted credit and the scores are set according to how they perform as good or bad risks. Since there is a population of those who either do not apply, expecting to be refused credit, or apply and are rejected, the score does not take into account the possibility that people on very constrained incomes nevertheless might manage to keep up with loan repayments. Some companies use reject inference to overcome this problem, but the accuracy of this is the subject of some debate 'in the scoring literature' (Bridges and Disney, 2001). Clearly this is another area that needs developing if unfair discrimination is to be avoided.

Control of unfair discrimination: credit

Statutory regulation

At the level of the individual, where data are recorded incorrectly or inaccurately, an applicant may be discriminated against and refused credit. The 1998 Data Protection Act addresses the question of the accuracy of information and its use. It allows people to look at their files in credit reference agencies and to correct records that are incorrect or to add statements to explain records that are correct but misleading.

The 1975 Sex Discrimination Act, the 1976 Race Relations Act and the 1995 Disability Discrimination Act prohibit discrimination in the offer and provision of services, which include banking and credit, on the grounds of gender, race and disability. Legislators have decided that in these cases fairness forbids firms taking data relating to them into account. However, since other discriminators, such as income or employment status, which may disproportionately affect women, people from minority ethnic groups or disabled people, are not outlawed, it is hard to see this as anything other than a statement of principle.

Self-regulation

There is a scheme of self-regulation that applies to credit scoring and that is enforced (at least in theory) by the licensing system to which lenders are subject under the 1974 Consumer Credit Act. The rules are contained in the Guide to Credit Scoring. The latest version is dated 2000 and was developed by the industry in conjunction with the Office of the Information Commissioner and the OFT[14]. It is not possible here to go into a detailed description of the rules. But, for example, a rule that might protect those who might be unfairly discriminated against is that credit grantors will check from time to time that the predictiveness of the scoring system is comparable with expectations. There is also a rule prohibiting redlining, that is, refusing credit simply on address only, although taking postal address into consideration, properly weighted, is permitted.

It is difficult to assess whether the guide is effective as self-regulation since there seems to be no central mechanism by which it is enforced, except where the OFT is considering licensing questions. I have seen no evidence that the two rules have given rise to any enforcement action. The British Bankers Association's Banking Code Guidance for Subscribers, March 2003[15], says that subscribers should comply with the Guide to Credit Scoring, but also points out that the Banking Code Standards Board, which monitors compliance, does not monitor compliance with the guide (see www.bba.org.uk/public/consumers/40883/1974).

A reflection of the provision in the guide on checking predictiveness appears in a leaflet published by the Finance and Leasing Association (FLA), a trade association in the credit industry. The leaflet is for member firms to hand out to applicants and is called 'Your Credit Decision Explained'. In this document, under the question 'Is credit scoring fair?', the following statement appears: "We test our credit scoring methods regularly to make sure they continue to be fair and unbiased". However, this is prefaced by a statement that a decision to grant credit is determined by policy and will reflect commercial experience and requirements.

This is not part of the FLA consumer code, so it cannot be tested by a challenge. But in any case, it is clear that fairness can be overridden by commercial needs.

Unfair discrimination: insurance and genetic testing

In the late 1980s, the development of genetic tests for certain diseases appeared to be leading towards a crisis in insurance. There was a concern that those seeking life insurance (and to a lesser extent critical illness and income replacement insurance) who might be at risk of a genetically transmitted disease, would be required to take a test and reveal the result to the insurer. Much concern was raised about the emergence of an uninsurable underclass as a result of those carrying certain genes being unable to get life insurance (see, for example, NCC, 2001). It was also said that they would be excluded from buying their own homes. It was felt that those carrying genetic markers for a disease, which they might never develop, could be unfairly discriminated against, because insurers, unfamiliar with the science, would assess the risk as if everyone with the gene would develop the disease. It seemed a matter of unfair discrimination that those with genetic markers should be excluded from normal life insurance pooling. As Onora O'Neill (2002) points out, the practice of life insurers until now has been to allocate individuals to inclusive pools, 95% of applicants being offered standard terms, even though the risk between applicants must vary considerably, even allowing for different premium rates related to age.

Control of unfair discrimination: insurance

Statutory regulation

Anti-discrimination legislation applies, at least in theory, to insurance. The 1976 Race Relations Act prohibits discrimination on grounds of race and ethnic origin in insurance. There is no exception. The 1975 Sex and 1995 Disability Discrimination Acts, however, prohibit discrimination but allow it where justified on statistical or actuarial information on which it is reasonable to rely. Since gender and disability often bring with them risks related to health and life expectancy, the effect of the Acts is considerably neutralised[16]. The 1995 Disability Discrimination Act could apply to the genetic testing issue, if it could be shown that those with genetic markers are treated less favourably than those with a similar level of risk. I have not come across any suggestion that it has been used in this way.

Self-regulation

Following previous initiatives, in March 2003 the Association of British Insurers agreed to a moratorium until November 2006, under which, for life insurance under £500,000, and health insurance under £300,000, insurers will not require an applicant to take any genetic test available or to reveal the results of a test if taken. Above these levels, insurers may ask for the result of the test if it has been taken, but only where the test has been certified by an independent government committee (the Genetics and Insurance Committee) as properly predictive of the likelihood of getting the disease. This was to deal with the question of the lack of experience of insurers in interpreting data from new tests. To date[17] only one test has been certified, that for Huntingdon's Chorea.

At a recent meeting of interested parties[18] to discuss what might happen when the moratorium comes to an end, the following points emerged:

- life insurance is rarely demanded as a condition of getting a mortgage;
- susceptibility to genetic disorders may show up in family history, which insurers have long asked about;
- there are not likely to be many cases where there is a single mutation in a cell carrying the likelihood of getting a disease;
- there may be inter-reaction between genes, which may increase or decrease the likelihood of getting some diseases, but these will not show up in a predictive single test, so an explosion of genetic tests relevant to insurance is unlikely;
- families with a member who has a genetic disorder, which would be the reason for taking the test in the first place, are often hard pressed, through other calls on their income, to buy life insurance.

So while the approach of the ABI is to be commended, it appears that the problem may not have been as acute as it at first appears.

Genetic testing got attention because it was a new problem. But if it is thought that life insurance is so desirable (although not essential) that it merits intervention on behalf of those who are unfairly discriminated against as a result of genetic disorders, surely this should be the case for anyone unfairly discriminated against, for whatever reason?[19] If some diseases are seen to require the insurance industry to show that risk pooling is fair, why should it be limited to those presently selected for this treatment? A principle of fairness in data use is needed to make sure that high-profile problems do not get attention while others are ignored.

Conclusion

This chapter has looked at three areas of risk in an expansion of data use in credit and insurance: of unfair exclusion, unfair targeting and unfair discrimination. The unfairness in this information use does not lie in privacy considerations. Indeed if privacy considerations were taken too far, modern credit and insurance would be severely restricted since they depend heavily on data use for assessing the risks involved in the products. Too much privacy could result in less accessibility.

I have tried to show the extent to which data use is causing unfair outcomes and the variety of approaches there are to mitigating unfairness. Some involve regulatory or self-regulatory controls on the use of data, while others attempt to improve accessibility for those excluded from mainstream products, through alternative, non-commercial, provision. The fact that there is such a variety of approaches indicates that government, regulators, trade bodies and providers acknowledge a concern. It is, however, very difficult to assess how effective they are, especially as the self-regulatory schemes are not properly open to scrutiny. Some solutions only give benefit to a limited number of people, while others rely on individuals who are affected taking court or other action to enforce rights, which may be beyond their means.

More needs to be known about: whether making firms alter their behaviour under self-regulation works better than making non-commercial provision; whether prohibiting discrimination has any effect if it has to be challenged by an individual enforcing rights, rather than a regulator in a policing role; and whether in countries with central regulators for data sharing some of the problems around responsible lending are tackled. The effect on competition of compelling further data sharing needs to be explored. Privacy considerations also have a role to play.

The label 'unfair' in the three categories examined above reflects a wider societal view of what is just, that is:

- people should have access to goods and services essential to everyday life;
- without some protection[20], people should not be sold goods or services that are harmful to them;
- people should not be refused goods or services as a result of discrimination on the grounds of personal characteristics that are irrelevant to the goods or services in question.

In the case of essential services, policy considerations on how access should be achieved cover much wider ground than merely the question of data use. The NCC (2002) has examined these and I do not propose to explore this further, except to say that data use could have a role to play where it is thought that consumer cross-subsidy is an appropriate way of funding access.

In the case of unfair targeting and unfair discrimination, however, there are principles relating to data use that would mitigate some of the problems and that are implicit in the existing self-regulatory and regulatory responses.

I want to argue here for consideration of a more coherent approach to fair data use, beyond the privacy-based approach of the 1998 Data Protection Act. The first data protection principle requires data to be fairly and lawfully processed. But fairness is interpreted in relation to processing and use as it affects individuals and privacy, rather than other outcomes. For example, in deciding fairness, "regard is to be had to the method by which they are obtained, including in particular whether any person from whom they are obtained is deceived or misled as to the purpose or purposes for which they are to be processed"(1998 Data Protection Act, sch 1).

The solutions and responses to perceived problems described above reveal an underlying concern with fairness, rather than merely privacy, whether or not they are successful in their aims. The Principles of Reciprocity state that the purpose of sharing data is to improve responsible lending, thus preventing targeting those to whom further debt might be harmful. As we have seen, the OFT Guide to Credit Scoring requires credit grantors to check from time to time that the predictiveness of the scoring system is comparable with development expectations. Discrimination on the grounds of race, gender and disability is prohibited. So is discrimination on raw postcode data. The response to the problems of those with markers for genetic diseases requires scientific proof of the relevance of those markers.

But fairness in data use is likely to have wider implications than the categories of problems set out above and certainly a wider application than in financial services. Much work is being done at present on unfair commercial practices. The EU is close to enacting a duty 'not to trade unfairly' in the Unfair Commercial Practices

Directive[21]. The Financial Services Authority requires the firms it regulates to pay due regard to the interests of their customers and to treat them fairly[22]. This thinking should be applied explicitly to data use, not just by commercial users but by public bodies as well.

Notes

[1] In some cases, regulatory pressure is adding to this. The effect of the Basel II Capital Accord on regulatory requirements for all international banks is likely to increase the risk-based pricing of credit, as banks will have to show regulators that their capital is adequate for the risks of their credit portfolios.

[2] The Registry Trust is a not-for-profit organisation, which maintains a register of county court judgements for England and Wales, including administration orders, for the Lord Chancellor. It also keeps registers for Scotland and Northern Ireland. The register is public. It is governed by a Board drawn from the consumer credit trade sector, with a consumer representative.

[3] These requirements have been developed by the Information Commissioner as a result of the 1998 Data Protection Act. The Information Commissioner works with the industry to make the consent form transparent, so that applicants know what information will be shared.

[4] Consumers taking out insurance may have to consent to insurance companies sharing data on claims in order to prevent fraud.

[5] Recent research commissioned by the DTI found that low-income households have an irreducible need for credit and households with constrained resources the greatest need for credit (Policis, 2004). This might be seen as an argument for more generous benefits or a higher minimum wage, but this point is not argued here.

[6] A super-complaint (defined by Section 11 of the 2002 Enterprise Act) is a complaint to the OFT that features of a market for goods or services harm the interests of consumers.

[7] Interestingly, in the US, credit checks are sometimes made on those applying for insurance. In the UK it is, according to the rules of the Principles of Reciprocity described, not possible to check with closed user groups in credit reference agencies for the purposes of deciding on granting insurance, although the industry-wide database CIFAS is open to insurers.

[8] Since writing this chapter, a news story has featured Vanquis, a subsidiary company of Provident Financial, which offers credit cards to those refused credit, at rates of interest between 50 and 70%. It was originally stated that the company obtained data on customers to target from Experian, but a spokesperson for Experian said that they were not informed when credit was granted and so had no list of customers refused credit. It would be interesting to know whether, without breaching the 'responsible lending' principle of SCOR, it would be possible to obtain a list of those with poor credit histories (rather than those refused credit) from a credit reference agency.

[9] Cattles has now announced in its annual report for the year ending December 2003 that it has ended the pilot as not enough new customers have been referred.

[10] In March 2004 the OFT announced the result of the study. Better financial awareness among consumers, and clear, accurate and relevant information from credit providers are required to make the use of debt consolidation fairer and more transparent. The study will inform the OFT's enforcement of the 1974 Consumer Credit Act.

[11] The Consumer Credit Bill, which resulted from the White Paper, is currently (March 2005) before Parliament. There are no proposals for controlling data collection or use, but there is provision for a general control by the court of unfair relationships between lenders and borrowers. A relationship may be unfair because of things done or not done by the lender before or after the making of an agreement. Some control of unfair targeting might be achieved, if the DTI codified the triggers for overindebtedness, for use in court challenges using this clause.

[12] The principles are, however, subject to scrutiny by the OFT for potential breaches of competition law and the most recent version has been signed off by the OFT. The rules provide for new entrants accessing data for a period before they are in a position to contribute their own, which allows competitors to enter the market.

[13] Under the 1998 Data Protection Act, a borrower could demand a copy of his or her file with this kind of lender, to show to an alternative loan company, which would not otherwise be able to get access to it.

[14] A copy of the Guide to Credit Scoring can be found on the Experian website at www.experian.co.uk/corporate/compliance/creditscoring. It is referred to frequently on other websites of the trade organisations which agreed it, but a copy cannot always be accessed on these websites. At the time of originally writing this chapter, it was available on the OFT website, but this is no longer the case (March 2005). The difficulty in obtaining a copy gives some indication as to how inadequate the Guide is as a self-regulatory scheme.

[15] The Guidance is available on the Banking Code Standards Board website at www.bankingcode.org.uk/home.htm

[16] Although the original text proposed that discrimination in insurance on the grounds of gender should be prohibited, the final text of the EU Gender Directive (http://europa.eu.int/scadplus/leg/en/cha/c10935.htm), adopted in December 2004, provides that gender may be used as a basis to assess risk in insurance, if objective data can justify the difference.

[17] No other tests have been approved, but on 28 March 2005 the government announced that the agreement with the ABI will continue until 2011.

[18] 'Insurance, genetics and fairness', joint reading of the Genetics and Insurance Committee and the Human Genetics Commission, 22 September 2003.

[19] A similar response from the ABI to discrimination on the grounds of tests and other data that might reveal HIV status is beyond the scope of this chapter. A change in the original position taken by the ABI was published for consultation in September 2003. The final draft version can be seen at www.abi.org.uk/Display/File/86/response_to_responses_FINAL.pdf

[20] For example by warnings or information that enables them to take precautionary measures. In some cases there is a complete prohibition on harmful/unsafe goods.

[21] Proposal for Unfair Commercial Practices Directive, Com (2003) 3J6 final.

[22] Principles for businesses, Financial Services Authority. Available at http://fsahandbook.info/FSA/handbook.jsp?doc=/handbook/PRIN/2/1

References

6, P. and Jupp, B.(2001) *Divided by information?: The 'digital divide' and the implications of the new meritocracy*, London: Demos.

ABI (Association of British Insurers) (2003) *Statement of principles on the provision of flooding insurance*, London: ABI.

ABI (2004) *A Changing climate for insurance*, London: ABI.

Bridges, S. and Disney, R. (2001) *Modelling consumer credit and default: The research agenda*, Nottingham: Experian Centre for Economic Modelling, University of Nottingham.

Datamonitor (2003) 'UK non-standard and sub-prime lending', London: Datamonitor DMFS 1506.

DTI (Department of Trade and Industry) (2001) *Report on the Task Force on Tackling Overindebtedness*, London: DTI.

DTI (2003) *Fair, clear and competitive: The consumer credit market in the 21st century*, Cm 6040.

Jappelli, T. and Pagano, M. (2000) *Information sharing in credit markets: The European experience*, Salerno: Centre for Studies in Economics and Finance (CSEF), University of Salerno.

Kempson, E. and Whyley, C. (1999) *Extortionate credit in the UK*, London: DTI.

Kempson, E., Collard, S. and Taylor, S. (2002) *Social Fund use among older people*, London: DWP.

Kempson, E., Collard, S. and Whyley, C. (2000) *Saving and borrowing*, London: DSS.

NCC (National Consumer Council) (2001) *Whose hands on your genes?*, London: NCC.

NCC (2002) *Meeting basic needs*, London: NCC.

NCC (2004) *Home credit*, London: NCC.

OFT (Office of Fair Trading (1997) *Non-status lending: Guidelines for lenders and brokers*, London: OFT.

O'Neill, O. (2002) *Autonomy and trust in bioethics*, Cambridge: Cambridge University Press.

Policis (2004) *The effects of interest rate controls in other countries*, London: DTI.

Whyley, C., McCormick, J. and Kempson, E. (1998) *Paying for peace of mind*, London: Policy Studies Institute.

7

Personal information in the National Health Service: the demise or rise of patient interests?

Jonathan Montgomery

Introduction

Information is essential to effective healthcare. Patients need to know that the health professionals caring for them are taking decisions based on accurate information about them as individuals and about the available treatments for their health problems. Over the past few years, the National Health Service (NHS) has put considerable effort into improving the management of information. The establishment of the National Institute for Clinical Excellence has furthered the drive to ensure that care is based on sound scientific evidence about effectiveness. Monitoring of mishaps and learning the lessons has been systematised, both in local NHS organisations and through the National Patient Safety Agency, so that patients can be better protected from human error. The National Programme for Information Technology for the NHS is now seeking to improve the way in which personal information is managed and protected.

The vision is for a single system of personal health records that can be accessed electronically from NHS facilities anywhere in the country when needed for patient care. Wasted appointments because the records are not available should become a thing of the past. The frustrations of having to tell health professionals the same things many times over will be dissipated. These are significant issues. One survey of patient experience across five countries found that patients in the UK were significantly more likely to find that their results or records were not available to doctors in time for their appointments than their counterparts in Australia and New Zealand. Twenty-three percent of those surveyed had encountered this problem in the UK. Almost half of the patients in the survey (49%) had to tell the same story to multiple health professionals (Blendon et al, 2003; see also Health Which? and NHS National Programme for Information Technology, 2003, pp 7-8). One of the results of the new system should be improvement in these areas, with benefits for the quality of care. Patients will also be able to check information to ensure that it is accurate. They will be able to exercise some control over who gets to see which parts of their records and be far better able to check that records are used in the way that they wish. Thus, services should become more responsive to patients' wishes and more focused on serving their individual needs.

Yet such a vision of a modernised information-based service carries risks. Health information is particularly personal and strong commitments to confidentiality have long been seen as an essential pre-requisite, giving patients the reassurance that they need before they are comfortable sharing sensitive information with professionals. Matters of health are closely connected with self-esteem, reputation and personal identity. Health status can be highly significant in relation to employment prospects, access to insurance (and loans such as mortgages) and, in some contexts, social standing. The increasing sophistication of genetics means that personal health information is increasingly significant in predicting future health, raising the stakes further in respect of potential misuse. It also offers prospects of benefits, particularly better-targeted drugs, as pharmacogenetics opens up the possibility that drugs can be tailored to be most effective for a specific individual rather than a population.

Personal health information is not only significant for the delivery of services to immediate patients. It also provides opportunities for use for wider purposes. These range from the efficient management of the health services that patients are accessing, such as enabling care to be audited to ensure that it is effective, to commercial exploitation. There is an economic value to health information in lots of diverse ways: from the direct marketing of continence products to those who need them, to medical research, and even the exposure of celebrities to sell newspapers. There are also potential public health benefits from understanding the patterns of ill-health and the efficacy of treatments that may be gained from the collation of data held within the NHS. Similarly, retail industries routinely use aggregated information on consumer choices to predict demand and enhance the responsiveness of their stores or marketing operations.

However, there is both confusion and concern from the public over the accessibility of data within the NHS. In research carried out to support a national consultation on the new NHS model for confidentiality, 23% of participants did not know how the NHS used their personal data and 7% of participants incorrectly believed that the Secretary of State for Health could access their personal health records (Consumers' Association et al, 2002, p 19)[1]. Further research into views on the proposed electronic record system elicited general but not universal support in principle, but also identified areas of concern. Advantages of the new system were seen to include ready access to information by health professionals, easier access to patients' own records and the ability to contribute to them if they wished. The main concerns were about the security of the system and the possibility of non-health professionals accessing material (Health Which? and NHS National Programme for Information Technology, 2003).

The management of personal information within the NHS needs to ensure that current patients' interests are met in a number of key respects. Accurate information needs to be readily available when needed and must be held securely so that patients' privacy is protected. This is not merely an issue of sound systems. Patients need to have confidence in these areas in order to entrust their information. A stronger partnership between the NHS and patients is required to ensure that information management delivers its potential benefits.

There are also broader interests. All citizens have a stake in their health services being well managed, so that they are accessible when needed, and based on sound research, so that they are effective when needed. These could be seen as people's interests as potential patients. Citizens also have interests as taxpayers in services being as cost effective as possible. The NHS needs to develop a model for handling personal health information that can meet these consumer needs.

Imagining confidentiality

The idea of medical confidentiality has implanted itself in parts of the public imagination on the basis of a cosy nostalgic image of the gentleman general practitioner (GP), seeing patients in the front room of his comfortable home, keeping their secrets in his head or perhaps in a dusty filing cabinet. It is intimate and personal, and the reassurance of privacy is built on a lifelong relationship of trust. The reality is very different, and long has been. Delivering healthcare is a complex business in which accurate information, its timely retrieval and the increasing demarcation of roles based on specialist skills are essential to delivering what patients expect of services. The relationship between a patient and his or her GP is most likely to be with a 'practice' – doctors in partnership supported by other health professionals – rather than the single-handed practitioner. While most healthcare continues to be provided in primary care, it is increasingly delivered with support and advice from hospital specialists. Patients expect to be able to move effortlessly into secondary care and are surprised when they have to repeat information that they have already provided. While general medical practice remains outside the NHS in contractual terms, patients expect healthcare to be slickly integrated.

Maintaining the traditional image of confidentiality leads to considerable dissonance with the reality that many professionals receive personal information as members of multi-disciplinary teams required to deliver complex modern care. Some have argued that confidentiality is a myth and pretending that it exists is a confidence trick, a breach of trust. Reliance on professional ethics and personal integrity as the guarantees of privacy has led to concern in the light of growing awareness of the bureaucracy of information management. Anxiety is exacerbated by the crisis in trust in the health professions that has followed a series of scandals – Bristol, Alder Hey, and Shipman[2]. If confidentiality depends on doctors being trustworthy, then is it built on shifting sands? Further, the emergence of a range of ways of accessing NHS services – general medical practice, NHS Direct, NHS walk-in centres – has meant that there is no longer a single professional who can expect to know all of a patient's health affairs. The refocusing of the NHS on patient experience and the advent of 'patient choice' as a key service value also imply the ending of the GP as the lynchpin of the system. Patients now expect to have a relationship with the NHS as a comprehensive and consumer-friendly service, not merely with a benign but powerful gatekeeper holding the keys to the treatment room.

If we cling on to the traditional image of confidentiality, then these changes threaten to leave patients naked, without protection. If there is nothing other than the personal guardianship offered by the professionals whom patients consult, then these developments seem either to put the safeguarding of confidentiality beyond their power (the expansion of healthcare teams) or to make their protection worthless (mistrust of the professionals on whom we rely). In fact, there is no need to be so pessimistic. There are other mechanisms to protect the interests of patients, more powerful in the context of these developments in the provisions of health services, which have been obscured by the persistence of the traditional image of confidentiality. Re-imagining the nature of medical confidentiality can bring these mechanisms to the fore and enable us more easily to assess their strength and identify the improvements that are necessary. It is possible to fight a forlorn rearguard action to hold on to the old paradigm that is rapidly being overtaken by the modernisation of the NHS. However, it would be far better to embrace the change and exploit the new agenda, which offers a more robust basis for placing patients' interests at the core of the system. Clinging to the old model of patient confidentiality does more to protect traditional professional power than to promote patients' interests.

The most promising new paradigm for protecting the privacy of patients in the context of health services is provided by data protection law. This incorporates the value of confidentiality, through the first data protection principle that data must be processed fairly and lawfully, but it goes much further. It ensures that responsibility for protecting patients' interests lies with those who have the power to do so – the organisations ('data controllers' in the language of the new paradigm). It is organisations that must take steps to ensure that data are kept secure – the main obligation of confidentiality under the old paradigm (making sure that information does not leak, or get 'disclosed' to third parties). The responsibilities of data controllers under the 1998 Data Protection Act go far beyond this, however – as has been discussed in Charles Raab and John Borking's chapters (Chapters Two and Three in this volume). Unlike the confidentiality model, data protection obligations extend to ensuring that the information held is fit for purpose. It must be relevant and not excessive (the third data protection principle). It must be accurate and up to date (the fourth data protection principle). Unlike the concerns of the confidentiality model, this paradigm can help ensure that information can only be used in the way that patients want and expect, not merely to prevent it being obtained by those who should not have access to it.

Most significantly, the data protection model draws attention to one of the most important blind spots created by the traditional conception of the issues. This is the way in which information is used within health services. The first data protection principle is elaborated by requiring that data can be processed only when certain justifications are present[3]. Health information is given a high level of protection as one example of the category of 'sensitive personal data' so that the types of justifications that are recognised are more limited than in relation to other types of information (although there is a general recognition of the legitimacy of 'medical purposes' to which I shall return). All processing of information, every time it is accessed, has to be justified against these principles, not merely the passing of it to other people or organisations. Therefore the NHS has had to examine whether the internal use it makes of its data is acceptable, not merely whether it is keeping data secret from outsiders.

The traditional model was strong on the limits of confidentiality – identifying when confidentiality could be breached. Professional guidance and to a more limited extent judicial analysis expounded the types of justification that could serve to override the obligation of confidentiality. Thus, for example, extensive discussions could be found of whether the Driver and Vehicle Licensing Agency (DVLA) could be informed if a patient was unfit to drive. Did the public interest in securing road safety override the patient's right to have his or her confidential information kept secret?

However, the model did not make it easy to consider what happened to information within the 'circle of confidentiality'. The essential obligation of confidentiality was to ensure that information was only made available to those within the community to whom it had been entrusted by the patient. In the mythology of confidentiality, this would have been only the GP, although it is doubtful that this would ever really have been the case. In the light of the emergence of healthcare teams, this became broadened to incorporate other health professionals involved with the patient's care. Provided confidential information was not released beyond this ever widening circle, then it continued to be thought that confidentiality was being preserved. Little attention, however, was given to the use made of information within this circle.

Professional concern was raised, especially by the British Medical Association (BMA), at the use of patient information by health service managers[4]. To the BMA, this seemed to be a breach of confidentiality – passing information beyond the magic circle of confidentiality to non-professionals. NHS leaders would have understood it as widening the circle, while still preserving confidentiality (because the information was secured within the NHS). The real issue, however, is whether the *use* to which information was being put was justified.

There is an instructive analogy with the ethics of organ retention after post-mortem that came to light following the Alder Hey and Bristol inquiries. When it became known that significant numbers of organs from deceased children had not been replaced in their bodies before burial or cremation, the public was scandalised. But we have to be careful to analyse the nature of the offence committed by the professionals concerned. At least one of the doctors involved practised with a disregard for professional ethics (Redfern, 2001). However, the vast majority of them, over the long history that the inquiries examined, believed that they were acting for the best and did so in good faith. With the advantage of hindsight it can be seen that they could have been more open with the families. At the time that many of the organs were retained, it probably seemed a cruel additional burden to impose on grieving families to ask their permission to keep material from their children's bodies for scientific analysis. Pathologists and others saw retention as a normal activity in relation to material that had been properly obtained. We now see that use as abnormal and a betrayal of trust. The 2004 Human Tissue Act will make specific consent essential for all tissue retention to prevent 'professional usefulness' being any longer seen as a legitimate justification.

The analogy with health information concerns the mismatch of understanding of what uses are legitimate between professionals and the wider community. The 1961 Human Tissues Act on human tissue concerned itself with whether its removal from the body was justified, by consent of the deceased patient, their relatives or the coroner. It was silent about the legality of retaining it once the specific purpose for removal (usually in this context in order to ascertain the cause of death) had been served. From the point of view of professionals, it appeared that this made it legitimate to make additional use of the material when this was in the broader public interest. This did not seem a major ethical issue as the tissue was not understood to comprise part of the identity of the deceased person and its use did not appear connected to their family. For the bereaved relatives, however, the same activity struck them as an abuse of trust, an offence to the memory of their loved ones and an intrusion into their own family life.

Similarly in relation to health information, the traditional model concerned itself with a particular stage of transaction, the passing on of information, not with the use of information itself. Provided that information was jealously guarded within the circle of confidentiality, it seemed that patient interests were properly protected. Yet as public awareness of the way in which information is used within that circle has been raised, it has become apparent that greater scrutiny needs to be given to how the internal use of information can be justified, particularly in relation to health services management (already seen as problematic by health professionals), epidemiology and research (both regarded as legitimate under the old model as keeping the information within the fold).

The results of these shifts in the structure of health services, the fixing of responsibility for compliance on organisational management and the replacement of the paradigm of 'confidentiality' with that of data protection should not be seen as damaging. The 'new NHS' is becoming more patient focused than the traditional model, with the emerging agenda around patient choice promising a more consumer-led service. As information is contained in records that need to be made more widely accessible to those caring for patients, health service organisations have greater power to protect patient confidentiality and privacy than individual professionals could ever hope to do. Making the organisations accountable for this fixes responsibility where the ability to deliver it lies. Done effectively, the new data protection world has the potential to benefit patients as consumers of the service. What needs to be considered now is whether the structures that are being put into place are sufficient to ensure that this benefit materialises.

Managing patient information in the new NHS

Over the past five years, the NHS has invested considerable efforts in the process of engaging the public and health professions in discussions over the way in which personal health information should be protected and used. A major consultation was undertaken by the NHS Information Authority (2002) on the model for the use of such information. This was reinforced by scrutiny and subsequently guidance from the Information Commissioner on the application of the 1998 Data Protection Act to personal health data. The processes culminated with the issuing by the Department of Health in November 2003 of *Confidentiality: NHS code of practice* (DH, 2003) along with endorsements from the Information Commissioner, General Medical Council, BMA and Medical Research Council.

The model (Consumers' Association et al, 2002) is based on a linked records system providing NHS staff with broad access to information on a 'need to know basis' that is justified by implied patient consent following extensive publicity on the way in which information is handled and a guarantee of patient confidentiality. Patients will be able to opt out from the general basis of staff access and sharing between NHS organisations, subject to some specified circumstances when their restrictions could be overridden. This will be achieved through a virtual 'sealed envelope' in which patients can place information that they do not wish to be generally available to those caring for them. The circumstances when the sealed envelope could be opened without specific patient consent are not yet fully worked out, but will probably concern contexts such as emergency care, where the 'vital interests' of the patient are at stake (an exception to the need for consent recognised in the 1995 European Data Protection Directive and the 1998 Data Protection Act that implements it). Patients would be ensured rights of access to and correction of their records, subject to specific legal limitations as at present. The system will also be able to generate an audit trail of who accesses patient data so that NHS organisations can ensure that staff have acted properly and patients can satisfy themselves that their rights have not been compromised.

Broadly speaking, this model is to be welcomed and regarded as a sound protection of patients' rights. The Information Commissioner has confirmed that the processing of personal health information to provide healthcare is consistent with the 1998 Data Protection Act provided that it is necessary for that purpose (Office of the Information Commissioner, 2002). The difficulties that have emerged concern the use of information beyond the purpose of providing immediate care for the patients whom it concerns. The Department of Health (DH) has shown itself to be committed to protecting confidentiality through an extensive review of the flows of patient information, leading to the setting up of Confidentiality Guardians (Caldicott Guardians, as discussed in Bellamy et al, Chapter Five, this volume) in each NHS organisation (Caldicott, 1997). It has also resisted in the courts attempts for non-NHS researchers to access patient information[5]. This review and litigation established that it is legitimate to use anonymised information for broader health services purposes. However, concerns remain over some areas where it is proposed to use personal information from which patients can be identified. In most circumstances, consent can be sought, but the DH remains of the view that there are circumstances in which it is necessary to use identifiable patient information without specific consent in order for the NHS to function effectively and efficiently.

The main focus for these issues to be explored has been the debate over the use of powers under Section 60 of the 2001 Health and Social Care Act to provide for use of patient-identifiable data without specific consent. Regulations under that section have been used in relation to communicable disease surveillance and cancer registries. Some use of such data can also be made to enable analysis, such as the anonymisation processes themselves (which are carried out on identifiable records but need to be done to secure anonymity), identification of contact details so that patients can be invited to consent to the use of their data in research, or linkage checks to validate data before they are used anonymously. Such uses are overseen by the Patient Information Advisory Group, set up to review the use of Section 60 powers.

The issues raised by such use of patient information go to the heart of what it means to be a patient of the NHS and a citizen of the UK. One line of argument builds on the individual's right to privacy and suggests that any use of information that may affect an individual should be prohibited without his or her consent. That consent might be implicit, in the sense that the patient was aware that the information might be used and raised no objection. However, to make it acceptable to rely on such an implicit consent there must be some confidence that patients were aware of both the possible use and also the opportunity to opt out. Such an approach fits well with the DH's commitment to increased public awareness of how the NHS uses information and also to the fact that Section 60 of the 2001 Health and Social Care Act is to be a temporary measure, with patient consent becoming the normal justification for the use of information. It could not yet be said that the conditions for implicit consent are fully in place.

This model, while strongly protective of the individual rights of existing patients, raises difficulties when the interests of citizens as possible future patients are considered. If patients are entitled to opt out of the use of information for epidemiological purposes, for example to trace the spread of infectious diseases or to monitor the incidence of cancer, then as a society we will be less able to understand those health conditions and prepare accordingly. In a voluntary context, it would seem wholly legitimate to offer 'members' of a health system a choice between opting in to an organisation that offers benefits in the form of treatment in return for agreement to the use of information for the improved effectiveness of the service as whole. This would equate to the agreement that a bank can process information for its own internal purposes. In such a context patients could choose to join a more efficient health service provider, but give up a degree of privacy, or to maintain greater privacy but at the expense of some service advantages. Such an argument of mutual burden and benefit works well where membership is a matter of choice, but is problematic where there is a universal service such as the NHS. It may be that the concept of citizenship could imply some loss of personal freedoms, including the use of data for public health purposes. However, there is no current consensus on which this could be based.

Protecting patient interests

Patient-led remedies

One of the results of the confidentiality paradigm was its dominance by professional control. The obligation fixed itself on the health professional and it was an obligation to keep things secret. Patient records were a place in which this information was stored, but they were not the property of patients. From the professional point of view, those records were the property of the professionals and contained information gleaned, created and interpreted by their professional skills. They existed as support for the professionals carrying out their job and were not seen as a constituent part of patients' identity.

The transformation of understanding can be traced through developments in the law relating to access to records. The traditional common law position was that patients had no right of access to their records, even though they contained important information about them[6]. The judicial position is shifting as a result of the recognition that people's rights to respect for their private and family life cannot be met unless they have access to their past and that often accessing health and social care records can be an essential part of understanding their personal identity. Thus, the European Court of Human Rights has ruled that a person brought up in local authority care is entitled to access his records in order to be able understand this past[7]. The change of perspective from one based on the (limited) obligations of professionals to one that identifies the importance of records to individual identity and autonomy is to be welcomed from a consumer perspective.

The gradual acceptance of statutory rights of access to records has been grudging but no less important. Private members' Bills in the 1980s secured rights of access to social care, employment and insurance medical reports and finally in 1990 health records more generally (1987 Access to Personal Files Act; 1988 Access to Medical Reports Act; 1990 Access to Health Records Act). Access rights are now provided by the 1998 Data Protection Act. Patients are entitled to be informed when their personal information is being processed, why it is being processed, and with whom it will be shared (Section 7). This transparency is a direct consequence of the extension of data protection law to all health records and is one of the drivers for the creation of the new 'compact' between patients and the NHS described in the previous section. Patients are also entitled to a copy of their records in an intelligible form, a continuation of the rights hard won in Parliament (Section 8). Importantly, if they find that information is inaccurate, they can ask that it be rectified, although they may find that all that they are given is the inclusion of their views as to accuracy alongside the opinions of the professionals (Section 14)[8].

There remain, however, vestiges of the old professionally dominated paradigm in the limitations of rights of access. Patients may be refused access to information within their records that would be likely to cause serious harm to the physical or mental health of the patient or of any other person (2000 Data Protection [Subject Access Modification] [Health] Order, SI 2000, no 413, art 5). The protection of third parties is a limitation that is entirely compatible with human rights principles – rights to respect to private life have to be balanced against the rights and freedoms of others. However, to deny patients access on the basis that it would be bad for them even though they wish to have it is a paternalistic justification that is more difficult to reconcile with a consumer-focused service. It implies that the health professionals are better placed than the patient to decide what is in the patient's interests. The exceptions to access rights are under review at present and it can be expected that the paternalistic grounds for refusal of access will be removed[9]. It is perhaps significant that the Department for Constitutional Affairs, not the DH, is leading the review as it indicates that the matter is one of legal rights rather than service provision.

There are some dangers in the development of the NHS national records system, which aims to ensure that professionals caring for patients can link together information currently held separately in different parts of the health service. It may make it possible for health professionals to piece together a picture of patients that cannot be seen by the patients themselves. Without seeing the same picture as the health professionals, it will be difficult for patients to correct false impressions. At present, each NHS organisation has a separate data controller, so patients must apply separately to every body that holds records to obtain access to all the information held by the NHS about them. It is difficult to justify creating a system for comprehensive access by clinicians without doing the same for patients, but it is not yet clear how this will be achieved.

One development that could emerge in the future out of the establishment of a national electronic records system would be an especially interesting tool for placing patient choice at the centre. The DH has undertaken to ensure that all NHS patients will have access to their own Internet-based 'health space' in which they can record their own health information such as health appointments, questions that they want to ask, and medication (www.healthspace.nhs.uk). This provides the basis for direct open access to their health records when they wish. It would be a small step from this to move to a national NHS records service in which the principal client was the patient. It would be the patient who unlocked that record to health professionals, either by an implicit authorisation when seeking care or by a specific grant of permission. This would get close to making patients the owners of their personal records, not merely passive objects of the gaze of the health professions.

Governance structures

There remains a major omission in the NHS vision for records management in the future. While standards of information governance are emerging, there is no overall framework for quality assurance in relation to confidentiality to reassure patients that the benefits rather than the risks of the vision for patient information services will be realised. The system for patients to call NHS organisations to account for their handling of information is fragmented and limited to ordinary complaints mechanisms and the use of the Information Commissioner. Fragmentation will become increasingly a problem as the NHS uses more providers from the independent sector, some of whom may be based abroad. A far more integrated quality assurance system is required. The development of national standards of information governance needs to be completed. It would be helpful for it to be led by a single identifiable champion for patients' interests, a form of internal NHS information commission. This would give patients a point of contact that could cut through the complexity of NHS providers, with the responsibility to ensure that patients' rights are protected by the system as a whole. There is too great a risk that the fragmentation of the current system will lead to no one having the responsibility to deal with problems because they are passed between different organisations rather than resolved.

Greater clarity is required of the responsibilities of local NHS bodies, from GPs to NHS Trusts, to comply with information governance standards. Commissioners' duties to secure compliance by service providers with NHS standards, whatever their status, need to be made more explicit. Common standards will be essential on data security, processes for informing patients about the use of information and recording the consents that they give, including any restrictions they wish to impose. These are not yet apparent.

Above all, there is an exciting possibility obscured in the future development of NHS records. At present, the system seeks to bring together existing records held by separate NHS providers and will be as good, or as poor, as the sum of those records. The real prize would be in a system in which the sum – a complete record – is greater than the current component parts. There is no clarity yet about whether the records service will remain limited to coordinating linkage between separate databases or whether a national service will emerge containing the patient records. If it does, there is the potential for patients to become the main client, acting themselves as the gatekeepers to their health records, not reliant on NHS staff to decide who should see the information. That would become a truly patient–focused system.

Conclusion

This chapter has considered recent developments in the handling of patient records by the NHS and has argued that they are broadly to be welcomed as supporting a move towards a service more focused on individual patients' needs. While there are clear causes for concern over the implementation of the new integrated records system, the vision is one that patients should see as better able to protect their interests and less dominated by the convenience of health professionals than the current system. The move from a narrow concern with confidentiality to a broader respect for proper data protection makes the NHS better placed to protect the interests of patients. Patients will be better informed about the way in which their records are used and given more say over who is permitted to access them. The direction of travel thus offers the prospect of better confidentiality governance and greater patient control. Nevertheless, there are still many gaps in the picture that is unfolding that need to be painted in before patients can be sure that the system will deliver its promise.

The most important would seem to be as follows:

1. The NHS needs to continue to take steps to ensure that patients understand how it protects and uses personal information.
2. A public debate needs to take place about the extent to which citizenship entails some restriction of choice over limiting the use of personal health information for 'public purposes'.
3. A comprehensive framework of confidentiality governance, with a national lead to ensure consistency, should be developed for the NHS to give patients the assurance that their information is being properly protected.
4. Standards are needed to ensure consistently high quality of data in the national records system.
5. The national records system needs to be structured around patients rather than providers, so that patients can readily access their

records, check them for accuracy and satisfy themselves that the
NHS staff accessing their records have a legitimate purpose.
6. A single access point should be established for complaints about
the use of personal information in the NHS so that patients can
easily and promptly have concerns addressed.

Notes

[1] This may have been influenced by scare stories in some national
newspapers suggesting that new legislation under the 2001 Health
and Social Care Act was aimed at permitting such access.

[2] Bristol concerned the mismanagement of children's cardiac services,
Alder Hey the inappropriate retention of children's organs after post-
mortem examinations, and Shipman the failure to detect a medical
mass murderer.

[3] These are set out in Schedules 1 to 3 of the 1998 Data Protection
Act.

[4] See, for example, the attempt to secure a Bill legislating on
confidentiality in the 1990s. Extracts are reproduced in *Bulletin of
Medical Ethics* (1994) vol 100, pp 13–17.

[5] *R v Department of Health, ex p Source Informatics Ltd [2000] 1 All ER
786.*

[6] *R v Mid-Glamorgan FHSA, ex p Martin [1995] 1 All ER 356.*

[7] *Gaskin v UK [1990] 1 FLR 167; MG v UK [2002] 3 FCR 289.*

[8] This continues the position established in the 1990 Access to Health
Records Act.

[9] No proposals have yet emerged for reform at the time of writing
(April 2005).

References

Blendon, R.J., Schoen, C., DesRoches, C., Osborn, R. and Zapert, K. (2003) 'Common concerns amid diverse systems: health care experiences in five countries', *Health Affairs*, vol 22, no 3, pp 106–21.

Caldicott, F. (1997) *Report of the review of patient-identifiable information*, London: DH.

Consumers' Association, NHS Information Authority and Health Which? (2002) *Share with care! People's views on consent and confidentiality of patient information – qualitative and quantitative research: final report*, London: Consumers' Association in association with NHS Information Authority, Birmingham and Health Which?.

Health Which? and the NHS National Programme for Information Technology (2003) *The public view on electronic health records*, Health Which? and NHS National Programme for Information Technology.

DH (Department of Health) (2003) *Confidentiality: NHS Code of Practice*, London: DH.

Office of the Information Commissioner (2002) *Use and disclosure of health data: Guidance on the application of the Data Protection Act 1998*, London: Office of the Information Commissioner.

Redfern, M. (2001) *The Royal Liverpool Children's Inquiry Report*, London: The Stationery Office.

Part Four: NCC's agenda

8

The new personal information agenda

Susanne Lace

E-PUBLICATION REAL TIME REPORTING SYSTEM
DATE: 13 December, 2007
READER ID NUMBER: 295079
BOOK: *The glass consumer*
READER STATUS: Now reading
TIME SPENT ON CURRENT PAGE: 15 seconds
PAGES READ: 207
AVERAGE TIME PER PAGE: 52 seconds
READER INTELLIGENCE LEVEL: High
PRIMARY MOTIVATOR: Career
(Adapted from Kasanoff, 2001)

Introduction

Bruce Kasanoff has predicted that soon we will read books on digital publication readers. Our reading habits will be recorded in companies' databases and we will have agreed to this, encouraged by some sufficiently appealing offer.

But whether or not digital readers take off, much of our own lives already are an open book. Authors in this volume have described how our lives are constantly recorded and scrutinised – how we have become 'glass consumers'.

The personal information economy does represent a new world in formation. It forces a fresh exploration of what our rights and responsibilities are. And yet the full contours of change remain far from clear. The economy is an elusive being, its existence marked often by absence rather than presence – the lack of supermarkets in deprived areas, the withdrawal of businesses. Its shape is further obscured by the opacity of organisational practice.

This book therefore set out to illuminate some of the darker corners of this economy. We have traced its most recent history and explored its operation in both public and private sectors. This chapter now moves on to discuss the National Consumer Council's (NCC) own agenda for change, to promote positive ways in which responsible information use can advance consumer interests.

Moving to a risk-based framework

The NCC's recommendations are shaped for the world into which we are moving. They focus on the importance of how information is used – it is not argued that information should rarely be collected, although much will always depend on the circumstances. Instead, we argue that personal information issues should be conceived and managed with much greater sophistication. We are living in a world in which, more than ever before, our personal information defines our opportunities. It is now time to reappraise our assumptions, adjust our expectations and challenge the old rules.

We need to appreciate but move beyond the traditional demarcation lines of privacy debates to recognise the broader benefits and risks of using personal information. In the future, policy will be formed less exclusively on the battlegrounds of privacy but on those of risk and of accountability. Privacy itself will need to be promoted as a social (rather than primarily an individual) value that supports democratic institutions.

It is interesting that some writers believe the most potent threat to liberty in the future will be overweening nannyism, built on the detailed analysis of consumers' behaviour. Lashmar (2004, p 31) recently argued that if

you have an obesity problem but cannot resist slipping ... half a dozen
doughnuts into your supermarket trolley, expect trouble at the
checkout. It is not too far-fetched to believe that the supermarket,
under mandatory government regulations, will have programmed your
storecard to stop you buying food with a high fat content.

Whether or not this comes to pass, the potential is certainly there for technology to underpin policies that would give many of us pause for thought. Yet consumers have accepted some products (such as mobile telephones) that have worried civil liberty campaigners (because of telephones' tracking technology), precisely because they appreciate the benefits. That is why the NCC's agenda acknowledges those benefits but also considers how we can recognise and address risks. One of the challenges will be to make organisations much more accountable for the (often hidden) decisions they take.

Implementing this vision does conjure diverse responsibilities. Regulators will need to refocus and strengthen their work, organisations must treat personal information lawfully and fairly, and consumers will need to develop a wider appreciation of the significance of their information. Governments, above all, must recognise and respond to the broad impacts of the personal information economy, particularly those affecting the less advantaged in society.

This will not be easy. There is no magic bullet to dissolve the complexity of fashioning a way forward. Policy makers will continue to face difficult choices – it is unrealistic to assume that new developments and competing interests will not bring challenges. Professionals, too, will need to exercise their own judgement when confronted with complex personal information issues, even if all parts of the NCC's agenda were in place.

But realising this vision would make a huge difference. Moving forward, the NCC's agenda revolves around six core principles:

- risk-based information policy;
- responsible innovation;
- open access;
- fair use;
- tackling poor practices;
- informed choice.

Each section in this chapter opens with a quotation – these are statements made in 2004 by the NCC's Consumer Network, members of the public who report their everyday experiences as consumers to us.

Risk-based information policy

"[A company] held incorrect information on a catalogue
transaction against my name. It took over a year to resolve –
a case of guilty until proved innocent. The mistake prevented me
getting credit."

The 'democratised' surveillance society

Before we can begin to appreciate the risks of the personal
information economy, we need some understanding of the
economy's nature.

Allusions to Big Brother scrutiny are becoming dated – instead,
we now are moving towards a society of 'little brothers'. Gibson
(2003) has written that the acceleration of computing power and
connectivity (and the simultaneous development of surveillance
systems) is leading to a state of "... absolute informational
transparency, one in which 'Orwellian' scrutiny is no longer a
hierarchical, top-down activity, but to some extent a democratized
one".

The spread of technologies such as camera-phones and web-
cameras in nurseries (allowing parents to monitor their offspring
and carers) marks the rise of lateral forms of citizen surveillance.
Mann calls this 'sousveillance', as most cameras no longer watch
from above but from eye level (*The Economist*, 2004).

But ubiquitous surveillance challenges privacy and creates risks
of its own. Lyon has defined surveillance as any collection and
processing of personal data for the purposes of influencing or
managing those whose data have been garnered (2001, p 2) and has
spoken of its dangers (2003a, p 142):

> In the past few years, surveillance has become algorithmic,
> technological, pre-emptive, classificatory, in every way broadening and
> tightening the net of social control and subtly stretching the categories
> of suspicion. It thus tends to undermine trust and, through its emphasis
> on individual behaviors, to undermine social solidarity as well. At the
> same time, it augments the power of those who institute such systems,
> without increasing their accountability.

The rise of the little brother society does create a need for greater awareness (among government, business and consumers) of the importance of personal information and the challenges it poses. Key to these debates, as will be discussed in this chapter, should be appeals to the principles of social justice and distributional fairness, quality of life and the notion that privacy in particular can be socially beneficial.

The risks

To tease out the challenges further, the book's introduction considered the importance and benefits of the personal information economy. The economy has generated new services, driven product innovation and promoted cost-efficiency. At the same time, key risks were highlighted, which may lie in the collection and manipulation of information or in the outcome of information use itself. The following five points summarise risks discussed throughout this book:

- *Injustice* – this includes using inaccurate or out-of-date information, making unjust inferences, function creep (when information is used for a different purpose from that for which it was collected) and the reversal of the presumption of innocence.
- *Lack of control of information* – such as the inability to find out what is held or where data are collected from, unjustified surveillance and data collected without consent.
- *Loss of dignity and autonomy* – this may result from the absence of transparency, the absence of anonymity or unjustified disclosure.
- *Inconvenience* – such as making a substantial effort to find out what information has been collected, how it has been used or to secure the correction of data.
- *Risks to life chances* – as the private sector concentrates on people and areas that present the best risks.

These risks have yet to be fully appreciated and addressed.

Re-imagining privacy

Privacy still forms the central plank in most defences against information misuse but it often has proved insufficient to counter the risks of information use. If it is to provide a more robust defence, then privacy needs to be reconceived.

Although defining privacy is problematic, Westin (1967) provided the influential definition that privacy was the claim of an individual to determine what information about him- or herself should be known to others. Drawing on Westin, Margulis (2003, p 246) has argued that privacy is important as it supports normal psychological functioning, stable interpersonal relationships, and personal development:

> It is a basis for the development of individuality. It protects personal autonomy. It supports healthy functioning by providing needed opportunities to relax, to be one's self, to emotionally vent, to escape from the stresses of daily life, to manage bodily and sexual functions, and to cope with loss, shock, and sorrow.

So if privacy is depleted, our development may be constrained. How significant a threat this is to our growth is, however, still unclear. The developmental aspects of privacy are under-researched and social scientists know too little about how people respond to being constant subjects of surveillance (Lyon, 2003a, p 153). However, one fear is that people may become more conformist in future, as they suppress their individuality to avoid drawing too much attention to themselves (*The Economist*, 2004).

But even if we did know more about this, how far would policy makers increasingly recognise the importance to individuals of privacy? After studying congressional policy making, Regan (1995) found that framing privacy as an individual right (as a value, an interest) had a weak impact on decisions, so to more effectively promote the value of privacy in policy-making debates, privacy should be presented as a social/societal value.

Privacy does have value beyond the individual – it supports democratic political systems by providing opportunities for political expression, political choice and freedom from unreasonable police interference (Margulis, 2003, p 246). It also provides opportunities for people and organisations to prepare and discuss matters 'in private'. Westin (2003, p 434) argues that:

> If we are switched on without our knowledge or consent, we have, in very concrete terms, lost our rights to decide when and with whom we speak, publish, worship, and associate. Privacy is therefore a social good in democratic societies.

Yet even if reformulating privacy primarily as a social value would bolster its persuasive power, the difficulty of quantifying privacy in the past has contributed to its marginalisation. As Richard Thomas (the Information Commissioner, the regulator charged with protecting personal information in the UK) has argued (2004):

> It is relatively easy to put a price on crime, to add up the stolen property and the fraudulently claimed benefits.... The value of privacy, though, is more difficult to calculate – what units do we use to measure it? How much loss of privacy is justified by a 10% reduction in crime?

So while other social policy objectives can be measured with some accuracy, arguments against excessive levels of surveillance often must be advanced in terms of abstract rights and fears of hypothetical consequences (Bennett and Raab, 2003). However, this should not lead us to reject privacy as a useful defence. The challenge is to develop credible arguments that recognise the personal and collective value of privacy and to articulate more cogently the broader risks of information use.

Reconciling competing interests and articulating risks

Over the last three decades, many developed countries have responded to concerns about privacy and information risks by providing for 'fair information principles' (as discussed in Charles Raab and John Borking's chapters, Two and Three, this volume) in data protection law. How well the law has stood up to the task will be discussed later in this chapter. At this stage, it is useful to look a little more closely at the context in which fair information principles operate.

Stewart (2004) has argued that data protection standards have reconciled, rather than balanced, competing interests (largely as it is difficult to quantify privacy benefits). Democratic societies do need to ensure that information is sometimes disclosed, whether that is to promote objectives such as the responsible conduct of public affairs or to support fair dealing in business (Westin, 2003, p 432).

But the tension between such conflicting interests is often immensely difficult to reconcile. When should a competing interest (say, a public good such as public health) trump privacy? Who should ultimately control consumers' information?

It is difficult to be prescriptive about these debates, perhaps invoking a simple matrix that would resolve all problems. Privacy is closely related to social legitimacy, so when a society does not accept certain conduct, it may deny private choice and privacy claims. As a result, debates over privacy are unlikely to go away, as they are tied to changes in the norms of society as to what kinds of personal conduct are regarded as beneficial, neutral, or harmful to the public good (Westin, 2003, p 433). And there will be no easy answers or short cuts that will do away with the need for skilled judgments in difficult cases.

We also need to recognise that the language of risk can be problematic. All risks are not alike and it is not easy to estimate the different degrees and kinds of risk inherent in transactions involving personal information (Bennett and Raab, 2003, p 227). The objective and subjective dimensions of risk cannot be separated easily, nor can their relationship be described clearly: "No easy distinction can be drawn between 'real risks' and 'mistaken perceptions', nor can it be supposed that science can determine the former and explode the fallacies of the latter" (Bennett and Raab, 2003, p 227). So regulatory policy in this field must be geared to people's perceptions and fears as much as (or even more than) any 'objective' calculation of risk, even if such a calculation were possible.

In effect, we need to recognise the complexity of privacy and information risks and continue to develop our understanding of their distribution, impacts and resolution.

Responsible innovation

"Data protection, I feel, often works against the consumer rather than
the other way round."

As we have seen, privacy and data protection law is a primary source
of protection against information risks. But this has proved to be of
limited effect. Data protection law has operated reactively and rights
often have been narrowly defined and poorly implemented,
undermining their scope and efficacy.

As Charles Raab notes in this volume, data protection law is hugely
challenged when attempting to control the desire of organisations
to amass ever increasing levels of information. 'Fair information
principles' are shot through with a liberal political theory that places
faith in procedural and individual remedies to excessive intrusions
(Rule et al, 1980). Hence some commentators have argued that
data protection rights only marginally impact on surveillance
societies or, worse, serve to legitimise new personal information
systems and thus extend social control.

While the NCC does believe that data protection law has a part
to play in providing protection against risks (and recommendations
are made in this chapter about how it could be strengthened), there
is a clear need to engage with information risks much earlier in
decision-making and policy processes.

Encouraging public involvement in the development of new systems and technologies

An environment where the law takes a backseat role favours the
dominance of the large technology companies that develop
sophisticated technologies exploiting consumer data, for which the
reactive constraints of data protection law may only be of limited
hindrance. As a result, the abilities of democracies to protect personal
information may be as dependent on decisions made in the
laboratories of these corporations as in the offices of regulators
(Bennett and Raab, 2003).

In spite of an increasing awareness among public policy makers
of the benefits of public engagement in issues of science and

technology (Wilsdon and Willis, 2004), we have yet to witness similar recognition among companies. A recent Royal Society of Arts report (RSA, 2004) found low levels of awareness of the need for public engagement and little action.

There is a very strong case to be made for consumer involvement in decision making on information risks. The most obvious danger is a backlash against new developments (witnessed so starkly in the debates on genetically modified food and discussed in the NCC's work on radio frequency identification technology – Lace, 2004). Vehicles for involvement are numerous. Work published by the NCC, and more recently by the think tank Demos, discusses how consumers can become involved in decision-making processes (NCC, 2003; Wilsdon and Willis, 2004).

If organisations are to take engagement seriously, they also need to recognise the constraints of those groups within civil society that make the case for privacy and data protection. Beyond the activities of regulators, who are significantly constrained by their own resources, the wider privacy movement is a shifting assemblage of players who often come together to work on particular issues, then break apart. Their funding is usually limited or precarious, which particularly militates against concerted campaigning. Paid, longer-term consumer representation is one way forward (as discussed in another NCC [2002] publication, *Consumer representation: Making it work*).

The responsibility of technology professionals and organisations

At the level of individual technologists, recognition of the social importance of their role has been developing for some time – the organisation Computer Professionals for Social Responsibility has existed for over 20 years, codes of conduct (such as that of the Association for Computing Machinery) have been promoted and academic research centres do investigate computing and social responsibility. Yet organisations, whether in the public or private sector, are key and it would be naïve to expect too much of professional autonomy if set against a hostile organisational culture.

The lead taken by Microsoft is insightful. In 2002, it appointed

Caspar Bowden, co-founder of the Foundation for Information Policy Research (a think tank that has campaigned to limit surveillance), as their Senior Privacy Strategist. The apparent aim was to bring an understanding of privacy issues into organisational thinking. Similarly, Cambridge University's Nanoscience Centre recently appointed a lab-based sociologist to help colleagues reflect on the social and ethical implications of their research (Wilsdon, 2004).

Looking forward, the NCC supports the recent Royal Society recommendation (in its report on nanoscience and nanotechnologies, – RS, 2004) that the Department of Trade and Industry should establish a group from a wide range of stakeholders to look at new and emerging technologies and to identify potential issues of concern (including social and ethical issues). It also agrees with the Royal Society that the research councils should ensure that the social and ethical implications of advanced technologies form part of the formal training of research students and staff.

Promoting tools to assess information risks and build protection into systems

Privacy impact assessments (PIAs)

Technical instruments do exist to help decision makers assess information risks and build protection against them into systems. PIAs comprise a methodology to identify privacy issues, impacts and risks that may be associated with proposals to develop technologies, services or products. They aim to ensure that good information-handling practices are considered throughout the design or redesign of programmes or services. They are premised on the belief that individuals have a right, subject to the explicit provisions of other legislation, to control the collection, use and disclosure of their personal information.

In May 2002, the Canadian federal government became the first jurisdiction in the world to make PIAs mandatory for new programmes and services (Bennett and Raab, 2003). Interestingly, a major reason behind this was to tackle people's concerns about e-government.

PIAs do not assume that there are necessarily correct answers to their questionnaires, which cover key data-handling principles. Instead, they aim to ensure that issues of personal information collection, retention, use, disclosure and so on are considered and debated by top-level decision makers (Bennett and Raab, 2003). Institutions must document their evaluation of privacy risks, the implications of those risks and their discussions of possible remedies, options and recommendations to avoid or mitigate such risks. In Canada, the results of the PIA are included in project briefs that seek funding for projects. Institutions must provide a copy of the PIA to the Privacy Commissioner at an early stage, prior to implementation.

Experience with PIAs so far has been in the public sector; this has shown some success (Flaherty, 2004). It is now time for governments elsewhere and companies to use PIAs. This could help build more responsible and accountable systems and crucially help foster risk-sensitive information practices. The Cabinet Office could act as a catalyst in the UK, initially by convening a conference to learn from international experience in this field.

Privacy-enhancing technologies (PETs)

In this volume, John Borking has made a persuasive case for PETs. He has shown how they can be used in many ways, from designing anonymity and subject access into hospital record systems to applications that promote consumer choice on the web.

The NCC agrees that there is considerable merit in the use of technologies such as PETs, particularly at the design stage of new systems and products. Governments, in particular, have a strong role to play in procurement exercises to ensure that they specify the use of PETs in system design. However, it is difficult to reach definitive conclusions more widely about PETs' role, as the diversity of technologies militates against sweeping generalisations. For example, those PETs that facilitate individual choices on the web do place the onus on the individual to know about and buy any necessary protection. As Lyon (2003b, p 7) argues, this disadvantages less informed and affluent consumers: "Another division emerges, based this time on awareness and, in some cases, ability to pay".

This is not to say that PETs do not have a rightful place at the policy table – it is more that we should consider how they can empower different groups of consumers, rather than just the most advantaged. The NCC seconds Borking's calls for their further research and development.

Responsible innovation: recommendations

The NCC *recommends* that:

- Companies creatively engage with social and ethical issues at an early stage in their research and development cycle, from involving consumers and their representatives to appointing privacy officers and other staff to recognise and act on the social implications of innovation.

- The UK government and companies use PIAs when designing new, or substantially redesigning, information systems. The 1998 Data Protection Act should be amended to ensure that government uses PIAs and provides the results of the PIAs to the Information Commissioner. Copies of the results of PIAs should be made available to the public.

- The Office of the Information Commissioner promotes the responsible use of PETs and the Department of Trade and Industry sets aside a significant proportion of its innovation funds for investment in this field. The Office of Government Commerce should also consider PETs in reviews (under the 'Gateway Review' system) of procurement projects.

Open access

"On taking goods to the check-out ... I was asked if I had a saver card. Not having a card, I was asked to pay a higher price."

Since its election in 1997, the UK's Labour government has paid much attention to social exclusion and has launched a cavalry of

initiatives to tackle problems. A treatise on the success of those
initiatives is beyond the remit of this book – instead, the aim here is
to focus on how the use of personal information may impact on
consumers' life chances and how this may be addressed.

There is increasing concern that the use of personal information
can reinforce social exclusion (Lyon, 2001; 6 and Jupp, 2001).
Evidence suggests that the poor in the UK are becoming
progressively more concentrated in certain areas (Lupton and Power,
2002); the fear is that the use of consumers' information may be
contributing to this. In this volume, Perri 6 (Chapter One) discussed
a geography of information exclusion, showing how geo-
demographic data profiling systems may restrict social mobility.
Harriet Hall also discussed personal information and financial
exclusion (see Chapter Six).

To recap, the box below summarises how authors have categorised
these risks.

Risks to life chances and constricting markets

Withdrawal of investment and limits on competition – drawing on
detailed information, organisations may focus only on the most
profitable customers and withdraw investment from areas where
less profitable customers live. This might not matter if there was
sufficient innovation by those offering 'downmarket' services to
make lower-income groups profitable, but in some areas this may
not be the case.

Another concern is that if focusing on the most profitable
consumers reduces the range of products available for others,
then there may be anti-competitive effects.

Offering unfavourable terms – some consumers may only have access
to products and services on terms that are less favourable than
those offered to higher-value consumers.

Targeting the worst-off – data systems may be accurate enough to
enable companies to target the worst-off consumers and heavily
market goods and services to them that will worsen their position.

Unjust discrimination – the converse problem is that information systems may not be accurate enough to enable this kind of focusing on the profitable. Instead, there will be problems of unjust discrimination based on the use of crude categorical information (such as postcodes) or on false or out-of-date information or from matched data where matching produces misleading information.

Perhaps first it is worth re-emphasising the point Hall makes in her chapter that the more effective use of personal information can open up access to goods and services (as it widened access to credit and insurance in the past). Using personal information to inform business practices, including policy on pricing, may benefit the majority of consumers.

But as 6 and Jupp argue (2001), underneath the fear of 'database discrimination' lies the issue of which goods and services society thinks everyone, not just the majority, ought to be able to consume. Our ongoing work at the NCC (under the banner 'Why do the poor pay more?') is exploring which goods and services are essential to meet consumers' basic needs. We have found that those with limited incomes pay more, or get less, for a range of goods and services. The reasons for this do vary, but some relate to how personal information is used. As Hall discussed, this may be because disadvantaged consumers are perceived to be, or actually are, higher-risk consumers. In the former case, providers may not know enough about particular groups and so price services too highly or restrict access to them.

To the extent that companies are taking decisions on insufficient data (and wrongly perceive certain consumers to be of higher risk), this highlights the economic value of good data, and how inaccurate or inappropriate uses of personal information can pollute commerce. This and good information-handling practices are discussed in the next section of the chapter.

Some commentators (such as Gandy, 1993) have argued that complex technology that collects and analyses information about individuals can produce discriminatory outcomes. Consumers are sorted into categories on the basis of routine measurements but those measurements are often incomplete, as assessments about status are divorced from circumstance. So the fact that you did not pay one credit card bill is logged but not why – and this can mean that decision making is unduly crude and unforgiving. Bias may be institutionalised as this missing evidence is "compensated for by a common tendency to fill in the missing with the familiar or with that which is expected" (Gandy, 1993, p 16). Lyon (2003a, p 34) has argued that:

> The increasingly automated discriminatory mechanisms for risk profiling and social categorising represent a key means of reproducing and reinforcing social, economic and cultural divisions in information societies. They tend to be highly unaccountable.

But even if companies are using consumers' information in segmenting the market, making commercially rational and accurate decisions, this too raises the issue of exclusion. Danna and Gandy (2002) have argued that one of the basic tenets behind customer relationship management, based on the Pareto Principle, is that 80% of any firm's profit is derived from 20% of its customers. This may lead companies to discriminate on price, targeting the most profitable and providing them with discounts or subsidies. Consumers also may be excluded from the market if profiles are used to determine whether certain goods or services are offered to them at all (Danna and Gandy, 2002, p 382):

> In an e-commerce setting, it is commonplace for consumers to receive differential access to goods and services as a result of collaborative filtering or observational personalization techniques. Consumers who fit into a particular profile may not be offered certain goods as readily as those who fit into other profiles. Discrimination in access and service based on a constructed profile has consequences for people in physical spaces like neighbourhoods as well as in administrated spaces like Web sites.

The question now is what the respective roles of the state and the private sector should be in taking responsibility for those who are classified as 'bad risks' (6 and Jupp, 2001). 6 and Jupp list the following as tools used by liberal democracies when the consequences of contractual decisions about risk have led to disadvantage:

- *Direct government compensatory action* – that is, targeting those who have been disadvantaged by the rational decisions of the private sector and assisting them with taxpayers' money (as in the cash benefits system).
- *Regulation preventing the use of sanctions and adverse outcomes* – one example is regulation preventing water companies from disconnecting supplies due to debt.
- *Regulation preventing certain considerations from being taken into account* – as when the private sector is prevented from using certain characteristics in risk assessment (for example, prohibitions on using genetic information).
- *Regulation requiring 'positive discrimination'* – for example, regulations requiring the Royal Mail to charge the same for letter delivery throughout the country.

Ultimately, the policy choice is a trade-off between the value to a society of the benefits to the intended group of beneficiaries and the scale of the potential costs falling upon others. If we consider that access to a range of basic services is necessary to achieve reasonable life chances for everyone, then actuarial fairness will not be enough (6 and Jupp, 2001).

It is interesting in this regard to look to the example of the 1977 Community Reinvestment Act (and related legislation such as the 1975 Home Mortgage Disclosure Act) in the US. The legislation obliged banks to report on their lending records in poorer areas that they previously had redlined (by deciding not to do business there). The open disclosure of their records spurred banks to look at what more they could do and also encouraged non-profit and state organisations to help build the credit-worthiness of local residents. As a result, US banks have invested an additional $1 trillion since 1977 in the poorest areas – and on a profitable basis.

Such creative responses to exclusion will need to evolve continuously in the future. Our own work at the NCC has included developing a tool to help decision makers evaluate policies aimed at funding improvements in access to essential goods and services.

Certainly, ongoing research and evaluation is vital to promote a better-informed policy debate – the impacts of the personal information economy are not always easy to predict. We need to know much more about whom it affects, how and when. The NCC would encourage the research councils and the Social Exclusion Unit to carry out/sponsor longer-term research on the impact of the personal information economy on social exclusion.

Fair use

"Personal information regarding my income and benefits entitlement was divulged to a third party by a local council officer without my knowledge or permission."

Appreciating fair information principles

In the UK, now is a particularly difficult time to champion the cause of privacy and data protection law: it frequently has acted as a scapegoat for other failures.

But being cast, however wrongly, as the whipping boy of lost causes has not won data protection friends. The perception lingers, apparently within significant swathes of the public and private sectors, that privacy and data protection law is a problem and not a solution: it places unnecessary burdens on organisations, undermining their effectiveness and confidence in their work. Yet whether this is borne out in reality is difficult to prove – studies of the costs and benefits of data protection are in their infancy and the results of regulatory impact assessments and other studies are inconclusive or contradictory (Harris, 2004).

However, studies on compliance with the law do indicate that data protection is not taken seriously by many organisations, whether in the public or private sector. Research in this field is limited, but most studies reveal that many organisations fail to comply with existing privacy and data protection legislation. In the EU, the European Commission (CEC, 2003) has reported anecdotal evidence suggesting that organisations across Europe comply very patchily with the 1998 Data Protection Directive, the most importance piece of European legislation in this field. A 2002 study of website compliance with the Data Protection Act (which implemented the Directive in the UK) also reported widespread failure to comply with the Act (OIC, 2003). Similarly, a survey of compliance practices with the Privacy and Electronic Communications Regulations (*Privacy Laws & Business*, 2004a) found that nearly half of the top 50 companies in five sectors were breaching the regulations.

This does mask differences between and within sectors. The incentives for a bank, for example, to comply with legislation may not be the same as those of an airline or retailer. And incentives may be higher or weaker depending on what type of information is handled (consumer, employee, client, and so on – Bennett and Raab, 2003).

Some organisations also may be unaware of their responsibilities under data protection legislation. The Information Commissioner did find (OIC, 2003) that smaller private sector organisations would welcome training to help them comply with the law (and the NCC certainly would encourage the Commissioner to promote the provision of low-cost training packages).

That said, even data security – that part of the data protection canon that would seem to nest most closely with an organisation's self-interest – has had a rocky history. According to Steven Adler of IBM, privacy- and security-related incidents in 2003 cost the global economy the colossal sum of $250 billion in direct damages and lost productivity (*Privacy Laws & Business*, 2004b). Improved information handling practices could save organisations millions.

Unsurprisingly, attempts have been made to appeal to the economic benefits of treating information seriously, citing increased efficiency, competitiveness and the facilitation of international trade. Good information-handling standards can enhance trust and so strengthen both commerce and relations with the public sector. In this vein and in the name of 'enlightened self-interest', the Information Commissioner recently called upon organisations to take data protection seriously (Thomas, 2004): "How can we be competitive if organisations hold inaccurate information, have poor security or have lost the trust of the public?".

In other words, bad data pollutes systems and privacy and data protection regulation is about keeping systems clean.

The Information and Privacy Commissioner in Ontario (IPC,

2003) also has written of the costs and benefits to business of implementing sound privacy policies and practices. Her arguments are condensed into Table 8.1.

Table 8.1: Costs and benefits to business of implementing sound privacy policies and practices

Lack of attention to privacy/data protection can result in:	Careful attention to privacy/data protection can result in:
Violation of privacy laws	Business development through expansion into jurisdictions requiring clear privacy standards
Damage to an organisation's reputation and brand	A more positive organisational image and a significant edge over the competition
Physical, psychological and economic harm to customers whose personal information is used or disclosed inappropriately	Enhanced data quality and integrity, fostering better customer service and more strategic business decision making
Financial losses associated with a deterioration in the quality and integrity of personal information, due to customer mistrust	Enhanced customer trust and loyalty
Loss of market share or a drop in stock prices following a 'privacy hit' resulting in negative publicity, or the failure or delay in the implementation of a new product or service due to privacy concerns	Savings in terms of time and money

The NCC agrees that fair information practices do have a role to play in addressing information risks, along with other initiatives. Consumer confidence and economic efficiency, at the very minimum, can be promoted by responsible information practices. Still, even in itself, data protection as it currently works is inadequate – reform is needed.

The 1995 Data Protection Directive and the 1998 Data Protection Act

As discussed in several places in this volume, the 1998 Data Protection Act (DPA), implementing the Data Protection Directive (95/46), is the most important piece of legislation regulating the collation and use of personal information in the UK. Unfortunately, it is not the tightest piece of legislation ever drafted – critics consistently have pointed to the ambiguity of key terms, which render uncertain what is, and crucially what is not, allowed.

Simplifying data protection

The Better Regulation Taskforce (BRTF, 2004) has argued that the Data Protection Directive should be reviewed on its 10th birthday in 2005, with the aim of simplification. While the NCC does not support a number of their recommendations, we agree that a review is necessary and timely. As the BRTF propose, the review should have clear objectives, a plan and a timescale.

Closer to home, the DPA should be reviewed and simplified. It is a lengthy and often ambiguous piece of legislation that many find hard to understand. This may contribute to the poor compliance with the legislation discussed earlier.

Simplification would enable the legislation to set out key fair information principles more clearly and help organisations comply with both the spirit and the letter of the law.

Poorly defined terms, practical problems and gaps in protection

To consider specific problems with the legislation, one example of a key term that is not defined in the DPA is that of consent, although it was defined in the mother legislation, the Data Protection Directive. A major problem is what constitutes implicit consent; this leaves organisations considerable scope to limit consumer involvement in decision making. Consumer involvement is also constrained as companies are allowed to use opt-out provisions for many forms of direct marketing. This puts the onus on consumers to remember to tick boxes or to spend time trying to understand what are often unclear options.

Other legislative terms with a difficult history include those of the 'relevant filing system' and what exactly constitutes 'personal information' (particularly following the recent Court of Appeal decision, in *Durant v FSA*, which limited the definition). Across Europe, the European Commission (CEC, 2003) also found that greater clarity was needed on what 'legitimate interests' are. The processing of non-sensitive personal information is allowed without consent provided that the 'legitimate interests', rights and freedoms of the individual are not overridden. As legitimate interests are poorly articulated within the legislation, this undermines appropriate consumer protection.

A further problem arises under the Data Protection Directive across Europe when organisations inform regulators about why they are collecting information. They can specify these purposes very broadly and effectively create databanks of extremely detailed information that consumers know little about (and which can be disclosed to others). Further, although the Directive gives consumers access to their information, its wording allows organisations to disclose only the 'classes of recipients' (broadly defined) with whom data are shared. This can reveal little, but in some cases knowing with which specific organisations information is shared is important; for example, a consumer may wish to be reassured that details of pharmaceutical products bought are not shared with named financial service providers. The NCC thinks consumers should be able to access this information, without being rebuffed by commercial confidentiality defences.

More generally, gaps in the Directive do exist. For example, Australian privacy law (National Privacy Principle 7) prevents private sector organisations from adopting an Australian government identifier (such as a national insurance number) as their own, to prevent function creep. Such a provision is absent from the Directive. Other principles missing from the Directive include a provision mandating organisations only to use true identities when absolutely necessary – this would force organisations to think about why they are collecting personal information; it may also act as a spur to the take-up of PETs.

A provision limiting or checking the use of algorithms also would be helpful. Many data-matching algorithms (formulae used by computers that generate decisions about consumers) are known to generate significant numbers of errors. Hence, where data matching is a basic tool in decision making, the possibility of misidentification is a concern. The NCC therefore thinks that regulators should be given the power to control the use of data-matching algorithms, to help limit incorrect assumptions.

More broadly, there is considerable scope for reviewing the laws of information use in England and Wales, including both statutory law and common law. At the time of writing, the human rights organisation Liberty was conducting a review of privacy in the UK. This should be built upon, to evaluate existing law and its power to regulate effectively in the face of rapidly evolving economic and technical developments.

Transfers of data internationally

Cross-border data transfer is one of the most contentious parts of the Directive. The operation of call centres provides the most well-known example of this. Whenever we call a customer service line in the UK, there is a strong likelihood that our call and data are routed around the world. Interestingly, and ostensibly in a bid to prevent the loss of call centre jobs to India, the trade union for employees of Lloyds Bank complained in the summer of 2004 to the Information Commissioner that transfers of data to Indian call centres were violating data protection rights, due to insufficient protection in India.

Under the Directive, transfers can take place only if recipient countries have 'adequate' levels of protection in place. The aim is to ensure that rights are not circumvented by exporting information to 'data havens'. However, it has proved extremely difficult to build systems that identify which countries have such protection and to construct practical mechanisms to facilitate compliant data transfer. Within Europe, different countries approach the export of data differently – for example, some require every export to be authorised in advance by the regulator (although there are doubts about whether this happens in reality).

As Charles Raab has shown, a key jurisdiction is the US, the only advanced Western industrial state without comprehensive data protection legislation. The Safe Harbor agreement between the US and the EU has provided one mechanism for effecting transfers to the US that would comply with the Directive, but it suffers from the fundamental flaw that companies voluntarily choose to sign up to the agreement (and many have not).

Another major concern is that national authorities lack the capacity to scrutinise the actual processing of data in another jurisdiction (as this would require on-site auditing of organisations' practices and also of a regulator's work). In his evidence to the House of Commons Select Committee on Constitutional Affairs in May 2004, the Information Commissioner stated that his own Office would not be able to scrutinise the arrangements in place in other countries. Since then, the European Commission has expressed dissatisfaction with the UK's approach (Chapman, 2004).

Looking ahead, the NCC agrees with the Better Regulation Taskforce (BRTF, 2004) that the European Commission should make more transparent the process and criteria for approving the adequacy of third-country protection.

The NCC also would like to see the further development of 'Binding Corporate Rules'. These are self-regulatory codes of practice, developed jointly by an organisation exporting data and a regulator, which aim to guarantee adequate protection for cross-border data transfers. Particular attention should be paid to the effective negotiation and oversight of codes. Monitoring is especially important, to ensure that organisations do what they say. The NCC's soft law principles (Lace, 2003a, 2003b) provide credible self-regulatory guidelines.

This is an area that will continue to spawn developments and controversy. Other initiatives to introduce global standards have so far failed (see Raab, Chapter Two, this volume), largely due to the resistance of business. Nevertheless, renewed activity on international standards is still welcome.

Public sector, personal information

The fair use of personal information has significant promise for public service improvement. The NCC is active in promoting more user-responsive public services and it is clear that the adaptation, or 'personalisation', of services and the delivery of e-government cannot advance far without the more effective use of personal information.

Certainly, public services are diverse in nature. In services that are collectively consumed, such as environmental health, personal information will have less value. But in services that are individually consumed (such as education and welfare), the careful use of appropriate personal information could offer considerable benefits, in facilitating the user–centred design and delivery of services. The electronic health record and the concept of personalised learning in education both illustrate an emerging approach to public services that is designed to value and enable the active participation of service users.

At the same time, both for services that are individually consumed and services that are enforced, there is a strong need to develop public trust. Rigorous systems that support the fair use of data can help build this trust. Each of the principles set out in the NCC's agenda has relevance for the public sector's use of personal information.

Within the UK, the NCC would welcome the introduction of senior managers who oversee how staff use personal information in all public sector organisations, effectively extending the model of Caldicott Guardians throughout the public sector.

Another key issue is whether legislation to facilitate public data sharing is needed. The European Information Society Group decided in 2004 to push for legislation for consent-driven data sharing powers as:

> ... the current situation, with fragmented data collection and updating often outsourced, and with sharing forbidden except when it is mandatory under legacy powers, gives the worst of all worlds: duplication, waste, error and confusion without credible protection against fraud or abuse. (EURIM, 2004, p 1)

The NCC has some sympathy with these concerns. Consumers are often annoyed at having to provide the same information to numerous public bodies and this can make it more difficult for vulnerable consumers to access the support they need. Consent-driven data sharing legislation may clarify the powers public bodies have.

Nevertheless, it will be extremely difficult to reach definitive legislative conclusions on when it is appropriate to share data, in the often complex circumstances in which data might be shared. As Bellamy and her colleagues concluded (Chapter Five, this volume), detailed codifications of permissions and prohibitions for sharing can never settle every case and it will not be possible to relieve frontline staff of the responsibility for what are often tough decisions. Legislation should be very carefully consulted upon (learning the lessons of the Cabinet Office's unsuccessful consultation in 2002 on data sharing – PIU, 2002) and drafted, with a full impact assessment carried out.

Fair use: recommendations

The NCC *recommends* that:

The European Commission carries out a major review of the Data Protection Directive, to include:

- Tightening key terms in the Data Protection Directive – this should include those of consent (clarifying what is meant by implicit consent and introducing opt-in provisions across all sectors), personal information, relevant filing system and legitimate interests.

- Enacting a data protection principle for the private sector not to use public sector identifiers, such as national insurance numbers.

- Enacting a data protection principle for organisations only to use true identities where absolutely necessary.

- Enacting a new power to limit/check the use of algorithms.

- Reform of the specification of data purposes, which would be informed by cross-national research on differences between national regulators in how strictly they control the specification of data collection purposes.

- Reform of access rights, to allow consumers to find out with which specific organisations information is shared.

The Department for Constitutional Affairs (following on from Liberty's forthcoming study) undertakes work on reforming information laws (including privacy and data protection legislation and the common law of confidence).

The Department for Constitutional Affairs consults on the simplification of the Data Protection Act.

The Department for Constitutional Affairs proposes consent-driven public sector data sharing legislation.

The Department for Constitutional Affairs carries out research evaluating the effectiveness of Caldicott Guardians, before they expand the use of senior professionals to oversee how staff use personal information in the public sector.

Companies and regulators continue to develop 'Binding Corporate Rules' and the International Organization for Standardization works on international privacy standards.

The Research Councils sponsor further research on the personal information economy, which would include developing evaluation frameworks for different policy tools and work on the public sector. In particular, a broad appraisal of the public sector's handling of, and relationship with, personal information should be commissioned. It would include evaluating the public sector's use of, and powers to access, personal information from the private sector. Equally, the public sector release or sale of personal data to the private sector should be examined.

Tackling poor practices

"I continue to receive phone calls [from personal injury claims handling firms, to take on my case] as I had an accident a year ago and somehow my details have been passed on."

National regulators play a key role as champions of fair information practices. Theirs is an extremely difficult task – unlike most regulators, they regulate practically every organisation in their country and often in a climate of antipathy towards data protection. Yet they are often under-resourced and have insufficient powers. This needs to change.

Limited enforcement, auditing and sanctions

One damning finding of the European Commission's (2003) report on the Directive's implementation in Europe was that enforcement was an under-resourced activity, accorded a low priority by most regulators. Auditing also is a limited activity – it is expensive and time-consuming and few regulators have the resources to carry it out regularly.

Although the Office of the Information Commissioner in the UK has announced that future enforcement work will be more strategic, it is hampered by limited powers. In its 2004 annual report, it has called for three additional powers:

1. 'Stop now' orders – these are injunctive powers to use against activities such as unsolicited marketing.
2. Powers of unannounced inspection for all organisations, public and private – currently the Office has to forewarn organisations before it can audit their practices.
3. Increased penalties – existing sanctions are inadequate so the Office is seeking the power to impose higher penalties.

The NCC is also concerned that the Office has insufficient resources to carry out its work effectively. In 2003/04, the Office's income (to cover its activities under both data protection and freedom of information legislation) was just over £10.5 million. Compare this to the sum spent on direct marketing expenditure in the UK in 2003/04, which the Direct Marketing Association estimated to be £13.66 billion (DMA, 2004). Seen as a percentage, the Office has only 0.07% of the budget of the UK's direct marketers. The importance of promoting good information-handling practices requires appropriate, and increased, funding: the NCC encourages the Department for Constitutional Affairs to review the Commissioner's resources.

The net result of all these failings is that for those organisations that do not comply with data protection law, the risks of getting caught are apparently low and sanctions are unlikely to act as a deterrent.

Advice and empirical evidence

The complexity of data protection legislation necessitates the provision of effective guidance and advice. This is a crucial area yet it is difficult to get the balance right between generic and specialist advice. So the NCC would encourage the Office of the Information Commissioner to further develop (and consult stakeholders on the effectiveness and delivery of) its guidance, particularly that offered on its website.

The UK's regulator also would benefit from a stronger empirical base for its work. The Office should sponsor more rigorous research and commission more papers on matters of interest (such as reports on new forms of technology, at an early stage in its development). It should consider establishing a dedicated research function, with specialist skills.

Regulating globally

Looking beyond Europe, is there a need for a supra-national regulator, or at least more formalised structures than those we have at present (such as the Article 29 Working Group, the forum for national regulators in Europe)? This is difficult to decide on the basis of available evidence, although the NCC does support the Better Regulation Taskforce's calls for the Article 29 Working Group to make its "deliberations more transparent" (BRTF, 2004, p 20). In the future, regulators must cooperate more closely than ever before.

Poor practices: recommendations

The NCC *recommends* that:

The Department of Trade and Industry and the Department for Constitutional Affairs ensure the introduction of increased sanctions, 'stop now' order powers and powers to carry out unannounced inspections for the Office of the Information Commissioner.

The Organisation for Economic Co-operation and Development initiates a forward-looking study to review existing regulatory structures and how these will need to evolve.

Informed choice

"I am particularly concerned about my mother who is elderly and seems to be targeted by ... firms with mail order catalogues, but also 'Christian' charities to which she has occasionally sent a donation. I am at a loss to know how to stop these catalogues and begging letters."

Surveys consistently have found that European consumers have poor knowledge of their data protection rights and do little to uphold them. Even the terminology of data protection is passive – the DPA calls consumers 'data subjects'. Consumer education is not strongly developed in this area. In fact, most of the time, most people comply with requests to disclose their information and do not appreciate what happens to their data and how it can be misused.

In the public sector, research carried out for the Department for Constitutional Affairs (DCA, 2003) found that the public's awareness of what personal information was held by public services was low, with 64% saying that they did not feel well informed. The NCC's own research similarly uncovered poor knowledge of information rights – for example, in 2004 only 3% of people were able to identify the Information Commissioner as the regulator of personal information.

This takes us to the thorny issue of what role we realistically can expect consumers to play in the personal information economy – and how they best can be supported?

Empowering consumers: a cautionary note

Appeals to the importance of issues such as data protection may fall on stony ground if they do not appear to tally directly with consumers' immediate self-interest. As Simon Davies of Privacy International has stated (Davies, 2002, pp 4-5):

> Traditionally, public reaction to privacy invasion has been contradictory and unpredictable. While opinion polls consistently indicate that people care about privacy, public opposition even to the most blatant privacy invasion is sporadic.

Will this change in the future? Prediction is extremely difficult but there is some evidence to suggest that consumer concern about how their information is handled is increasing (as noted in this volume's Introduction). Trust in the government's use of information via channels such as e-government may be particularly limited and may be influenced by privacy concerns; it would not be surprising if disappointment with take-up stimulates the use of tools such as privacy impact assessments and PETs in the public sector.

Be that as it may, it is certainly easy to talk about consumer empowerment, about creating a culture in which all consumers understand the importance of their data and actively participate in information decisions, challenging poor practices and exercising their rights. However, building this capacity across society is likely to be difficult and slow, even if consumer education and public information programmes are strengthened significantly.

This pessimism, or realism, relates partly to the intangible nature of information risks. It also relates to the limits of measures that seek to improve the information supplied to consumers, and which require consumers to take action to assert their rights. The economic rationality of consumers is limited; we often do not have the time or inclination to seek out information and make considered choices (Bush, 2004). Information and redress also can have negative distributive effects because they may benefit disproportionately more affluent and better-educated consumers, who are more able to protect their own interests. Consequently, they may conceal or even magnify existing injustice (Wilhelmsson, 1996).

This is not to contradict recommendations about providing consumers with access to their information. It is rather to sound a cautionary note on the limits of consumer empowerment and also to recognise that less advantaged consumers will need more support – and protection – than information alone.

Transparency and accountability

Too little is known about how the personal information economy works; much of the private sector's actions remain masked by commercial confidentiality and many organisations have yet to recognise the value of greater openness. As Martin Evans noted in Chapter Four, this does question the legitimacy of such a covert economy.

Greater transparency about how organisations collect and use data potentially could help consumers and interested stakeholders better understand the benefits and risks of information use. This would involve building mechanisms that allow consumers to access their data and provide ongoing choices about information use – in itself, this may engage some consumers more actively in decisions (as, for instance, it is hoped NHS plans to improve patients' access to their health records will increase their control over the sharing of their medical history).

Opting out of data collection should not be difficult or designed so that consumers will not exercise choices. This builds on the earlier recommendation that legal requirements for opt-in provisions be introduced across the board. Research has shown that consumers prefer opt-in provisions and often find privacy notices confusing (NCC, 1999). Reporting rules, which would ensure that organisations report on their compliance with legislation and good practice in this area, would also be welcome. But we still need to convince organisations that transparency and accountability mechanisms would be in their interests; some will be easier to convince than others. Onora O'Neill (in the 2002 Reith Lectures, www.bbc.co.uk/radio4/reith2002/) did warn against naïve calls to greater transparency:

> Transparency can encourage people to be less honest, so increasing deception and reducing reasons for trust: those who know that everything they say or write is to be made public may massage the truth.

So attempts to increase transparency may fail unless organisations are convinced of its importance – taking us back to the need to convince organisations of the value of fair information handling.

At this point, it is helpful to look to recent developments in the US. In October 2003, the national 'Do Not Call Registry' was established. The aim was to allow consumers to control the telemarketing calls they received at home. By registering online or by calling a free-phone number, they could register to have their details removed from the call lists of telemarketers. The service is managed by the Federal Trade Commission and enforced by state law enforcement officials. Companies can be fined for failure to comply.

Within *four months* of the Do Not Call Registry's operation, 91% of the US public said they had heard of it. Over half of US adults had signed up to the service and over 90% of them reported receiving fewer calls. Commenting on the findings, the Harris Poll (Harris Interactive, 2004) stated that the results were: "...remarkable. It is rare to find so many people benefit so quickly from a relatively inexpensive government program".

A service similar to the Do Not Call Registry has been available in the UK since 1999, via the Telephone Preference Service (TPS), which is funded by companies that subscribe to the TPS file of registered customer phone numbers. Companies' use of the TPS is a legal obligation, under the 1999 Telecommunications Regulations. In comparison with the US, the UK's results are modest – only 5.8 million numbers have been registered with the TPS over a five-year period. While awareness of the TPS and also the Mail Preference Service (MPS) is growing, there is a long way to go: the Direct Marketing Association (DMA), which manages these services, note in their 2004 annual report that only 35% of people were aware of the MPS (they did not provide figures for the TPS). Only 1.7 million households have joined this, despite the MPS (which is funded by the direct mail industry) having operated for over 20 years This service is not, however, statutory – it is a self-regulatory mechanism.

The NCC thinks that the Preference Services are not being promoted actively enough – there may be a conflict with the DMA's role as a professional association. We need evidence that companies are being monitored for compliance and that sanctions are delivered when companies fail to comply with the provisions. The DMA's annual report does not provide such figures so observers currently have to rely on their assertions that all is well.

As we reported in the Introduction to this book, the NCC's own research has shown that consumers are very concerned about the amount of material and calls they receive; 79% of the public agreed with the statement that "the sheer amount of marketing material I receive irritates me". Seventy-nine per cent also were in favour of fining companies that called people who had joined a service to stop receiving direct marketing calls at home. The following recommendations aim to strengthen their position.

Informed choice: recommendations

The NCC *recommends* that:

The Office of the Information Commissioner strengthens its consumer education role and works with other stakeholders on educational initiatives.

The Office of the Information Commissioner further develops awareness campaigns of data protection legislation.

The DMA boosts its campaigns to promote awareness of the Preference Services, publishes research on awareness with the different services and reports on compliance and sanctions delivered.

Public and private organisations holding personal data build mechanisms to allow consumers ongoing access to, and choices about, their data. The NCC agrees with Bellamy et al's 'right to know' recommendation in this book that e-government services should include online mechanisms to allow users to request (at no cost) what is known about them and what is shared. Condensed privacy notices, short documents drafted to offer consumers choices about how their information is used (Pedersen, 2004), should also be piloted by national regulators.

The Department of Trade and Industry should establish corporate reporting rules on compliance with relevant legislation and good practice in this field. In particular, and in a similar fashion to California's 2003 Security Breach Notification Act, it should be mandatory for organisations to notify consumers when an unauthorised person has accessed their personal data.

This, then, comprises the NCC's agenda for change. It is a demanding agenda — its realisation will demand the hard work and commitment of many.

The way ahead

At present, we are only slowly waking up to the realisation that personal information defines our experience as consumers. The personal information economy has offered us many benefits but only recently have we begun to recognise its broad impact. The challenge now is to capitalise on those benefits while recognising and tackling the risks. Increasingly, this will force us to look beyond nation states for solutions – as with many consumer issues, the NCC will need to work more effectively at a transnational level than ever before.

This will move us into a new phase of consumer policy making. From the 1960s and 1970s, the first generation of consumer policy and advocacy focused on product safety, from cars to toys. The second generation advanced a wider agenda on services, from travel to pensions. Both have achieved significant advances, updating tired policy models and playing their part in fostering a safer economy and more competitive businesses.

Today, we need to develop a new generation of consumer policy, capable of addressing in the interests of consumers the key drivers that underpin the economic system itself, from personal information through to intellectual property.

Until now, as Perri 6 earlier noted, many commentators have approached issues of information use by either raging against an economic or technological order they see as destroying all hope for privacy or by adopting a fatalistic resignation that 'privacy is history'. The NCC agrees that both reactions are misplaced. This book constitutes our attempt to move beyond a polarised debate, to look more widely at the opportunities and risks for consumers and to set out our own vision.

In so doing, we hope that we have shone some light on the workings of the personal information economy. We also hope we have convinced readers of the significance of personal information and of the necessity for ongoing, concerted action. We are keen to build alliances with others who are similarly concerned to work for positive change for consumers, particularly for the less advantaged. For the personal information economy tests not only our commitment to economic imperatives – it most fundamentally challenges our humanity.

References

6, P. and Jupp, B. (2001) *Divided by information? The 'digital divide' and the implications of the new meritocracy*, London: Demos.

Bennett, C.J. and Raab, C.D. (2003) *The governance of privacy: Policy instruments in global perspective*, Aldershot: Ashgate.

BRTF (Better Regulation Taskforce) (2004) *Make it simple, make it better*, London: BRTF.

Bush, J. (2004) *Consumer empowerment and competitiveness*, London: NCC.

CEC (Commission of the European Communities) (2003) *First report on the Implementation of the Data Protection Directive* (95/46/EC) 265 Final, 15.5.2003, Brussels.

Chapman, P. (2004) 'Bolkestein rebukes UK over lack of data privacy', *European Voice*, 15-21 July, p 1.

Danna, A. and Gandy, O.H. (2002) 'All that glitters is not gold: digging beneath the surface of data mining', *Journal of Business Ethics*, vol 4, pp 373-86.

Davies, S. (2002) '"Private virtue" in Big Brother: someone somewhere is watching you', part one of a *Guardian* supplement, 7 September, pp 4-5.

DCA (Department for Constitutional Affairs) (2003) *Privacy and data-sharing: Survey of public awareness and perceptions*, London: DCA.

DMA (Direct Marketing Association) (2004) 'The DMA census of the direct marketing industry 2003-2004' (www.dma.org.uk).

Economist, The (2004) 'Move over, Big Brother', *The Economist Technology Quarterly*, 4 December, p 26.

EURIM (European Information Society Group) (2004) 'Data sharing and matching: the law in practice' (www.eurim.org).

Flaherty, D. (2004) 'Privacy impact assessments: an essential tool for data protection', Speech at the *Privacy Laws & Business* Annual International Conference, Cambridge, 6 July.

Gandy, O.H. Jr (1993) *The panoptic sort: A political economy of personal information*, Boulder, CO: Westview Press.

Gibson, W. (2003) 'The Road to Oceania: reflections on the world since George Orwell' (www.gbn.com/ArticleDisplyServlet.srv?aid=7200).

Harris Interactive (2004) 'Do Not Call Registry is working well', Harris Poll 10, 13 February (www.harrisinteractive.com).

Harris, P. (2004) 'Is data protection value for money?', Speech at the 26th International Conference on Privacy and Personal Data Protection, Wroclaw (Poland), 15 September.

IPC (Information and Privacy Commissioner) (2003) 'Privacy and boards of directors: what you don't know can hurt you' (www.ipc.on.ca)

Kasanoff, B. (2001) *Making it personal: How to profit from personalization without invading privacy*, Cambridge, MA: Perseus Publishing.

Lace, S. (2003a) *Self-regulation: The National Consumer Council's position*, London: NCC.

Lace, S. (2003b) *Three steps to credible self-regulation*, London: NCC.

Lace, S. (2004) *Calling in the chips? Findings from the first summit exploring the future of RFID technology in retail*, London: NCC.

Lashmar, P. (2004) 'It's all for your own good', part three of a *Guardian* special supplement, 25 September, p 28.

Lupton, R. and Power, A. (2002) 'Social exclusion and neighbourhoods', in J. Hills, J. Le Grand and D. Piachaud (eds) *Understanding social exclusion*, Oxford: Oxford University Press.

Lyon, D. (2001) *Surveillance society: Monitoring everyday life*, Buckingham: Open University Press.

Lyon, D. (2003a) *Surveillance after September 11*, Cambridge: Polity Press.

Lyon, D. (2003b) 'Introduction', in D. Lyon (ed) *Surveillance as social sorting: Privacy, risk and digital discrimination*, London: Routledge.

Margulis, S.T. (2003) 'Privacy as a social issue and behavioral concept', *Journal of Social Issues*, vol 59, no 2, pp 243-61.

NCC (National Consumer Council) (1999) *Privacy in the information age*, London: NCC.

NCC (2002) *Consumer representation: Making it work*, London: NCC.

NCC (2003) *Involving consumers: Everyone benefits*, London: NCC.

OIC (Office of the Information Commissioner) (2003) *Study of compliance with the Data Protection Act 1998 by UK based websites*, Wilmslow: OIC.

Pedersen, A. (2004) 'Taking the confusion out of privacy notices', *Privacy Laws & Business*, international newsletter, April, p 27.

PIU (Performance and Information Unit) (now the Prime Minister's Strategy Unit) (2002) *Privacy and data-sharing: The way forward for public services*, London: Cabinet Office.

Privacy Laws & Business (2004a) 'Firms fail to comply with e-privacy regulations', UK newsletter editorial, May, p 4.

Privacy Laws & Business (2004b) 'US study reveals privacy spending trends', International newsletter editorial, April, p 6.

Regan, P. (1995) *Legislating privacy: Technology, social values and public policy*, Chapel Hill, NC: University of North Carolina Press.

RS (Royal Society) (2004) *Nanoscience and nanotechnologies: Opportunities and uncertainties*, London: RS.

RSA (Royal Society of Arts) (2004) *What's there to talk about? Public engagement by science-based companies in the UK*, London: RSA.

Rule, J., McAdam, D., Stearns, L. and Uglow, D. (1980) *The politics of privacy: Planning for personal data systems as powerful technologies*, New York, NY: Elsevier.

Stewart, B. (2004) 'The economics of data privacy: should we place a dollar value on personal autonomy and dignity', Speech at the 26th International Conference on Privacy and Personal Data Protection, Wroclaw (Poland), 15 September.

Thomas, R. (2004) 'Show and tell: is market competitiveness hindered by data protection law?', Speech to the Royal Society of Arts, London, 8 June.

Westin, A.F. (1967) *Privacy and freedom*, New York, NY: Athenaeum.

Westin, A.F. (2003) 'Social and political dimensions of privacy', *Journal of Social Issues*, vol 59, no 2, p 431.

Wilhelmsson, T. (1996) *Twelve essays on consumer law and policy*, Helsinki: University of Helsinki.

Wilsdon, J. (2004) 'Nanotech needs to listen to its public, and now', *Financial Times*, 1 September.

Wilsdon, J. and Willis, R. (2004) *See-through science: Why public engagement needs to move upstream*, London: Demos.

Index

References to boxes, figures and tables are in *italics*

and terrorism threats 87-8
types 76, 82-3
PETTEP research project 88
PIAs *see* Privacy Impact Assessment
(PIA) tools
PIU (Performance and Innovation
Unit) 38, 144, 232
PKI (public-key infrastructure) 80
Platform for Privacy Preferences
(P3P) 58, 83
population registers 144
see also Census data; electoral roll;
identity cards
Porter, D. 19
postal surveys, lifestyle/shopping 2,
107-8
postcodes 30, 106
and flood risk 166
preference services 7, 55, 122, 125,
239-40
awareness campaigns 124
prepaid cards 79
Prime Minister's Strategy Unit (2002)
38, 144
Principles of Reciprocity 160, 172-3,
181
privacy, definitions 212-13
privacy codes *see* standards and codes
of practice
Privacy Diagnostic Tool 89n
Privacy Impact Assessment (PIA) tools
89n, 217-18
NCC recommendations *219*
Privacy Incorporated Software Agent
(PISA) project (2000) 88
privacy knowledge engineering
(PYKE) 83-5
Privacy Laws & Business 225
privacy management systems 82
privacy protection 4, 8, 45-64, 51-64,
124-7
consumer demands 32-4
costs and benefits 224-6, *226*
evaluation methods 23-5, 26-7,
224-5
general principles 48-51
and liberalisation policies 36-7
regulatory methods 23-4, 25-8,
51-64, 225, *226*, 234-6
see also data protection legislation;
self-regulation measures
privacy regulators

background and history 20-1
funding and resources 26, 235
international networks 37
investigation methods 26-7, 52-3
NCC recommendations *219*, 235,
241
private sector employees 52-3
see also Office of the Information
Commissioner
privacy risk 21-8, 45-8, 121-3, 211-14
five domains 211
analysis 73-5, *74*, 89-90n
competing interests 213-14
conceptual frameworks 21-3
distribution in populations 25, 34,
46, 123-4
future directions 34-7, 212-13
and government policies 150-1
measurement of trends 23-8
mistakes and accuracy issues 5-6, 22,
23, 123, 146-7
trust and autonomy issues 8, 69-71,
89n, 118, 145
probation services 140
'problem-oriented policing' (POP)
136
professional bodies, and privacy
policies 55, 192-3
profiling 28
background and history 28-30
and genetic testing 34
life chances and social mobility
effects 7, 28-32
see also data-informed marketing
models; list industries
pseudo-identities 77-9
pseudoanonymity 91n
public perceptions 237-40
on genetic profiling 113
on health information systems 149,
189, 194
on information uses and privacy
risks 8, 21-3, 35-7, 48, 146-7, 149,
237
on relational interaction 116-17
on surveillance 111-12
on technology 215-16
public sector services 7, 18, 25, 46-7,
119-20, 133-51, 231-2
data sharing 50, 52-3, 134-43, 231-2
legislation 196-7, 198-9, 231-2
PET applications 80-2, 87-8